COLLECTION BESCHERELLE

Les verbes anglais

Formes et emplois

Gilbert Quénelle
Didier Hourquin

HATIER

AVANT-PROPOS

Le **Bescherelle** des verbes français a rendu, c'est notoire, d'immenses services – et il continue d'en rendre – à des générations de professeurs et d'étudiants désireux de trouver un guide sûr dans l'incroyable dédale de nos conjugaisons multiples et variées. Pensons aux perplexités de l'étudiant non francophone (sans compter les incertitudes et les doutes des francophones !) en découvrant que le verbe français du premier groupe le plus anodin – le verbe « aimer », par exemple – ne compte pas moins de trente-cinq formes différentes pour l'ensemble de ses temps. Le verbe « aller », champion des verbes irréguliers, n'en a, il est vrai que deux de plus, mais il donne à l'élève la joie de découvrir dans sa conjugaison pas moins de trois racines distinctes, tirées du latin (*ire* et *vadere* ayant fourni deux sources incontestables, mais la racine de l'infinitif « aller » restant à ce jour controversée quant à ses origines). Oui, sans aucun doute, le Bescherelle s'imposait !

La nécessité de concevoir un **Bescherelle des verbes anglais** était *a priori* moins évidente. Même si la linguistique de l'anglais et les études grammaticales quelque peu sérieuses n'ont pas de mal à montrer l'absurdité de la réputation de facilité parfois attribuée à la grammaire anglaise (et qui va jusqu'à l'affirmation pour le moins surprenante que la langue anglaise n'a pas de grammaire !), il reste vrai que la morphologie du verbe anglais, comparée à celle du verbe français est d'une singulière pauvreté. Le verbe *like*, comme le verbe *love*, les deux principaux équivalents de notre verbe « aimer », n'a que quatre formes en tout pour conjuguer tous les temps à toutes les personnes et pour produire les deux formes impersonnelles non conjuguées : *like*, *likes*, *liked*, *liking*. Et il en est ainsi de la grande majorité des verbes, qui se contentent des trois suffixes **-s**, **-ed**, et **-ing**. Mais, dira-t-on, vous oubliez les verbes irréguliers, qui sèment la terreur chez nos élèves francophones, petits et grands. La belle affaire ! L'équivalent *go* de notre épouvantable verbe « aller » – avec ses trente-sept formes et ses trois racines – ne peut aligner que quatre formes distinctes : *go*, *went*, *gone* et *going*. Et le recordman toutes catégories *be* ne dépasse pas huit ! Quelle pauvreté ! Et quelle audace de vouloir nous apprendre à conjuguer les verbes anglais ! C'était apparemment une gageure et une entreprise un peu vaine.

Conception maquette : Yvette Heller
Adaptation maquette et mise en page : Isabelle Vacher
Dessins : Corédoc

© HATIER – Paris – Juin 1997

ISSN 0990 3771 - ISBN 978-2-218-**71747**-5

Il faut pourtant féliciter les Editions Hatier d'avoir voulu montrer qu'un guide de type Bescherelle pouvait être tout aussi utile pour traiter, en dépit des apparences trompeuses, de la grande complexité du verbe anglais. Il faut surtout se réjouir que l'on ait fait appel pour cela à la compétence reconnue d'un Gilbert Quénelle, angliciste sûr et auteur talentueux de nombreux ouvrages pédagogiques. Avec son collaborateur Didier Hourquin qui lui a apporté entre autres choses le précieux appui d'un traitement informatique des verbes anglais, il s'est d'abord appliqué à concevoir pour l'anglais une démarche sensiblement différente et bien adaptée aux réalités du système verbal anglais, tout en conservant les vertus de rigueur et d'exhaustivité de l'original (sans prétendre vouloir tout traiter).

Les utilisateurs de l'ouvrage seront reconnaissants aux auteurs d'avoir ainsi considérablement réduit la partie consacrée aux traditionnels « tableaux de conjugaison » qui sont, nous venons de le voir, beaucoup moins utiles ici que pour le français et d'avoir en revanche analysé avec soin, dans la première partie intitulée « Grammaire du verbe », les trois phénomènes fondamentaux qui expliquent la richesse de significations et la vraie difficulté du système verbal anglais, malgré la relative pauvreté morphologique : le jeu subtil des **temps** et des **aspects**, celui de la **modalité** (grâce au rôle important des auxiliaires modaux), le rôle éminent que jouent en anglais les très nombreux **verbes à particules** dont on trouve une liste dans l'inventaire alphabétique de la troisième partie.

Le grand mérite de Gilbert Quénelle et de Didier Hourquin est d'avoir réussi à rassembler dans un seul volume une riche information qui fait parfois l'objet d'ouvrages spécialisés pour traiter un seul des éléments (comme, par exemple pour les verbes à particules ou pour le temps et l'aspect). Ils l'ont fait en tenant compte d'un vaste public non spécialisé, simplement désireux de comprendre tout en apprenant à puiser dans le vaste réservoir des verbes anglais.

Denis Girard
Inspecteur général honoraire
de l'Éducation nationale

SOMMAIRE

Tableaux de conjugaison   87

Index   115

COMMENT UTILISER CE LIVRE ?

Le **Bescherelle** n'est ni un livre de grammaire classique, ni un dictionnaire : c'est un outil de travail complémentaire qui vise à susciter une réflexion. Son utilisation permet de mieux comprendre la grammaire du verbe anglais comme le produit d'un système de pensée différent du système de pensée français.

En anglais, un petit nombre de formes verbales permet d'exprimer un grand nombre de sens. En effet, la personne qui parle (le locuteur) peut nuancer une même forme selon la durée relative de l'action (aspect) et selon son état d'esprit du moment (modalité).

De plus, grâce à l'emploi de particules, l'anglais peut multiplier à l'infini les formes et les sens à partir des formes de base.

À partir de ces constats, trois types d'outils sont proposés au lecteur, selon ses besoins du moment.

1 La grammaire du verbe

Elle permet d'analyser avec une précision suffisante la valeur des temps et des aspects du verbe en anglais en général et de ses auxiliaires ordinaires et modaux.

Elle explique aussi la formation et le sens des verbes à particules, la place et le sens des principaux types de compléments du verbe ainsi que l'importance de la forme passive.

Le texte est construit en doubles pages articulées en paragraphes courts auxquels il est facile de se reporter. Deux synthèses donnent une vue d'ensemble sur les temps anglais et sur la modalité.

2 Les tableaux

Ils présentent de manière synthétique toutes les formes possibles de la conjugaison, les contractions et les différents types de verbes irréguliers.

3 Les index

L'index général comprend tous les verbes (6 000 environ), réguliers, et irréguliers, simples ou à particules. Une telle richesse exclut la possibilité d'introduire toute traduction des verbes dans cet index.

Il a été enrichi des verbes nouvellement entrés dans la langue d'aujourd'hui.

Il est complété par des index spécifiques :
• index des verbes à complémentation ;
• index des verbes à particules ;
• index des verbes irréguliers.

Pour chaque catégorie, un renvoi est prévu aux pages correspondantes de la grammaire du verbe et des tableaux.

LISTE ALPHABÉTIQUE DES POINTS DE GRAMMAIRE ABORDÉS

LISTE ALPHABÉTIQUE DES POINTS DE GRAMMAIRE ABORDÉS

Grammaire
du verbe

À SAVOIR

Il y a temps *(time)* et temps *(tense)*

Pour évoquer le temps qui passe, qui s'écoule du passé au présent et du présent à l'avenir, c'est-à-dire le **temps chronologique** (en anglais : *time*), les langues se servent de formes appelées **temps grammaticaux** (en anglais : *tenses*).

Par exemple, pour le temps chronologique du passé, le français a le choix entre les quatre temps grammaticaux que sont l'imparfait, le passé simple, le passé composé et le plus-que-parfait. L'anglais, lui, dispose de trois temps grammaticaux : le *present perfect*, le *preterite* (en français : prétérit) et le *pluperfect*.

Deux pièges à éviter

- D'abord, il n'y a pas de correspondance parfaite, à l'intérieur de chacun des deux systèmes, entre temps chronologique et temps grammatical.
  On peut utiliser, par exemple, en anglais comme en français, un temps grammatical du présent pour parler de l'avenir.
  What are you doing tomorrow?
  Que faites-vous demain ?

- D'autre part, il n'y a pas de parallélisme entre les deux systèmes de temps grammaticaux français et anglais pour la même tranche de temps. Par exemple, pour traduire le verbe dans la situation suivante du passé :
  When she saw him in London...
  on peut se servir :
  – soit du passé composé *(quand elle l'a vu)*, si le moment de la rencontre n'est pas précisé par le contexte ;
  – soit du passé simple *(quand elle le vit)*, si les circonstances sont par ailleurs précisément indiquées ;
  – soit de l'imparfait *(quand elle le voyait)* si cette rencontre est habituelle.

La durée et l'aspect

Les Anglais ne ressentent pas le temps qui passe comme les Français. Ils ont presque toujours le sentiment que les temps chronologiques (le passé, le présent et l'avenir) sont liés l'un à l'autre dans une même durée, alors que les Français ont tendance à les séparer plus nettement entre eux.

C'est pourquoi, quand nous cherchons à comprendre un verbe anglais, il nous faut tenir compte de ce qu'on appelle son **aspect** : la **durée** de l'événement (action ou état) qu'il exprime, le fait qu'il vient de commencer, qu'il se répète ou pas. Cette notion, le verbe français ne peut l'exprimer tout seul ; il faut lui adjoindre une expression appropriée.

Par exemple, pour reprendre la situation précédente :

When Margaret saw him in London he was speaking to a policeman.

Quand Margaret le vit à Londres, il parlait avec un agent de police.

la forme *was speaking* donne à penser que cette conversation avait commencé avant que Margaret ne le voie et qu'elle a sans doute continué après. Ce que le français pourra rendre en adjoignant au verbe une expression comme « être en train de » : *Quand elle le vit, il était en train de parler à un agent de police.*

Mais regardons les choses de plus près pour chacun de ces temps qui se succèdent dans le temps chronologique *time*.

1. LE PRÉSENT

Le temps chronologique du présent s'étend en anglais bien avant et bien après ce qu'en français on nomme le moment présent ; c'est pourquoi les formes pouvant exprimer ce *present time* sont nombreuses.

La forme en *-ing*

- La forme en *-ing* (ou *continuous*) montre **concrètement, dans sa durée, une action en cours relativement longue**, dont on ne précise ni quand elle a commencé, ni quand elle s'achèvera.
  I'm reading a book by Agatha Christie.
  Je suis en train de lire un livre d'Agatha Christie.
  Plusieurs adverbes ou expressions adverbiales peuvent préciser le temps chronologique : *now, today, this week, for the time being,* etc.

- À cet aspect peut s'ajouter l'expression d'une **modalité** (cf. p. 34), par exemple une supposition dans :
  He must be reading it too.
  Il doit (être en train de) le lire aussi.

  En résumé, **la forme en *-ing* me permet de « m'impliquer » dans la description de l'action**.

La forme simple

En employant cette forme, l'anglais quitte le concret du moment présent, comme si l'action était « vue d'en haut », pour parler :

- d'un trait caractéristique d'un personnage ;
  He reads slowly. Il lit lentement.

- d'une habitude (le présent simple est alors accompagné d'un adverbe comme *often, never, generally, usually, always*, ou autres expressions appropriées) ;
  On Sundays he usually reads in bed.
  Le dimanche, il lit au lit.

- d'une référence à une autorité (*the dictionary / Shakespeare says...*) ;
  Some grammar books call this the simple present.
  Certaines grammaires appellent ceci le présent simple.

- d'un règlement, d'un usage ;
  The law forbids photocopying books.
  La loi interdit de photocopier les livres.
  The British send their greeting cards in the beginning of December.
  Les Britanniques envoient leurs cartes de vœux début décembre.

● d'une « vérité éternelle », en dehors de ma responsabilité.
  Birds of a feather flock together. Qui se ressemble s'assemble.

En résumé, **la forme simple me permet de parler de l'action avec détachement, comme si je n'y étais pas directement impliqué.**

Forme simple ou en *-ing* ?

Des verbes comme *know, love, believe, remember, think*, etc. ne résultent pas d'une action volontaire mais expriment des **processus mentaux, indépendants de la volonté.** Dans ce sens, ils **ne peuvent pas être employés à la forme en *-ing.***
  I think I love you.
  Je pense que je t'aime. (*think* = « avoir l'impression de »)
  I feel you're right.
  J'ai le sentiment que tu as raison.

Mais quand le verbe prend la valeur d'une action, la forme en *-ing* redevient possible.
  What are you doing? I'm thinking about you.
  Que fais-tu ? Je pense à toi. (ici, *think* = « évoquer », « réfléchir », et résulte d'une démarche volontaire)

Yes, but...

Telle est la **souplesse de l'anglais** que pour exprimer sa manière de voir à un moment donné, un Anglais se donne le droit d'inverser les rôles convenus et habituels des formes simple et en *-ing*.

● On trouvera un présent en *-ing* pour décrire, avec une nuance de regret, de reproche, ou d'irritation, une action habituelle.
  He's always borrowing my books!
  Il faut toujours qu'il m'emprunte mes livres !

● On trouvera un présent simple pour décrire une action en cours dans le présent, au lieu de la forme en *-ing*, à condition que cette action soit brève, et pour ne pas donner l'impression d'une sorte de « ralenti ».
  I put my pen down and get up: someone is knocking at the door.
  Je pose mon stylo et je me lève : on sonne à la porte.

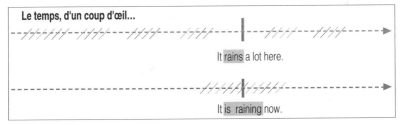

Le temps, d'un coup d'œil...

It rains a lot here.

It is raining now.

13

2. L'AVENIR

L'anglais n'a pas de forme spécialisée pour exprimer l'avenir, mais emprunte **différentes formes verbales**, accompagnées d'adverbes ou de compléments de temps comme *soon, tomorrow, shortly...*

Formes en *-ing*

> *Next week **I'm** visit**ing** the National Gallery.*
> La semaine prochaine, je visite / je visiterai la National Gallery.
> ***I'm going to** write a book about English painting.*
> Je vais écrire un livre sur la peinture anglaise.
> *People **are going to** like it.*
> Les gens vont l'aimer.

Avec le présent en *-ing* et la formule *be going to*, **l'avenir est considéré comme presque réalisé**, tant l'intention d'agir est forte, ou la probabilité ou l'imminence de l'action marquée. La forme en *-ing*, une fois encore, actualise le sens, rend plus concrète l'action envisagée. C'est « comme si c'était fait ».

Forme simple

> *OK... I get up early and work hard.*
> Bon, je me lève tôt et travaille dur.

Ici, comme toujours, la forme simple me montre plus en recul. L'action est envisagée comme **imminente** puisqu'elle paraît fermement décidée, mais **d'une manière plus abstraite**, comme si quelqu'un d'autre avait pris la décision. C'est « comme ça que cela doit se passer ».

L'auxiliaire *will*

> *We'll write / we'll be writing to you.* On vous écrira.

Will est ici un simple **auxiliaire du futur**. La forme simple et la forme en *-ing* sont à peu près équivalentes, la forme en *-ing* étant plus concrètement imaginable, la forme simple mentionnant seulement l'action comme devant se réaliser.

Les nuances modales

> *We will write to you soon.*

- Si *will* est mentionné en toutes lettres et non sous sa forme contractée, il prend une valeur modale et induit ici une nuance du type : « Vous pouvez compter sur moi. » À l'expression du futur, *will* ajoute une notion de **volonté** : « Soyez assuré que nous vous écrirons bientôt. »

- D'autres modaux comme *can, may, might,* etc. (cf. p. 40-41) placés dans un contexte de futur avec des adverbes appropriés (*tomorrow, next month,* etc.) permettent eux aussi d'exprimer l'avenir.

  I may write a chapter tonight.
  Il se peut que j'écrive un chapitre ce soir.
  I might write a chapter tonight.
  Il se pourrait que j'écrive un chapitre ce soir.

Dans ce même cadre, on peut placer :
- *be to* et l'infinitif, qui exprime une obligation inéluctable, provenant par exemple, d'un emploi du temps « imposé » ;

  I am to write the first chapter next week.
  Il est prévu que j'écrive le premier chapitre la semaine prochaine.
- *have to* et l'infinitif, qui suggère une obligation moins impérative.

  I have to write soon.
  Il faut que j'écrive bientôt.

Yes, but...

- En français, nous employons deux futurs dans une même phrase.
  Je partirai quand il viendra.

- En anglais, le verbe de la **subordonnée de temps** est dans ce cas au présent.
  I shall go when he comes.

- Mais, dans une interrogative indirecte, il n'est pas surprenant de trouver, en anglais comme en français, le futur dans les deux propositions.
  I'll ask him when he will come.
  Je lui demanderai à quelle heure il arrivera.

Le temps, d'un coup d'œil...

Tonight I'm listening to the weather forecast.
It's going to rain soon.
It will rain tonight.
It might rain tonight.

Le choix de la forme ne dépend pas du moment où se produira l'action mais de la manière dont elle est envisagée.

---

3. LE *PRESENT PERFECT*

C'est le temps grammatical du passé le mieux lié au présent chronologique : son nom ne contient-il pas le mot *present* ? Quand je l'emploie, je dispose même d'une gradation de moyens pour exprimer comment je ressens le passé.

Attention ! Le *present perfect* ressemble au passé composé français, mais il n'en est pas l'équivalent : il peut se traduire aussi par le présent de l'indicatif.

Un passé « vu d'en haut »

Quand je demande à un ami :
> *Have you (ever) played tennis with my brother?*
> As-tu (jamais) joué au tennis avec mon frère ?

je ne m'intéresse pas aux circonstances – quand ?, comment ?, où ?, pourquoi ?. Je veux simplement savoir si cette action a eu lieu ou non. De même, dans les exemples suivants :
> *We have visited San Francisco.*
> Nous avons visité San Francisco.
> *They have bought a new car.*
> Ils ont acheté une voiture neuve.
> *It's the first time I have met him.*
> C'est la première fois que je le rencontre.

En employant le *present perfect* dans sa forme simple, je suis comme « détaché » par rapport au fait en question.

Un passé vu de plus près

Si, à la question : *Have you (ever) played tennis with my brother?* mon interlocuteur se contente de répondre : *Yes, I have*, il n'est guère explicite. Mais il peut dire :
> *Yes, I have played with him since last spring.*
> Oui, je joue avec lui depuis le printemps dernier.

ou encore :
> *Yes, I have played with him for months.*
> Oui, cela fait des mois que je joue avec lui.

Grâce à l'emploi de *since*, de *for*, ou avec des mots ou expressions comme *lately, recently, up to now*, etc., **l'action semble se rapprocher** au point de presque « recouvrir » le présent, ses conséquences sont plus sensibles, elle est comme plus « chaude » dans l'esprit de mon interlocuteur.

Un passé « à portée de la main »

Si maintenant on me répond :
> *Oh! I have just played with him.* Oh ! Je viens de faire une partie avec lui.

le passé est si proche qu'il touche le présent, le joueur est, pour ainsi dire, encore essoufflé. De même dans, par exemple : *It has just rained* (sous-entendu : le sol est encore humide) ou *I have just poured your tea* (sous-entendu : bois-le tant qu'il est chaud).

Un passé... présent

La **forme en -*ing*** permet à un Anglais d'exprimer plus concrètement son opinion qu'avec la forme simple qui, pour l'expression du passé comme pour celle du présent, reste un peu abstraite... Ainsi, pour traduire : « J'ai joué au tennis », *I have been playing tennis* exprime plus d'effort que *I have played*.

> *I have been playing a good match.*
> J'ai joué une excellente partie.

ne peut être dit qu'avec chaleur, alors que *I have played a good match.* est bien moins vraisemblable. De même dans :

> *You have been smoking again!*
> Tu as encore fumé !

ou :

> *I have been working for ten hours.*
> Sous-entendu : C'est long ! Il n'est même pas nécessaire d'ajouter *hard*.

Yes, but...

Au lieu de dire : *Have you played tennis with him?* on aurait pu aussi poser la question : *Did you play tennis with him?*
Dans ce cas, mon interlocuteur a en tête une date qu'il peut donner. Il se sert du *preterite*, autre temps grammatical du passé, qui introduit une valeur différente.

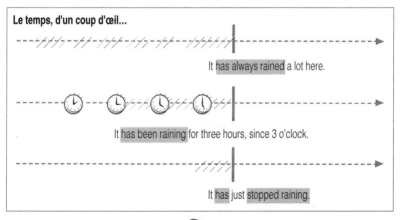

Le temps, d'un coup d'œil...

It has always rained a lot here.

It has been raining for three hours, since 3 o'clock.

It has just stopped raining.

4. LE PRÉTÉRIT

À la différence du *present perfect*, le prétérit (en anglais : *preterite* ou *past*) établit une **coupure nette avec le présent** chronologique.

Le temps du récit

- Le prétérit peut être traduit par l'imparfait, par le passé composé ou par le passé simple, mais dans tous les cas **les faits sont bien séparés du présent**.
  I lived in San Francisco then. When I met her, she told me this story...
  Je vivais alors à San Francisco. Quand je l'ai rencontrée, elle me raconta cette histoire...
  Leur durée, ici, n'intéresse pas : la période concernée peut être relativement longue (*lives, told*) ou courte (*met*).

- *Used to*, qui insiste encore plus sur l'aspect révolu de l'action ou de l'événement, peut teinter le passé d'une coloration affective.
  I used to have lots of friends there.
  J'y avais beaucoup d'amis. (sous-entendu : c'était le bon temps)

Un passé « à la loupe »

Contrairement au *present perfect*, **le prétérit incite à s'intéresser aux circonstances**.
C'est ainsi que l'on peut préciser, entre autres :

- le temps par une expression qui date bien l'action ;
  He bought his car last October / three months ago.
  Il a acheté sa voiture en octobre dernier / il y a trois mois.
  Remarquons au passage que *ago* exprime bien que le temps s'en est allé : dans *ago*, il y a *go*.

- la manière ;
  She called me from a phone box.
  Elle m'a appelé d'une cabine téléphonique.

- le lieu ;
  I met him in San Francisco.
  Je l'ai rencontré à San Francisco.

« Actions-points » et « actions-traits »

- Le **prétérit simple** peut aussi évoquer dans leur simplicité une **succession d'actions rapides** (actions-points) qui ponctuent la narration.
  I knocked at the door, someone opened, I saw Brian.
  J'ai frappé à la porte, on a ouvert, c'était Brian.
  On traduit par le passé simple, par le passé composé, ou par l'imparfait.

- **La forme en -*ing***, au contraire, décrit une **action qui s'inscrit dans une durée** (action-trait).
  "What were you doing, at ten p.m., when I tried to call you?" "I was working."
  « Que faisais-tu hier soir, à dix heures, quand j'ai essayé de t'appeler ? » « Je travaillais. »

  La forme en -*ing* avec le prétérit a donc la même valeur qu'avec le présent.

- On peut utiliser la forme en -*ing* pour l'expression du futur dans le style indirect.
  He told me he was going on holiday in a week's time.
  Il m'a dit qu'il partait en vacances dans une semaine.

- On peut introduire une modalité quand, au lieu de dire simplement :
  The house stood on the hill.
  La maison se dressait sur la colline.
  on ajoute une nuance affective.
  My parents' house was standing on the hill, you know.
  Tu sais, c'est la maison de mes parents qui était sur la colline.

Le prétérit modal

Les emplois de la forme simple et de la forme en -*ing* ne surprennent plus quand on en a bien compris le fonctionnement, mais ils sont plus subtils quand il s'agit d'exprimer une modalité particulière. Par exemple, le prétérit, appelé prétérit modal, est d'usage après *as if, as though*, ou encore dans *It's time...* ou *I wish...*

It's time we left.   *I wish he came.*
Il est temps que nous partions.   Je voudrais qu'il vienne.

C'est le subjonctif français qui correspond à ces attitudes subjectives.

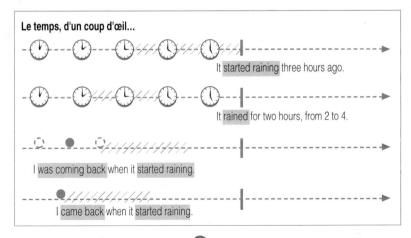

Le temps, d'un coup d'œil...

It started raining three hours ago.

It rained for two hours, from 2 to 4.

I was coming back when it started raining.

I came back when it started raining.

5. LE *PLUPERFECT*

Ce temps grammatical, appelé aussi *past perfect*, **joue par rapport au prétérit le rôle que le present perfect joue par rapport au présent chronologique.**

Un passé dans le passé

- Quand on l'emploie, on dispose donc d'une même gradation de moyens pour exprimer comment le passé est ressenti. Ce temps est très comparable au plus-que-parfait et au passé antérieur français. Il peut aussi se traduire par l'imparfait.

Suivons cette gradation, mais cette fois en partant du plus proche. Comparez :
> *I have just read a sci-fi book.*
> Je viens de lire un livre de science-fiction.
> *I had just read that book when the sequel was published.*
> Je venais de lire ce livre quand la suite a été / fut publiée.

L'événement : *I have just read that book* est seulement mentionné. Il est positionné par rapport à un autre événement : *the sequel was published*, qui sert de point de référence, évoqué par le prétérit.

> *I had been reading the first chapter when the light went out.*
> Je lisais le premier chapitre quand la lumière s'éteignit.

Ici, *I had been reading the first chapter...* évoque une durée plus évidente, plus concrète. Soit parce qu'elle apparaît encore « chaude » à celui qui parle, soit parce que l'action durait encore au moment de l'autre événement, *when the light went out*, qui sert de point de référence.

- On retrouve tout naturellement ce système au style indirect.
  - Style direct : *He said: "I have read it."*
  - Style indirect : *He said that he had read it.*

C'est le moment passé où les paroles sont prononcées qui sert de point de référence.

Une durée plus précise

Comme avec le *present perfect*, la durée de l'action est souvent précisée par un complément de temps (*for two weeks, since three o'clock*, etc.) ou une référence à un événement, un état de fait passé.
> *He had known her for three years (since the war) when he proposed to her.*
> Quand il l'a demandée en mariage, cela faisait trois ans qu'il la connaissait.
> (... il la connaissait depuis la guerre.)

Un passé qui s'éloigne à l'infini

It was after the Flood, but the Earth had not dried yet.
Le Déluge avait cessé mais la Terre n'avait pas encore séché.

Le *pluperfect* modal

Comme le prétérit, le *pluperfect* peut avoir une valeur modale (cf. p. 19).
I wish he had come.
J'aurais aimé qu'il vienne, je regrette qu'il ne soit pas venu.

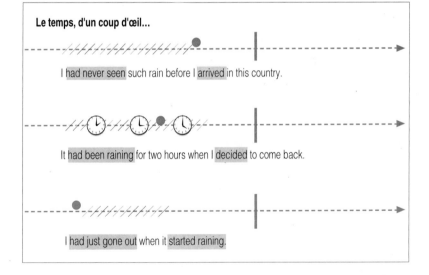

Le temps, d'un coup d'œil...

I had never seen such rain before I arrived in this country.

It had been raining for two hours when I decided to come back.

I had just gone out when it started raining.

Temps et aspects en anglais traduits par...		Plus-que-parfait	Passé antérieur
Pluperfect			
	I had seen him before.	Je l'avais vu auparavant.	
Il peut être rendu plus concret par la forme en *-ing*.	*I had just parked the car... / I had been parking the car when he arrived.*		Quand j'eus garé la voiture, il arriva.
Valeur modale : *I wish I had.*			
Preterite			
Tantôt « action-trait » : forme en *-ing*. Tantôt « action-point » : forme simple.	*I was parking the car when he arrived.* *When I came in I saw him immediately.*		
Valeur modale : *It's time we left.*			
Present perfect			
Très lié au présent. Il en est encore rapproché par *have just* et par la forme en *-ing*.	*I have known him for years, since 1990, in fact.* *We have met many times.*		
Valeur modale : *You've been smoking again !*			
Present			
S'étend souvent bien avant et bien après le moment où on parle. Encore prolongé par la forme en *-ing* mais ce n'est pas toujours possible.	*I often write to him.* *I'm meeting him tomorrow.* *I am writing him a letter but I write slowly.*		
Valeur modale : *He's always borrowing money.*			
Future			
Pas de forme spécialisée. Forme simple moins concrète que la forme en *-ing*. La contraction *'ll* a un sens moins fort que *will*.	*I'll write to him some time.* *I'll be writing to him sometime.* *I will always write.* *I will have seen him by then.*		
Valeur modale : tous les degrés de probabilité (cf. p. 44-45).			

Passé composé	Passé simple	Imparfait	Présent	Futur antérieur	Futur simple
		Je venais de garer la voiture quand il arriva.			
Je garais la voiture quand il est arrivé.		Je garais la voiture quand il arriva.			
Quand je suis arrivé, je l'ai vu tout de suite.	Quand j'arrivai, je le vis tout de suite.				
			Je le connais depuis des années, en fait depuis 1990.		
Nous nous sommes vus souvent.					
			Je lui écris souvent.		
			Je vais le rencontrer demain.		Je le rencontrerai demain.
			Je suis en train de lui écrire mais j'écris lentement.		
					Je lui écrirai un jour.
					J'écrirai toujours, c'est certain.
				Je l'aurai vu d'ici là.	

AUXILIAIRES ORDINAIRES
BE, HAVE, DO, LET
●●●

À SAVOIR

Certains **auxiliaires** – *be, have, do* et *let* – sont employés pour former la conjugaison des autres verbes. D'autres, dits auxiliaires modaux, donnent au verbe une « couleur » qui permet à celui qui parle de traduire ses intentions.

Emplois en tant qu'auxiliaires

● **Be** permet de construire toutes les formes en *-ing*.
> *What are you doing tomorrow?*
> *We'll be writing to you.* (cf. p. 14)

Il sert le passif (cf. p. 84).
> *I was born before you.* Je suis né avant toi.
> *I'll be laughed at.* On se moquera de moi.

● **Have** contribue à la formation de tous les temps composés (cf. p. 16-17 et 20-21).
- Le *present perfect.*
> *Have you ever obeyed your parents?* Avez-vous jamais obéi à vos parents ?
- Le *pluperfect.*
> *He had only met her three times before he proposed to her.*
> Il ne l'avait rencontrée que trois fois quand il lui a demandé sa main.

Mais il y a des situations plus complexes qui nécessitent aussi l'emploi de *be*.
> *What have you been doing?* Qu'est-ce que tu fabriquais encore ?

● **Do** est de règle pour toutes les formes interrogatives et négatives d'un verbe ordinaire à la forme simple (cf. tableaux p. 88-89).

● **Let** est au service de l'impératif.
> *Let us go! / Let's go!* Allons !   *Let him go!* Qu'il parte !

Emplois en tant que « suppléants »

● **Be** s'associe de plus à *here* et *there* : il permet de constater un état de fait.
> *There are no clouds in the sky today.* Il n'y a pas de nuages dans le ciel aujourd'hui.

● **Have** remplace *make* pour exprimer la cause.
> *I had my watch repaired.* J'ai fait réparer ma montre.

Have donne ici à la phrase un sens passif, mais il peut aussi lui donner un sens actif.

I had (ou I made) Dan repair my watch.
J'ai fait réparer ma montre par Dan.
They had Bill teach Marie some English.
Ils ont demandé à Bill d'enseigner un peu d'anglais à Marie.

- **Let** peut, comme *have*, prendre une valeur de cause.
They let Bill teach Marie some English.
Ils ont laissé Bill enseigner / Ils ont demandé à Bill d'enseigner un peu d'anglais à Marie.
They let him go. Ils l'ont laissé partir.

Emplois à part entière

- Chacun de ces auxiliaires ordinaires peut aussi se comporter comme un verbe à part entière.
Be est le verbe d'état par excellence, capable d'exprimer l'âge (*He is 13.* Il <u>a</u> treize ans.) ou l'état physique ou mental (*I am fine.* Je <u>vais</u> bien.).
Have est l'égal de *take* quand on dit : *Have a cup of tea.* (Prenez une tasse de thé.) ou *I had a good time.* (J'ai passé un bon moment.)
Do est aussi le rival de *make* et s'en distingue en plusieurs circonstances. On dit *to do business* (faire des affaires) et *to make a bargain* (faire une affaire).
I'm making an exercise which you will do tomorrow.
J'élabore un exercice que vous ferez demain.
Let a le sens de « louer ».
My house is to let.

- Par voie de conséquence, certains auxiliaires peuvent être... auxiliaires d'eux-mêmes.
Don't do that! Ne faites pas ça !
He has had his day. Il a eu son heure de gloire.

- Comme de nombreux autres verbes à part entière, ils peuvent aussi s'adjoindre diverses particules (cf. p. 46).
Be : *Are you up?* Tu es levé ?
Have : *Can I have my book back?* Puis-je récupérer mon livre ?
Do : *They did away with the witnesses.* Ils se sont débarrassés des témoins.
Let : *Don't let me down.* Ne me laisse pas tomber.

Emplois comme auxiliaires modaux

Be, have et *do* permettent même d'exprimer la modalité.
I am to write the first chapter next week. (cf. p. 15)
Il est prévu que j'écrive le premier chapitre la semaine prochaine.

You had better write to thank them.   *I do like grammar.* (*do* = forte insistance)
Tu ferais mieux de leur écrire pour les remercier.   La grammaire me passionne.

1. *BE*

Be joue un rôle très important pour les verbes anglais : il participe à leur fonctionnement et il est riche de valeurs propres. D'où la place qu'il tient dans les dictionnaires.

Verbe auxiliaire

- Grâce à ses huit formes différentes, pleines (*I am, he is, they are*, etc.) et contractées (*I'm, he's, they're*, etc.), et avec l'aide de *have, has, had*, ce verbe intervient presque partout dans la conjugaison, simple et en *-ing* (cf. tableaux p. 88-95).

- Il est à la base de la voix passive (cf. p. 84), comme équivalent du français « on », par exemple.
  I have been fired. On m'a renvoyé.

Verbe suppléant

- Employé avec *go*, *be* fait concurrence à *have*. Comparez :
  - *He's gone / He is gone: the door is locked.*
    Il est parti : la porte est fermée à clé.
  - *He's just gone / He has just gone.*
    Il vient de partir.

  Dans la première phrase, *is gone* exprime un état résultant d'une action, d'un événement. Dans la seconde, *has gone* est un simple *present perfect*.

- Attention : les deux formes contractées sont identiques. Ainsi la phrase : *He's gone to Leeds* se comprend-elle :
  - *He is gone to Leeds.* (sous-entendu : il y est parti définitivement, il n'en reviendra pas)
  - *He has gone to Leeds.* (sous-entendu : il y est parti, mais il en reviendra)
  Seul le contexte peut nous renseigner.

- Ne confondez pas non plus *has been* avec *has gone*.
    He's been to Leeds / He has been to Leeds.
    Il est allé à Leeds. (sous-entendu : il en est revenu)

- Emploi avec *here* et *there*.
    Here they are. Les voilà.
    There are ten people. Il y a dix personnes.
  Ces emplois (constatation d'un état de fait) peuvent parfois surprendre si l'on se place dans une logique française, mais sont cohérents dans l'esprit des Anglais : *be* se conjugue « normalement » sans être perturbé par la présence de *here* ou *there*.
    There being nobody else...
    Comme il n'y avait personne d'autre...

Shouldn't there be a policeman here?
Ne devrait-il pas y avoir un policier ici ?
Tom, could you please help me? There's a good boy!
Tom, sois gentil, tu peux m'aider ?

- *It is* est proche de *there is*, pour exprimer :
  - La distance : *How far is it to London?* On est à combien de Londres ?
  - Le temps qu'il fait : *It is foggy.* Il y a du brouillard.
  - La durée : *It is five years since he left.* (Surtout pas ~~there is~~.) Cela fait cinq ans qu'il est parti.

Verbe à part entière

- *Be* désigne ici un état, au sens plein du terme. Pensez au fameux : *To be, or not to be* de Shakespeare. C'est ainsi qu'il peut exprimer :
  - L'âge.
    How old are you?
  - La condition physique.
    How are you? I am fine, thanks.
  - Le fait d'exister.
    Shakespeare is the best playwright that ever was.
    Shakespeare est le meilleur dramaturge de tous les temps.

- Quand la phrase est sans ambiguïté, avec *when, if, though, unless, until,* on peut omettre verbe et sujet.
    When a boy, he used to be quite mischievous.
    Quand il était jeune, il était très espiègle.

- On voit donc que dans cet emploi, *be* peut être classé avec d'autres « verbes d'état » comme *appear, become, feel, get, go, grow, make, seem, smell, sound, taste,* etc.

Yes, but...

- Attention, on dira :
    There was (et non ~~there were~~) *ten minutes to wait.*
    Il y avait dix minutes d'attente. (sous-entendu une période de dix minutes, que l'on ne compte pas précisément)

    There's good children! (et non ~~There are~~)
    Soyez sages, les enfants !

- Notez par ailleurs que le français « il y a » ne se traduit pas automatiquement par *there is / there are.*
    What's the matter?
    Qu'est-ce qu'il y a ? Qu'est-ce qui se passe ?

2. HAVE

Have n'a que quatre formes pleines : *have, has, had* et *having*, mais attention aux formes contractées affirmative et négative, qui peuvent être confondues avec celles de *be* : *he's* peut se comprendre *he is* ou *he has* (cf. p. 26).

Verbe auxiliaire

Il permet de former le *present perfect* et le *pluperfect* de tous les verbes ordinaires (cf. tableaux p. 90-91).
> *Have you finished your tea?*
> Tu as fini ton thé ?

Verbe suppléant

- *Have* a un emploi « causatif » qui le rapproche de *make*.
  > *I had (ou made) Dan repair my watch.*
  > J'ai fait réparer ma montre par Dan.

- Mais attention à certaines ambiguïtés. Considérez la phrase :
  > *He had his watch stolen.*

  Détachée de son contexte, elle peut signifier, au sens passif :
  > On lui a volé sa montre.

  et, au sens actif :
  > Il a fait voler la montre de quelqu'un par quelqu'un d'autre.

- Attention aussi à l'ordre des mots. Comparez :
  > *He had his hair cut.*
  > Il s'est fait couper les cheveux.
  > *He had cut his hair.*
  > Il s'était coupé les cheveux.

Verbe à part entière

- Le premier sens plein de *have* est un sens statique : la possession.
  > *He has a phone in his car. Do you have one?*
  > Il a un téléphone dans sa voiture. Et vous ?

- Le deuxième sens plein est dynamique et exprime plusieurs notions équivalentes de :
  - **prendre**
    > *He is having a bath.*
    > Il est en train de prendre un bain.

I had tea at the Joneses' yesterday.
J'ai pris le thé chez les Jones hier.

- **donner**

  We had a party to celebrate Tom's success.
  On a donné une soirée pour célébrer le succès de Tom.

- **faire**

  I have a walk every morning.
  Je fais une promenade à pied tous les matins.
  Shall we have a ride on the moors?
  Et si on prenait le cheval pour aller dans la lande ?

- **recevoir**

  I had a telegram from him.
  J'ai reçu un télégramme de lui.
  I have that picture from my sister.
  C'est de ma sœur que je tiens cette photo.
  I have some trouble with my car.
  J'ai des ennuis avec ma voiture.

- **accepter**

  He won't have it that Paul is guilty.
  Il refuse d'accepter que Paul soit coupable.
  I won't have it!
  Je ne tolérerai pas ça !

● Il peut, comme quelque trois mille verbes à part entière, être accompagné de diverses particules (cf. liste des verbes à particules, p. 177).
  I'll have it out with him as soon as I see him.
  Je mettrai les choses au point avec lui dès que je le verrai.
  They had it in for me from the very beginning.
  Dès le tout début, ils en ont eu contre moi.

Auxiliaire modal

La « coloration » modale (ferme intention, opinion) est encore plus nette dans des tournures comme :
  You'd better apologise to him.
  Tu ferais mieux de t'excuser auprès de lui.
  I'd rather do it myself.
  J'aimerais mieux le faire moi-même.

3. *DO*

Do a cinq formes pleines : *do* pour l'infinitif et le présent (mais *does* à la troisième personne du singulier), *did* au prétérit, *done* au participe passé, *doing* à la forme en -*ing*. Ses formes contractées sont sans ambiguïté : *don't, doesn't, didn't*. Il se partage à peu près également entre son rôle d'auxiliaire et son rôle de verbe à part entière.

Verbe auxiliaire

Do et *did* ne font que marquer le temps et la troisième personne aux formes simples interrogative et négative (cf. tableaux p. 88-89).
> *Does / Did John play the piano?*

Verbe suppléant

● Dans une question ou une réponse, *do* **évite la répétition** du verbe.
> *You speak better than I do. So does she.*
> Vous parlez mieux que moi. Elle aussi.
> *They speak German. Oh, do they?*
> Ils parlent allemand. Vraiment ?
> *She plays the piano, doesn't she?*
> Elle joue du piano, n'est-ce pas ?
> *Does she play well? Yes, she does. / No, she doesn't. / No, she does not.*
> Elle joue bien ? Oui. / Non.

Remarquez que la forme pleine *does not* donne plus de force à la négation. On pourrait traduire par : Oh non !

● *Do* peut prendre une **valeur emphatique**, qui exprime un premier degré de modalité.
> *He <u>did</u> say it.*
> Il l'a bien dit.
> *John <u>does</u> play the piano beautifully.*
> John joue du piano vraiment merveilleusement. (on insiste sur le sens – l'excellence du jeu du pianiste)
> *He owns or <u>did</u> own a piano.*
> Il possède, ou du moins possédait jadis, un piano. (on insiste sur le temps – le passé)

De même avec l'impératif.
> *<u>Do</u> tell him that he'll be welcome.* Dis-lui bien qu'il sera le bienvenu.

Comme vous avez pu le constater dans les exemples, on peut, à l'écrit, souligner *do* et *did* pour bien indiquer qu'il s'agit d'une forme d'insistance. À l'oral, c'est une inflexion de la voix qui les met en valeur.

● *Do* a de nombreux emplois d'usage courant avec le premier sens de « **faire** » en général.
What are you doing?

Ces emplois très variés, peuvent être :
• Transitifs :
Do the meat (couper la viande), *do one's teeth* (se brosser les dents), *do one's hair* (se coiffer), *do one's shoes* (cirer ses chaussures), etc.
• Intransitifs :
I can't do without you. Je ne peux vivre sans toi.
Do as you would be done by. Ne faites pas aux autres ce que vous ne voudriez pas qu'on vous fasse.

Parmi ces emplois, un bon nombre appartiennent à la langue familière : *He's done for!* (Il est fichu !), *You've been done.* (Tu t'es fait avoir.)

N'oubliez pas que le traditionnel *How do you do?* n'est plus une question puisqu'on y répond par la même formule de politesse (à ne pas confondre avec *How are you?* qui attend généralement une réponse comme *I'm fine, thanks...*)

● *Do* et *make*
On dit *do business* mais *make a bargain*, comme nous l'avons observé plus haut. *Do* et *make* sont souvent proches, mais non interchangeables. *Make* exprime plutôt l'activité elle-même, d'une manière concrète, avec le sens original de « fabriquer ». *Do* exprime plutôt le résultat de cette activité.

Comparez :
• *To make money* (gagner de l'argent), *to make mistakes* (faire des fautes), *to make the best of it* (en tirer le meilleur parti), etc.
• *To do one's duty* (faire son devoir), *to do one's best* (faire de son mieux).

Autres emplois

Bien qu'il ne puisse pas être employé comme auxiliaire modal, *do* peut être, comme *be* ou *have*, très prolifique comme verbe à particules (cf. liste, p. 177) et, à ce titre, exprimer une certaine modalité. Voyez par exemple :
I could do with a cup of tea.
Je prendrais bien une tasse de thé.
Well done, Jim!
Bravo, Jim !
It isn't done.
Cela ne se fait pas.

4. LET

Avec *let*, nous nous rapprochons du domaine des verbes ordinaires : son rôle d'auxiliaire est en effet mineur par rapport à ses emplois à part entière et ses possibilités d'association avec des particules pour former de nombreux composés.
Il n'a que trois formes : *let, lets* et *letting*.

Verbe auxiliaire

- *Let* auxiliaire ne sert qu'à former le mode **impératif**.
  > *Let him stay here!*
  > Qu'il reste ici !
  > *Don't let him get out!*
  > Qu'il ne sorte pas !
  > *Let's go to the cinema.*
  > Allons au cinéma.
  > *Let them forget it.*
  > Qu'ils oublient tout cela.

  Il s'agit moins, on le voit, d'un ordre que d'un **conseil**, d'une **suggestion**, d'une **invitation**.

- Très employé à la première personne du pluriel, qui implique celui qui parle dans l'action proposée, *let* est beaucoup plus rare à la première personne du singulier, pour exprimer comme un encouragement qu'on se donnerait à soi-même.
  > *Let me think....*
  > Réfléchissons... Voyons...

  La troisième personne du singulier et du pluriel exprime une sorte de vœu ou parfois un acquiescement, une résignation.

  En somme, on trouve dans toutes ces formes **une valeur modale**, parfois un souhait, plutôt qu'un ordre.
  > *Let them be happy! May they be happy!*
  > Qu'ils soient heureux !

- À la **forme négative**, *let* existe dans un registre littéraire :
  > *Let us not waste our time.*
  > Ne perdons pas notre temps.

  et dans un registre familier avec *do* et *you* :
  > *Don't let me catch you again!*
  > Que je ne t'y reprenne pas !

Verbe à part entière

- Le sens de base de ce **verbe irrégulier** (*let* – *let* – *let*) est « laisser, permettre ».
  Who let you into the house?
  Qui vous a fait entrer dans la maison ?

- De ce sens, on passe à celui de « louer ».
  My house is now to let.
  Ma maison est à louer, maintenant.

  Un emploi intransitif est alors possible.
  A house that would let easily...
  Une maison qui se louerait facilement...

  Le mot existe aussi comme substantif dans :
  I'm looking for a short let for my flat.
  Je cherche à louer mon appartement pour une courte période.

- *Let* garde un peu de son sens impératif, dans par exemple :

  Let me help you.
  Permettez que je vous aide.

  Let me tell you this...
  Laissez-moi vous dire ceci...

  Don't let him go out!
  Ne le laissez pas sortir !

  Let him in!
  Faites entrer !

Locutions verbales

Let est riche d'emplois avec :

- Des adjectifs.
  Let him alone. Laisse-le tranquille.
  Let him loose / free. Libérez-le.

- Des particules (cf. p. 58-73).
  He let the cat out of the bag.
  Il a vendu la mèche.

  The engine let out a cloud of smoke.
  La locomotive cracha un nuage de fumée.

  Don't let me down.
  Ne me laisse pas tomber.

  Don't let on about the meeting.
  Ne dites rien sur cette réunion.

  You don't know what you're letting yourself in for.
  Vous ne savez pas dans quoi vous vous engagez.

A U X I L I A I R E S   M O D A U X

À SAVOIR

Définition

Il s'agit d'une dizaine d'auxiliaires qui, associés aux verbes simples ou composés, réguliers ou irréguliers, expriment la modalité, c'est-à-dire **l'attitude d'esprit de celui qui parle**, autrement dit son humeur (*mood* en anglais).

Comparez :
> *Do you want some tea?*

qui n'est qu'une sèche demande de renseignement, et :
> *Would you like some tea?*

qui exprime plus de chaleur et de sollicitude.

Caractères communs

À la différence de *be, have, do* et *let*, les modaux ne peuvent pas être utilisés seuls comme verbes à part entière.

À ce titre :
- ils ne sont jamais précédés de *to* ;
- ils ne sont suivis que d'un infinitif sans *to* ;
- leur forme interrogative se fait par simple inversion du sujet ;
- ils ne prennent pas de **s** à la troisième personne du singulier ;
- ils ne sont jamais précédés d'un auxiliaire ordinaire.

Peu de formes mais beaucoup de sens

Shall et *should*, *will* et *would*, *can* et *could*, *may* et *might*, *must* et *ought to* : les formes sont relativement peu nombreuses.
Mais les sens et les emplois sont très diversifiés – il y a par exemple deux emplois de *should* – et se recouvrent partiellement d'une forme à l'autre. On n'étudiera que les principaux modaux, en les séparant en trois groupes selon l'attitude de celui qui parle (le « locuteur »).

Shall / should, will / would

Avec ces auxiliaires, on imagine l'action comme si elle était réalisée. Il faudra pourtant distinguer *shall / should*, qui impliquent davantage l'idée d'un devoir à accomplir, et *will / would* qui ont plutôt le sens de « vouloir ». Dans les deux cas, on observera des modalités plus ou moins fortes.

Par exemple *will* est plus fort dans :
I will see him today. Je le verrai aujourd'hui. (sous-entendu : j'en ai la ferme intention)
que dans :
Will you come for a drink? Voulez-vous prendre un verre avec moi ?

Can / could, may / might

L'action paraît alors beaucoup plus libre : tout semble possible. Sa réalisation va dépendre des capacités du sujet, personne ou chose, de l'existence d'une opposition ou d'une autorisation extérieure, ou des circonstances qu'il va rencontrer sur sa route.

Par exemple si on dit :
I may go to England next year.
Il se peut que j'aille en Angleterre l'an prochain.
on est encore incertain, mais moins incertain que si l'on dit :
I might go to England next year.
Il se pourrait que j'aille en Angleterre l'an prochain.

Must, ought to, should, have to, be to

Ici, l'action est placée sous le signe de l'obligation dont la source peut être intérieure ou extérieure au sujet. Nous avons déjà rencontré *have to* et *be to*, p. 15.

Par exemple, quand je dis :
I have to read this book.
c'est parce qu'on me l'a demandé, alors que :
I must read this book.
supposerait que c'est un acte que je m'impose à moi-même.

Yes, but...

- Attention aux formes négative et interrogative : par exemple, la forme négative de *I have to go to England to practise modals* n'est pas *I have not to go* mais *I don't have to go...*

- En français aussi, bien sûr, nous disposons de moyens d'exprimer la modalité. Mais ce sont plus souvent des expressions que de simples auxiliaires. D'où, en anglais, toujours plus de rapidité, mais aussi parfois plus d'ambiguïté.

1. SHALL

Shall ne se rencontre plus qu'assez rarement dans la langue quotidienne actuelle. Ses trois emplois principaux peuvent être classés d'après la modalité qu'ils expriment, dans un ordre croissant.

Simple auxiliaire du futur

> Tomorrow I shall be 25.
> Demain j'aurai 25 ans.

Cet emploi, où shall est contracté en 'll, est réservé à la première personne du singulier et du pluriel. Il se confond aussi avec will, à la forme simple et à la forme continue : We'll be writing to you. (cf. p. 14)

À la forme négative, il devient shall not ou plus souvent shan't.

> We shan't be there before lunch.
> Nous n'y serons pas avant le déjeuner.

Proposition polie

> Shall we dance? Vous dansez ?

Réservé à la forme interrogative, shall traduit, sur un ton poli, une proposition ou une offre d'aide.

> Shall I open the window?
> Voulez-vous que j'ouvre la fenêtre ?
> I'll take three of them, shall I?
> Je vais en prendre trois, d'accord ?

Ordre impérieux ou interdiction formelle

> They shall not pass!
> Ils ne passeront pas !

Cet emploi, un peu archaïque, aux deuxième et troisième personnes du singulier et du pluriel se rencontre souvent dans la Bible.

> Thou (= You) shalt (=shall) not kill.
> Tu ne tueras point.

On le trouve encore aujourd'hui dans des textes de loi.

> The fine shall not exceed £100.
> L'amende ne devra en aucun cas dépasser 100 livres.

Il permet aussi d'exprimer une ferme détermination.

> You shall obey him! (sous-entendu : pas question de ne pas lui obéir !)

2. SHOULD

Should est plus courant et plus complexe. Il peut s'employer à toutes les personnes. Il se contracte en 'd, qu'il ne faut pas confondre avec la contraction de had.

Futur dans le passé

On l'emploie surtout dans les interrogatives indirectes. Comparez :
I don't know when we shall meet again. Je ne sais pas quand on se reverra.
I didn't know when we should meet again. Je ne savais pas quand on se reverrait.

Souhait, conseil, obligation

I should be on holiday by now! Je devrais déjà être en vacances !
I should write to thank them. Je devrais leur écrire pour les remercier.
Shouldn't you go and see her? Est-ce que vous ne devriez pas aller la voir ?

À ces emplois peut s'ajouter l'expression du regret ou du reproche.
I should have written to him. J'aurais dû lui écrire.
They should have told you, shouldn't they? Ils auraient pu te prévenir, non ?

Probabilité (moyenne)

He should win the game. Il devrait gagner la partie.
That shouldn't be John. It's too early. Ce ne devrait pas être John. Il est trop tôt.

Conditionnel

I should / I'd go with you if you invited me.
J'irais avec vous si vous m'invitiez.
I should have gone with you if I had had time.
Je serais allé avec vous si j'avais eu le temps.

Dans ces emplois on pourrait tout aussi bien utiliser *would* au lieu de *should*.
Dans la langue châtiée, en début de phrase, *should* renforce le caractère hypothétique de la situation : *Should he change his mind...* Au cas (peu probable) où il changerait d'avis...

Subjonctif

It is surprising that he should be so ignorant. C'est étonnant qu'il soit si ignorant.
Let's go now, lest he should / for fear that he should change his mind.
Allons-y maintenant, de peur qu'il change d'avis.

3. WILL / WOULD

Will et *would* ont plus de caractères communs que *shall* et *should* et seront étudiés parallèlement.
Will, dans son sens actuel, contient **l'idée de volonté, de désir**.
C'est ainsi qu'on dira de quelqu'un : *He has a strong will*. (Il a une forte volonté.)
Cela se retrouve dans le proverbe : *Where there is a will there is a way*. (Vouloir, c'est pouvoir.)
Ce qui conduit à commencer l'étude par le sens le plus fort.

Volonté, ordre, ferme intention

I will see him today.
Je le verrai aujourd'hui. (sous-entendu : j'y suis décidé)
On insiste en utilisant la forme pleine, que l'on prononce fermement. (Comparez avec : *I'll see him*, qui n'est qu'une forme neutre et indique un simple futur.)

De même pour exprimer un refus :
Little Tom won't go to bed before nine o'clock.
Le jeune Tom refuse de se coucher avant neuf heures.
My car won't start.
Ma voiture refuse de démarrer.

Il existe d'ailleurs un verbe à sens plein, d'un emploi relativement rare : *will* (vouloir) pour dire par exemple : *It is as God wills*. (Comme Dieu le veut.) ou *to will somebody's happiness* (vouloir le bien de quelqu'un).

Au passé, on peut dire :
I called him but he wouldn't answer.
Je l'ai appelé mais il n'a pas voulu répondre.

Invitation, requête

Will you please sit down?
Voulez-vous vous asseoir ?
Won't you come with us?
Et si vous veniez avec nous ?

L'emploi de *would* permettra de se montrer plus poli, plus prévenant.
Would you mind closing the window?
Puis-je vous demander de fermer la fenêtre, s'il vous plaît ?
Would you please sit down?
Veuillez vous asseoir...

Supposition, conjecture

> *She'll be about 70.* Elle doit avoir 70 ans.
> *Who's calling at this time of day? That will be the milkman.*
> Qui frappe à cette heure du jour ? Ce doit être le laitier.
> *It would have been about 10 p.m. when she came.*
> Elle a dû venir vers 10 heures du soir.

Répétition, habitude

● C'est ce qu'on appelle la « forme fréquentative », parfois difficile à rendre en français.
> *Every time I start speaking, she will interrupt me.*
> Chaque fois que je commence à parler, il faut qu'elle m'interrompe.
> *Boys will be boys.*
> Un garçon, c'est toujours un garçon.

N'employez dans ce sens que la forme pleine, pour ne pas confondre avec le simple futur.

● Au passé, faites la différence entre *would* et *used to*.
> *He would smoke a lot, then.*
> À cette époque, il fumait beaucoup.

Would laisse supposer qu'il recommencera peut-être à fumer, alors que *He used to* impliquerait qu'il a sans doute définitivement cessé de fumer.

Les valeurs propres de *would*

● Futur dans le passé.
Comparez :
> *He says that he'll come back.*
> Il dit qu'il reviendra.

> *He said that he'd come back.*
> Il a dit qu'il reviendrait.

● Auxiliaire du conditionnel.
• Présent.
> *He would go with you if you asked him.*
> Il irait avec toi si tu le lui demandais.

• Passé.
> *He would have gone with you if you'd asked him.*
> Il serait allé avec toi si tu le lui avais demandé.

● Pour *would* comme pour *should*, la forme pleine n'est obligatoire que dans les questions et les réponses du type : *Yes, I should... Yes, I would...*

4. CAN / COULD, MAY / MIGHT

Can / could et may / might introduisent l'idée que la réalisation de l'acte envisagé va dépendre soit des **capacités** de la personne ou de la chose, soit des autres à qui on demande une **permission**, à qui on fera une **suggestion**, soit des circonstances, ce qui déterminera une échelle de **probabilités**.

Capacité : can / could

● Au présent et au passé.
> *I could drive for hours before the accident, but now I can't.*
> Je pouvais conduire pendant des heures avant l'accident, mais maintenant je ne peux plus.

● Aux autres temps, on utilise *be able to*.
> *I'll never be able to read all this!* Je ne pourrai jamais lire tout ça !

Au passé, *could* et *be able to* peuvent avoir un sens légèrement différent. Comparez :
> *When I was young, I could drive for hours...*
> Quand j'étais jeune je pouvais conduire pendant des heures....
>
> *...but yesterday I wasn't able to drive for more than one hour.*
> ...mais hier je n'ai pas réussi à conduire pendant plus d'une heure.

Dans la première phrase, *could* exprime plutôt une capacité permanente, tandis que dans la deuxième, il s'agit d'une circonstance particulière, à un moment donné.

● Ces auxiliaires sont particulièrement employés :
• Avec les verbes de perception.
> *Can you hear me?* se traduit simplement par : Vous m'entendez ?

• Pour exprimer un savoir-faire.
> *She can speak Italian.* Elle parle l'italien.

● Retenons enfin que la forme négative peut exprimer une impossibilité ou un fait hautement improbable.
> *He can't be dead!* C'est impossible ! Il n'est pas mort !

Permission : can / could / may / might

● Au présent, ils s'emploient pour demander une permission, selon la progression suivante : *can < could < may < might*. Comparez :
> *Can I / could I / may I borrow your book?* Je peux / Pourrais-je / Puis-je t'emprunter ton livre ?

Might, lui, s'emploie avec le sens de permission seulement :
• Au style indirect pour rappeler des paroles passées.
> *He said you might borrow his book.* Il a dit que tu pouvais emprunter son livre.

- Pour exprimer un excès de politesse teinté d'ironie.
    Might I borrow your book? Pourrais-tu me faire l'honneur de me prêter ton livre ?

● Au passé et au présent, on pourra utiliser l'équivalent *be allowed to*, avec encore une fois une nuance.
    When I was younger I could stay up until 10 o'clock.
    Quand j'étais jeune, j'avais le droit de veiller jusqu'à 10 heures.
    Yesterday I was allowed to stay up until midnight.
    Hier soir, j'ai eu le droit de veiller jusqu'à minuit.

Ici encore, l'équivalent *be allowed to* insiste plus sur le caractère circonstanciel, momentané, de la modalité.

● Dans les autres cas, seul un équivalent est possible.
    I don't know if he'll be allowed to / if he'll have the right to come.
    Je ne sais pas s'il aura le droit de venir.

Attention : si la forme négative *can't* peut exprimer un refus, la forme négative de *may* ou *could* serait *mustn't*.
    You can't / mustn't come.
    Je t'interdis de venir.

Suggestion : *can / could / might*

    We can / could go to the cinema.
    Nous pouvons / pourrions aller au cinéma.
Les deux formulations sont à peu près équivalentes, mais *could* est plus courant.

Can et *could* peuvent s'accompagner d'une vraie hypothèse.
    We can go to the cinema, if you feel like going out.
    Nous pouvons aller au cinéma, si tu as envie de sortir.

Might peut laisser planer un léger doute.
    We might go to the cinema... (Peut-être pourrait-on...)

Probabilité : *can / could / may / might*

● *Can, could, may* et *might* permettent une gradation du plus au moins probable selon l'appréciation de celui qui parle.
    He can win the game : il a toutes les chances de gagner la partie.
    He could win the game : pourquoi pas, mais cela va dépendre.
    He may win the game : ce n'est pas exclu.
    He might win the game : il y a vraiment peu de chances.

● Si l'appréciation porte sur une action en cours, ils sont suivis de la forme en *-ing*.
    He can / could / may / might be working.

● Au passé : *He can / could / may / might have missed his bus.*

5. OUGHT TO / MUST / NEED / DARE

Avec ces modaux, la réalisation de l'acte paraît obligée. Cette **obligation** peut venir du sujet lui-même, ou des autres, ou encore d'une loi morale supérieure. Il n'est donc pas étonnant que ces auxiliaires expriment aussi des degrés de probabilité plus élevés.

Obligation : *ought to / must*

> *I ought to write to my father.*
> Je devrais écrire à mon père.

Le sens est proche de : *I should write* (cf. p. 37).

- Pour exprimer une nécessité plus forte, on aura recours à *must*, **au présent**, si elle est **d'origine interne**.
  > *I must read this book.*
  > Il faut que je lise ce livre.
  > (sous-entendu : c'est un acte que je m'impose à moi-même, j'en ai décidé ainsi)

- Si cette nécessité **vient de l'extérieur**, on utilisera un équivalent comme *have to*.
  > *I have to read this book.* (sous-entendu : parce qu'on me l'a demandé).

- *Have (got) to, be to, be obliged to* sont des formules presque équivalentes qui peuvent servir à d'autres temps que le présent.

Attention ! Il y a deux réponses possibles à la question : *Do you think I must wait for her?*
> *No, you don't have to (wait).* ou *No, you needn't (wait).*
> Non, ce n'est pas nécessaire.
> *No, you mustn't.*
> Non, je te l'interdis.

Probabilité

- Pour exprimer une probabilité moyenne, il existe un deuxième emploi de *ought to*.
  > *They ought to be here soon.*
  > Ils devraient bientôt arriver.

- Si l'on emploie *must*, il s'agit même d'une quasi-certitude.
  > *It must be very cold outside.*
  > Il fait certainement très froid dehors.

La forme négative serait : *It can't be cold outside* (c'est impossible qu'il fasse froid...).

- Au passé :
  > *He must have borrowed this book from Jane.*
  > Il a certainement emprunté ce livre à Jane.

- Il existe un nom correspondant à ce sens.
  > *This book is a must.*
  > Il faut absolument lire ce livre.

Need et *dare*

Ils ont tous les deux un emploi modal et un emploi à part entière.

- L'emploi de *need* modal est limité en anglais moderne aux seules formes négative et interrogative.
  > *You needn't wait for me.*
  > Inutile de m'attendre.
  > *Need I wait for you?*
  > Faut-il que je t'attende ?

- *Need*, verbe ordinaire, régulier, a le sens de « avoir besoin ».
  > *I don't need to read this.*
  > Je n'ai bas besoin de lire ceci.
  > *This car needs to be repaired / needs repairing.*
  > Cette voiture a besoin d'une réparation.
  > *When I needed some advice, I always called him.*
  > Quand j'avais besoin d'un conseil, je l'appelais toujours.

- *Dare* modal obéit aux mêmes usages, avec le sens de « oser ».
  > *How dare you say such things?*
  > Comment osez-vous dire des choses pareilles ?
  > *How dare you!*
  > Vous avez du culot !
  > *I dare not speak to him.*
  > Je n'ose lui adresser la parole.

- Comme verbe ordinaire, régulier, *dare* peut être suivi de l'infinitif avec ou sans *to*.
  > *I don't dare (to) go alone.*
  > Je n'ose pas y aller seul.
  > *I dare say she's about 40.*
  > Je lui donne dans les 40 ans.

AUXILIAIRES MODAUX

Modalités	Shall	Should	Will	Would
Suggestion, invitation	Shall we dance?		Will you please sit down?	Would you please sit down?
Interdiction	They shall not pass!		You will speak to nobody!	
Conseil, souhait, obligation		I should write to them.		
Probabilité plus ou moins grande		He should win the game.		
Impossibilité, fait très improbable				
Volonté, ferme intention			I will see him today.	He wouldn't answer.
Supposition, conjecture			That <u>will</u> be the milkman.	It would have been about 10.
Répétition, habitude, forme fréquentative			He will talk for hours.	He would smoke a lot then.
Capacité				
Permission				

Ce tableau ne reprend que les principaux exemples d'emplois des dix principales modalités analysées.

Can	Could	May	Might	Ought to	Must
We can go to the cinema.	We could go to the cinema.		We might go to the cinema.		
					You mustn't smoke here.
				I ought to write to them.	I must read this book. (ou have to)
He can win the game.	He could be working.	He may have won the game.	He might win the game.	They ought to be there soon.	He must be reading your book.
He can't be dead!					
I can drive. (ou am able to)	I could drive for hours.				
Can I borrow your book? (ou Am I allowed to)	Could I borrow your book?	May I borrow your book?	He said you might borrow it.		

Observez les modalités les plus nuancées et les auxiliaires les plus sollicités. Une richesse qui ne va pas sans ambiguïté.

À SAVOIR

La moitié des verbes anglais sont beaucoup plus riches de sens qu'il ne le paraissent. Comment en profiter ?

Richesse d'un seul verbe

● Prenons, un verbe très courant, comme *go*. Il peut signifier :
 • se déplacer
   We've gone three miles from the station.
   Nous avons fait cinq kilomètres depuis la gare.
 • évoluer
   How are things going at the sea-side?
   Comment ça va au bord de la mer ?
 • convenir
   These colours don't go with your new shoes.
   Ces couleurs jurent avec tes nouvelles chaussures.

Observons-le maintenant au centre d'un « carrefour » de phrases possibles et cherchons-en le sens, en commençant par *when*.

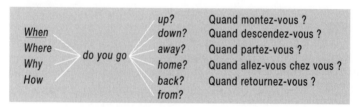

When		*up?*	Quand montez-vous ?
Where	*do you go*	*down?*	Quand descendez-vous ?
Why		*away?*	Quand partez-vous ?
How		*home?*	Quand allez-vous chez vous ?
		back?	Quand retournez-vous ?
		from?	

● Même si toutes les combinaisons ne sont pas possibles (on ne peut poser la question ~~When do you go from?~~), les sens du verbe se multiplient grâce à l'association de petits mots invariables.
À l'origine, ce sont le plus souvent des adverbes comme *out*, ou des prépositions comme *from*, mais parfois aussi des noms comme *home*, ou des adjectifs. Par souci de simplification, nous les appellerons ici **particules**.

Certains verbes, très « prolifiques », peuvent s'associer ainsi à dix, vingt particules différentes pour former des *phrasal verbs* ou « verbes à particules ». Richesse d'autant plus grande que chaque association peut avoir parfois plusieurs acceptions !

Richesse de trois mille verbes

À côté de *go*, existent de nombreux verbes de mouvement comparables, comme *walk* (marcher), *move* (se mouvoir), *glide* (glisser), *flow* (couler), etc. Ils sont prêts à s'associer avec à peu près les mêmes particules.

> *He shuffled back to his bed.*
> Il regagna son lit en traînant des pieds.

Sur plus de six mille verbes que compte la langue anglaise, environ trois mille, particulièrement productifs, peuvent s'associer chacun à cinq, dix, vingt, voire plus de trente particules différentes, si bien que l'ensemble des « verbes à particules » ainsi formés atteint un total d'une douzaine de mille.

Comment les utiliser ?

Devant un tel foisonnement de sens, il ne faut ni se « jeter à l'eau » en espérant deviner le sens juste, ni recourir systématiquement au dictionnaire.

Nous proposons plutôt l'approche suivante :
– apprendre à reconnaître les verbes « de base » (cf. la liste, page 115) ;
– étudier de plus près une dizaine de verbes parmi les plus utiles et les plus « prolifiques » : leur sens de base, les particules avec lesquelles ils s'associent le plus souvent, et quelques expressions idiomatiques courantes mais pas toujours prévisibles ;
– étudier particulièrement une dizaine de particules parmi les plus usuelles : nature, fonction, place, ainsi que quelques expressions idiomatiques.

L'immense terrain occupé par ces verbes ne saurait être entièrement couvert, mais au moins ces indications vous aideront-elles à ne pas vous perdre.

1. BE

Le verbe de base

Nous avons étudié *be* comme « auxiliaire » et « suppléant » (cf. p. 26-27). Nous avons observé qu'il est aussi un verbe à part entière. Dans cet emploi, c'est le verbe d'état par excellence, qu'on peut rapprocher de verbes comme *appear, become, feel, look*, etc.

Les particules

● *Be* compte donc parmi les verbes pouvant s'associer à un grand nombre de particules qui lui donnent son dynamisme. Les dictionnaires spécialisés dénombrent un très grand nombre de cas. Les autres classent plus souvent les expressions avec chaque particule, puisqu'elles conservent avec *be* leur sens propre. L'ordre de fréquence est à peu près le suivant.

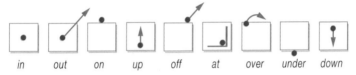

in   out   on   up   off   at   over   under   down

● La particule a parfois une valeur adverbiale.
Is the nail in?   *The tide is out.*
Le clou est-il enfoncé ?   C'est marée basse.

● Elle a parfois aussi une valeur prépositionnelle.
Is she on a diet? On the pill?
Est-ce qu'elle suit un régime ? Est-ce qu'elle prend la pilule ?

● Parfois adverbe et préposition s'associent.
It's up to me.   *Be off with you!*
Cela dépend de moi.   Allez-vous-en !

Expressions idiomatiques

That's him all over.   *Why are you down on me?*
C'est tout-à-fait lui.   Pourquoi m'en voulez-vous?

It's all over with him.   *He's beyond caring.*
Il est fichu.   Il ne s'en fait plus du tout.

He's always at her.   *He is under the water.*
Il la harcèle sans cesse.   Il n'est pas très bien en ce moment.

2. STAND

Le verbe de base

Stand est aussi un verbe de position. Il exprime l'idée d'« être » mais la prolonge : c'est « être debout », « s'élever », « se dresser », « se maintenir » pour les êtres vivants et pour les choses, au propre et au figuré, aux emplois transitif et intransitif.

He stood the child on the chair.
Il a mis l'enfant debout sur la chaise.

The child has learnt to stand now.
L'enfant sait se tenir debout maintenant.

Les particules

Comme pour *be*, chacune d'elles greffe sur le verbe son sens propre pour préciser la position ou suggérer un mouvement.

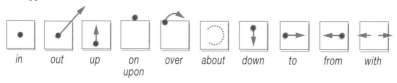

in out up on upon over about down to from with

To, from et *with* servent souvent à préciser un mouvement par rapport à quelqu'un ou quelque chose d'autre. Toutes les autres particules – auxquelles on peut ajouter *by, off* et *for* – sont utilisables à peu près à égalité d'emploi.

They stood up when he came in.
Ils se sont levés quand il est entré.

He stood down in her favour.
Il s'est désisté en sa faveur.

His figure stood out on the landscape.
Sa silhouette se détachait du paysage.

He stands up for human rights.
Il défend les droits de l'homme.

He won't do anything good if I don't stand over him.
Il ne fera rien de bon si je ne suis pas sur son dos.

All the soldiers are standing by.
Tous les soldats sont en état d'alerte.

Expressions idiomatiques

If he hits you again, stand up to him!
S'il te frappe encore, fais-lui face !

She stood me up.
Elle m'a posé un lapin.

I doubt very much that her story will stand up to questioning.
Je ne suis pas du tout sûr que son histoire tiendra si on l'interroge.

Notons au passage des noms composés comme *a stand-in* (un remplaçant, une doublure), ou *a standby* (une personne sur qui on peut compter).

3. GO

Le verbe de base

Go a deux familles de sens plutôt dynamiques.

- L'une est de valeur concrète : « aller », « se rendre à », « fonctionner ».

  We've gone three miles. *How are things going?*
  Nous avons fait cinq kilomètres. Comment ça va ?

- L'autre est de valeur abstraite, figurée : « convenir », « devenir ».

  These colours don't go. *He's going bald.*
  Ces couleurs jurent. Il devient chauve.

Les particules

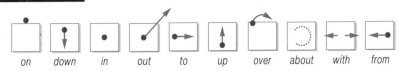

| on | down | in | out | to | up | over | about | with | from |

Les emplois les plus nombreux se font avec *on* et *down* qui soulignent la continuité, l'inflexion ou l'arrêt d'un mouvement, au propre et au figuré.

What's going on here? *Work goes with success.*
Qu'est-ce qui se passe ici ? Le travail va de pair avec le succès.

The idea didn't go down well. *She goes about with a soldier.*
L'idée n'a pas été bien reçue. Elle sort avec un soldat.

On trouve aussi, associés à *go*, d'assez nombreux adjectifs ou noms qui jouent ainsi le rôle de particules.

go bad : mal finir *go easy* : y aller doucement
go slow : faire une grève perlée *go halves* : partager

Expressions idiomatiques

That won't go down with me. *Go for it!*
Ça ne prendra pas avec moi. Fonce !

He's going in for president. *Will he go up?*
Il est candidat à la présidence. Va-t-il passer dans la classe supérieure ?

He went out when he saw the blood. *And then the balloon went up.*
À la vue du sang, il perdit conscience. Et c'est alors que les ennuis ont commencé.

She's going all out in her studies.
Elle se donne à fond dans ses études.

4. *COME*

Le verbe de base

Come a essentiellement un sens dynamique, propre (venir, arriver) et figuré (devenir).

Come and have a drink!
Viens prendre un verre !

To come and go.
Aller et venir.

Come to think of it, you're right.
Tout bien pesé, tu as raison.

Come what may.
Advienne que pourra.

Les particules

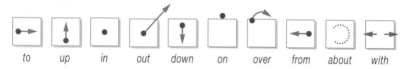

| to | up | in | out | down | on | over | from | about | with |

- Très nombreuses sont les associations avec quatre particules de mouvement : *to, up, out* et *down*, aux sens propre et figuré, avec des particules adverbiales ou prépositionnelles, et assez souvent les deux successivement.

  Please come up to me.
  Montez me rejoindre, s'il vous plaît.

  How did the issue come up in the first place?
  D'abord, comment se fait-il que la question soit venue sur le tapis ?

  He often comes up with good ideas.
  Il sort souvent de bonnes idées.

- Peu d'emplois avec les autres particules. Citons cependant :
  Tell me how it all came about. Explique-moi comment tout ça s'est produit.

- À noter ici encore l'usage assez fréquent de noms ou d'adjectifs jouant le rôle de particules adverbiales.

  come alive : s'animer
  come good : bien finir malgré tout
  come true : se réaliser

  come home : « redescendre sur terre »
  come full circle : changer complètement d'avis

Expressions idiomatiques

She came down with the flu.
Elle a attrapé la grippe.

Your idea came in handy.
Votre idée s'est avérée utile.

Come off it!
À d'autres ! Mon œil !

Come on!
Tu plaisantes !

À noter un nom composé : *a comeback* (un retour sur scène) qui est passé en français.

5. RUN

Run a une dizaine de sens différents, tous dynamiques, aussi bien comme intransitif que comme transitif. À côté du sens premier de « courir », on trouve ceux de « fonctionner » et « faire fonctionner ».

He left the engine running.
Il a laissé tourner le moteur.

They're running a new bus line.
Ils ont ouvert une nouvelle ligne d'autobus.

Dans un contexte politique plutôt américain, on trouvera :

They plan to run two candidates.
Ils ont l'intention de présenter deux candidats.

He's running for president.
Il se présente à la présidence.

Les particules

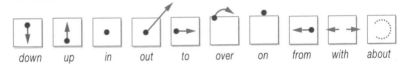

| down | up | in | out | to | over | on | from | with | about |

Elles n'ont pas beaucoup à apporter sauf dans les sens figurés.

There's no need to run all my ideas down.
Ce n'est pas la peine de dénigrer toutes mes idées.

Running in.
En rodage.

He runs himself to death.
Il se tue à force de travail.

The price of coffee is running up.
Le prix du café s'envole.

Time is running out.
Il nous reste peu de temps.

She runs to fat.
Elle se laisse grossir.

Expressions idiomatiques

I'll run over to her soon.
Je ferai bientôt un saut chez elle.

Last time I saw her she ran on at great length about herself.
La dernière fois que je l'ai vue, elle n'en finissait pas de parler d'elle.

But I didn't let my temper run away with me.
Mais j'ai su me dominer.

Well, I'll run off a short letter to her.
Bien, je lui enverrai un mot en vitesse.

6. FALL

Le verbe de base

Fall exprime évidemment, au sens propre, un mouvement vers le bas, une chute. Au sens figuré, il évoque une sorte de commencement.

I'm going to fall asleep.
Je vais m'endormir.

He fell silent.
Il se tut.

Les particules

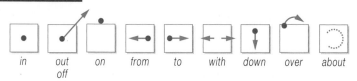

On peut ajouter à ces particules, à la place de up, des mots comme away, back ou behind.

- In peut avoir une valeur adverbiale aussi bien que prépositionnelle, au sens propre et au sens figuré.

  The roof has fallen in.
  Le toit s'est effondré.

  His cheeks have fallen in.
  Ses joues se sont creusées.

  She fell in love with him immediately.
  Elle est immédiatement tombée amoureuse de lui.

- Fall out n'exprime pas seulement une sorte de chute, de retombée. Il rend aussi l'idée d'arriver, de devenir.

  Everything fell out as we had hoped.
  Tout s'est passé comme nous l'espérions.

- Les emplois avec on sont multiples, selon le lieu de la « chute ».

  He always seems to fall on his feet.
  Il semble toujours retomber sur ses pieds.

  He fell on his knees and thanked God.
  Il tomba à genoux et remercia Dieu.

Expressions idiomatiques

Most married people fall out over money.
La plupart des couples ont des querelles d'argent.

He fell for her immediately.
Il tomba amoureux d'elle immédiatement.

All the guests fell about when he told them his story.
Tous les invités éclatèrent de rire quand il leur raconta son histoire.

7. TAKE

Le verbe de base

Les sens issus de *take* (prendre) sont nombreux. Citons :
- mener
  He'll take you to the station. Il vous conduira à la gare.
- consommer
  Do you take sugar in your tea? Vous mettez du sucre dans votre thé ?
- utiliser
  It takes two people to do this job. Il faut deux personnes pour faire ce travail.
- soustraire
  Take two from six... Six moins deux...
- occuper
  Take a seat, please. Asseyez-vous, s'il vous plaît.
- choisir
  What are you taking next year, maths or physics?
  Tu choisis quoi, l'an prochain, les maths ou la physique ?
- contenir
  This bus takes 50 people. Ce bus a une capacité de 50 personnes.

Les particules

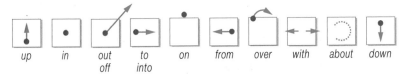

| up | in | out off | to into | on | from | over | with | about | down |

Pour mieux prendre conscience de la diversité des sens, regardons de plus près *take up*.

Who will take breakfast up to your mother?
Qui montera le petit-déjeuner à ta mère ?

When did you first take up golf?
Quand t'es-tu mis au golf ?

All the children took up the song.
Tous les enfants ont repris en chœur.

I'll take you up on that.
Je vous prends au mot.

Expressions idiomatiques

Shall we take in Eton?
On passe par Eton ?

Don't take it out on me!
Ne t'en prends pas à moi !

I think people will take to the streets.
Je pense que les gens vont descendre dans la rue.

Noms composés : *takeaway food* (plats préparés), *the take-home pay* (le salaire net).

8. *GET*

Le verbe de base

● Verbe transitif, *get* a de nombreux sens issus du premier : « obtenir ».
Did you get the bread? Tu as acheté le pain ?

● Le plus remarquable est dit « causatif ».
I must get my hair cut. Je dois me faire couper les cheveux.

● Comme intransitif, il a souvent un sens « résultatif ».
He's getting old. Il vieillit.

Les particules

Elles sont nombreuses à s'accrocher à ce verbe, exprimant des mouvements divers et abstraits.

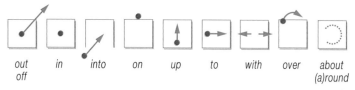

out	in	into	on	up	to	with	over	about
off								(a)round

She must have got out of bed on the wrong side.
Elle a dû se lever du pied gauche.
The scandal has got out.
Le scandale a éclaté.
He got off with a fine.
Il s'en est tiré avec une amende.
I couldn't get a word in.
Je n'ai pas pu placer un mot.
They got into trouble.
Ils se sont attiré des ennuis.

The car had difficulty getting up the slope.
La voiture n'arrivait pas à monter la pente.
I can't get over the fact that he got through.
Je n'en reviens pas qu'il ait réussi.
Let's get down to work.
Mettons-nous au travail.
She knows how to get (a)round people.
Elle sait s'y prendre avec les gens.

Expressions idiomatiques

He's always getting at me.
Il ne cesse de s'en prendre à moi.
He's getting on for 50.
Il approche la cinquantaine.

He's always getting up to mischief.
Il ne peut s'empêcher de faire des bêtises.
I'll get my own back on him.
Je lui rendrai la monnaie de sa pièce.

Encore quelques noms composés : *the getaway* (la fuite), *a get-together* (une réunion).

9. PUT

Put n'a le plus souvent que le sens de « poser », « mettre ».
> *He put a lot of money in real estate.*
> Il a placé beaucoup d'argent dans l'immobilier.

Le sens peut aussi être figuré.
> *How shall I put it?*   *Let's put it he is innocent.*
> Comment dire ?   Mettons qu'il soit innocent.

Out, que l'on peut associer à *off*, de même que *in* et *up* sont de loin les plus fréquentes. *From, over, about* sont quasi absentes, remplacées par *away, back* et *through*.

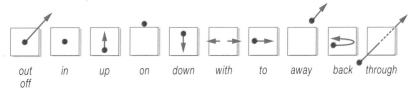

out   in   up   on   down   with   to   away   back   through
off

> *Don't forget to put out / off the fire.*
> N'oublie pas d'éteindre le feu.
>
> *She's always putting herself out for them.*
> Elle se met toujours en quatre pour eux.
>
> *Put it off till tomorrow.*
> Remets ça à demain.
>
> *My accident put me off swimming.*
> Mon accident m'a dégoûté de la natation.
>
> *"He's loyal," she put in.*
> « Il est loyal, » fit-elle remarquer.
>
> *Posters have been put up all over the town.*
> On a collé des affiches dans toute la ville.

> *The argument he put up is not valid.*
> L'argument qu'il a avancé ne tient pas.
>
> *Can you put on the light?*
> Peux-tu allumer ?
>
> *Don't put on an English accent.*
> Ne fais pas semblant d'avoir l'accent anglais.
>
> *I put down my name for the mixed doubles.*
> Je me suis inscrit pour le double mixte.
>
> *He put his mistake down to overwork.*
> Il a attribué sa faute au surmenage.

> *I won't put up with this!*   *Can you put me up for the night?*
> Je ne le tolérerai pas !   Vous pouvez me loger pour la nuit ?

10. SET

Le verbe de base

Set peut être considéré comme terminant une série d'actes. Comparez : *get* (obtenir une chose), *take* (la prendre), *put* (la mettre quelque part) et enfin *set* (l'installer).

Au sens propre :

My village is set on the top of a hill.
Mon village est situé au sommet de la colline.

She had her hair set.
Elle s'est fait faire une mise en plis.

Au sens figuré, *set* a parfois une valeur causative.
It set me thinking. Cela m'a donné à réfléchir.

Les particules

Elles ne modifient pas beaucoup le sens premier, déjà « fixé » (*set*), mais elles le précisent ou l'infléchissent.

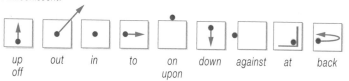

| up off | out | in | to | on upon | down | against | at | back |

He set up in business in Liverpool.
Il a monté une affaire à Liverpool.

They set up house together.
Ils se sont mis en ménage.

The dress does not set off her eyes.
Cette robe ne met pas ses yeux en valeur.

Come before winter sets in.
Viens avant que l'hiver ne s'installe.

They set to with their fists.
Ils en sont venus aux mains.

Shall I set you down at the corner?
Je vous dépose au coin de la rue ?

Set it down on my account.
Mettez ça sur mon compte.

Set on, quant à lui, entre dans de nombreuses expressions.

Set something on foot.
Faire démarrer.

Set one's hands on something.
Prendre possession de quelque chose.

Expressions idiomatiques

It's no use her setting her cap on him: he's only set on his work.
Elle a bien tort d'essayer de vouloir mettre le grappin sur lui : il ne s'intéresse qu'à son travail.

He'll never set the Thames on fire. Il n'a pas inventé la poudre.

VERBES À PARTICULES
LES PARTICULES
●●●

À SAVOIR

Ces petits mots (ou groupes de mots), associés à un grand nombre de verbes, forment de multiples expressions verbales (*phrasal verbs*), de sens très variés.

Nature de la particule

- Elle peut être un adverbe.
  I can't put the lid on, the box is too full.
  Je ne peux pas mettre le couvercle, la boîte est trop pleine.

- Ce peut être une préposition, qui donc introduit un complément.
  Put the plates gently on the table, please.
  Mettez les assiettes doucement sur la table, je vous prie.

- Le même verbe peut être suivi d'un adverbe, puis d'une préposition.
  I know who put him up to cheating. Je sais qui l'a poussé à tricher.

- La particule peut être aussi, mais plus rarement, un pronom comme *it*, qui devient donc ainsi une sorte d'adverbe.
  He took it out on John.   *He lords it.*
  Il s'est défoulé sur John.   Il agit en maître.

- Ce peut être encore un adjectif, ou un nom.
  I hope my dreams will come true. J'espère que mes rêves se réaliseront.
  When will you phone home? Quand téléphoneras-tu chez toi ?

- Le verbe, enfin, peut être suivi de plusieurs mots, traditionnellement associés, et former des « idiomatismes ».
  He has a tendency to get above himself.
  Il a tendance à avoir une trop bonne opinion de lui-même.
  Silence fell when the subject got beyond a joke.
  Le silence se fit quand le sujet devint trop sérieux pour en plaisanter.

La fonction la plus apparente et la plus commune de la particule est de **dynamiser** le verbe de base.

- Elle le dynamise d'autant plus nettement que le sens de ce verbe est plus vague. C'est le cas, par exemple, de *get*, avec lequel elle prend son sens plein.

  He got up at ten o'clock.　　　　　　　*He got on the chair and jumped.*
  Il se leva à dix heures.　　　　　　　　Il monta sur la chaise et sauta.

  I'll get off at the next stop.
  Je descendrai (du train, du métro, de l'autobus, etc.) au prochain arrêt.

- Lorsque le verbe est déjà porteur d'une idée de mouvement, celui-ci est précisé par la particule. C'est le cas, par exemple, de *drive*, de *walk* ou de *jump*.

  He first drove to the station, then (drove) away, then (drove) back and finally decided to drive home.
  D'abord il roula vers la gare, s'en éloigna, revint en arrière et enfin décida de revenir chez lui.

- Elle peut même transformer un verbe de position en verbe de mouvement.

  I'll lie down for a while. Je vais m'allonger un moment.

- Quelques verbes formés à partir du nom d'un objet n'existent pas sans particule.

  The boat keeled over. Le bateau chavira. (*a keel* = une quille)

- Avec un verbe intransitif, la particule se place presque toujours immédiatement après le verbe.

  Come in and sit down. Entrez et asseyez-vous.

  Parfois elle se place en tête de phrase, pour insister sur la rapidité du mouvement.

  Off we go. Et nous voilà partis.

- Avec un verbe transitif, il convient de faire la différence entre particule adverbiale et particule prépositionnelle.

  • Particule adverbiale.
  Si le complément est un groupe nominal court, on la trouve soit avant, soit après.

  Bring up the chair. Bring the chair up. Remonte la chaise.

  Si le complément est un pronom, elle est toujours placée après.

  Bring it up. Remonte-la.

  Elle ne peut se trouver séparée du verbe par un complément long.

  Bring up the chair that you put yesterday in the garden.
  Remonte la chaise que tu as mise hier dans le jardin.

  • Particule prépositionnelle.
  Elle se place évidemment avant le complément, sauf dans une proposition relative et à la forme interrogative.

  This is the person (whom) I brought the chair for.　　*Who(m) shall I give the chair to?*
  Voici la personne pour qui j'ai apporté la chaise.　　À qui vais-je donner la chaise ?

À LA RECHERCHE DU SENS

Complexité

Ce qui rend la recherche du sens plus difficile, c'est que les particules peuvent non seulement caractériser un mouvement ou un état, mais se rapporter à des êtres animés aussi bien qu'à des objets, et donner au verbe un sens concret, propre, ou un sens abstrait, figuré. Il faut donc essayer de repérer, d'après le contexte, dans quelle direction fonctionne la particule.

Le fonctionnement le plus simple

Ce n'est pas tant le verbe que le rôle de la particule qui pose problème. On donnera donc la priorité à celle-ci en traduisant d'abord le résultat de l'action exprimée par la particule. On traduira ensuite le verbe qui décrit la manière dont l'action est accomplie.

Les idiomatismes

● Dans l'usage, la fonction dynamisante de la particule n'est pas toujours clairement reconnaissable. Les dictionnaires généraux, selon leur ambition, donnent, à la suite de chaque verbe ordinaire, une liste d'emplois avec telle ou telle particule. Il existe aussi plusieurs dictionnaires spécialisés dans les *Phrasal Verbs*. Seul le recours à ces ouvrages permettra d'élucider le sens de certains verbes à particule : si le sens de *go up* est évident, auriez-vous pu deviner, par exemple, celui de *make up* ?

> *She spends a lot of time making herself up.*
> Elle passe beaucoup de temps à se maquiller.
>
> *He's made up the whole story.*
> Il a inventé toute l'histoire.
>
> *We'll have to make up for lost time.*
> Il nous faudra rattraper le temps perdu.
>
> *Let's make it up!*
> Si on faisait la paix ?
>
> *Make up your mind.*
> Décide-toi.

- Nous avons retenu dix particules très fréquentes, qui feront l'objet d'une étude détaillée dans les pages suivantes. Les voici dans leur ordre de fréquence : 1. *up*, 2. *out*, 3. *in*, 4. *down*, 5. *on*, 6. *over*, 7. *with*, 8. *to*, 9. *from*, 10. *about / (a)round*.

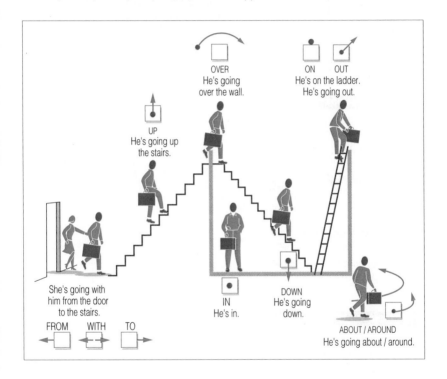

- Pour les vingt autres particules les plus fréquentes, cf. p. 72.

1. UP

Up exprime le plus souvent un mouvement, dans le sens concret vers le haut, ou une position « en hauteur », pour les êtres vivants comme pour les choses. Dans les sens abstraits et figurés, il s'agit plutôt de mouvements ou de positions approchant d'un paroxysme, de la perfection, de l'achèvement d'une action.

He threw the ball up. Il a jeté la balle en l'air.
He drove up the street. Il remonta la rue en voiture.

Les associations

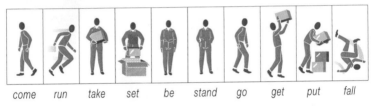

come   run   take   set   be   stand   go   get   put   fall

I like watching the sun come up.
J'aime voir le soleil se lever.

He's quite taken up with her.
Il ne pense qu'à elle.

The ship has run up the red flag.
Le navire a hissé le drapeau rouge.

I'll take that up with him.
Je lui en parlerai.

Expressions idiomatiques

Don't try to come up!
N'essaie pas de faire le malin !

It's up to you to decide.
C'est à toi de décider.

What is he up to?
Qu'est-ce qu'il fabrique ?

He's up to no good.
Il prépare quelque sottise.

I don't feel up to it.
Je ne m'en sens pas le courage.

He's well up in grammar.
Il connaît à fond la grammaire.

Cette particule est si robuste qu'elle peut même assumer le rôle d'un verbe à elle toute seule.
I upped and told her what I thought of her.
Sans plus attendre, je lui dis ce que je pensais d'elle.

Retenez le nom composé *setup*, qui signifie « situation » ou « installation ».
I don't like that setup at all.
Je n'aime pas du tout l'allure de tout ça.

Programme setup.
Installation du logiciel.

2. OUT

Au propre comme au figuré, *out* apporte l'idée de « dehors », de « à l'extérieur ».

The ball is out.
La balle est sortie du terrain.

He lives out of town.
Il ne vit pas en ville.

Out with it!
Dis ce que tu as à dire !

He feels out of it.
Il se sent en marge.

Les associations

get   put   set   fall   be   stand   take   come   go   run

- Elles se font surtout avec les verbes rendant compte de positions et de mouvements de personnes ou de choses, en particulier *get*.

The news has just got out.
La nouvelle vient de paraître.

That wasn't what I set out to do.
Ce n'est pas ce que je voulais faire initialement.

- Les sens sont nombreux avec *be*.

The secret is out.
On a vendu la mèche.

We've run out of petrol.
On est tombés à court d'essence.

Our apple tree is out.
Notre pommier est en fleurs.

It came out that he was penniless.
Il s'avéra qu'il était sans le sou.

Expressions idiomatiques

L'expression *fall out*, par exemple, a de quoi surprendre. À côté du sens de « retombée nucléaire », elle a le sens de « se passer », « arriver », « avoir pour résultat ».

It so fell out that they were not to meet again.
Il se trouva qu'ils ne devaient plus se rencontrer.

Fall out a aussi le sens de « se quereller ».

They fall out every two weeks but their quarrels never last.
Ils se font une scène tous les quinze jours mais leurs disputes ne durent jamais.

On retrouve ce mot comme préfixe dans de nombreux composés : *outdated* (suranné), *outlive* (survivre), etc. (cf. p. 75).

3. IN

Sens de base

- Avec *in*, il s'agit surtout de décrire des positions à l'intérieur d'un lieu, d'une période, de circonstances.

  Is there somebody in? Il y a quelqu'un ?
  Come in! / Get in! Entrez !

- Il y a beaucoup d'emplois au figuré.
  We're in the money. Nous sommes riches.

Les associations

| be | stand | fall | take | get | put | come | go | run | set |

- Il n'est pas étonnant de voir cette particule le plus souvent utilisée avec les verbes de position *be* et *stand*, ainsi qu'avec *fall*.
  I fall in very well with your plans. Votre décision cadre avec mes projets.

- Autres exemples :

  I wasn't in on it.
  Je n'étais pas dans le coup.

  The train is in.
  Le train est en gare.

  We took in Stratford on our way home.
  Nous avons visité Stratford au retour.

  He didn't take in the situation.
  Il n'a pas bien compris la situation.

  He's got in with bad company.
  Il a de mauvaises fréquentations.

  I put in three hours a day looking after him.
  Je consacre trois heures par jour à m'occuper de lui.

  She has come in first.
  Elle a le premier prix.

  He doesn't go in for reading very much.
  Il ne s'intéresse pas beaucoup à la lecture.

  The rain has set in for the night.
  Il va pleuvoir toute la nuit.

Expressions idiomatiques

  She is in.
  Elle a été élue.

  He was in for the teacher.
  Il était dans les petits papiers du professeur.

4. DOWN

Sens de base

- Au sens propre, *down* exprime un mouvement vers le bas jusqu'à un effet d'anéantissement ou d'échec.

  I'm sure he fell down.   *Down with the tyrant!*
  Je suis certain qu'il est tombé.   À bas le tyran !

- Au figuré, *down* indique une diminution, une réduction.

  Please, slow down. Ralentis s'il te plaît. (mais on dira aussi : *slow up*...)
  Prices seldom go down.   *It's time I stood down.*
  Les prix vont rarement à la baisse.   Il est temps de démissionner.

Les associations

go   run   come   put   get   set   take   stand   be   fall

She feels a little run down.   *I took down all that you said.*
Elle se sent à plat / mal fichue.   J'ai pris en note toutes vos paroles.
I put him down as a crook.   *I am down on my luck.*
Je le prends pour un escroc.   Je n'ai pas de chance.
Don't let things get you down.   *He fell down badly this time.*
Ne te laisse pas abattre.   Il a vraiment raté son coup cette fois.

Expressions idiomatiques

He's down and out.   *They put me down to wash the dishes.*
Il est sans le sou.   Il m'ont désigné pour faire la vaisselle.
The idea suits me down to the ground.   *She's down on you, I'm afraid.*
L'idée me convient parfaitement.   Elle t'en veut, j'en ai peur.

Remarquez l'emploi de *down* dans certains mots composés comme *a down-to-earth person* (une personne qui a les pieds sur terre) ou *down-under* (aux antipodes).

Enfin, comme *up*, le mot peut être un verbe à temps plein.

They downed tools. Ils ont cessé le travail. Ils se sont mis en grève.

5. ON

Sens de base

- Au sens propre, *on* évoque un état de contact.

  Put your hat on.   *Don't throw it on to the table.*
  Mets ton chapeau.   Ne le jette pas sur la table.

- Au sens figuré, on dira :

  She put a good face on. Elle a fait bonne figure.

- *On* exprime aussi une progression, une continuité.

  Read on. Continuez à lire.   *I'll follow on after you.* J'enchaînerai après vous.

Ne confondez pas les deux sens de *on*. Comparez :

  Go on! Continue !
  The police had no clue to go on. La police n'avait aucun indice sur quoi s'appuyer.

Les associations

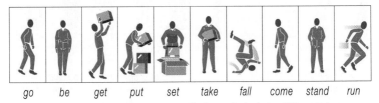

go   be   get   put   set   take   fall   come   stand   run

On est le plus souvent associé aux verbes décrivant plutôt des positions et des mouvements.

We'll come on the 1st of May.
Nous viendrons le premier mai.

"Get on!" the station-master said.
« Montez ! » dit le chef de gare.

The Old Vic has put "Macbeth" on.
On joue « Macbeth » à l'Old Vic.

They set the police on the wrong track.
Ils ont mis la police sur une fausse piste.

I'll take on the responsibility.
Je prendrai la responsabilité.

They put me on to a good hotel.
Ils m'indiquèrent un bon hôtel.

Expressions idiomatiques

We had a drink on the house.
Le patron a offert la tournée.

He's back on cigarettes.
Il s'est remis à fumer.

She's on the pill.
Elle prend la pilule.

You're on.
Tope là.

Noms composés : *onlooker* (badaud, spectateur), *on-line* (en réseau), *onshore* (à terre).

6. OVER

Sens de base

- Au sens propre, *over* ajoute l'idée d'un mouvement par dessus ou d'une position au-dessus de quelque chose.

  The plane was flying over London. L'avion survolait Londres.

- Au figuré, *over* décrit souvent une évolution dans le temps ou ce qui reste à la fin d'une période.

  Over the last ten years he has travelled a lot.
  Il a beaucoup voyagé ces dix dernières années.

  Take what is left over. Prenez ce qui reste.

  Game over. Fin de la partie.

Les associations

| go | come | run | fall | get | take | put | stand | set |

Let's go / run over the events of that period.
Révisons les événements de cette période.

What came over her?
Qu'est-ce qui lui a pris ?

Their dog had just been run over.
Leur chien venait de se faire écraser.

The chair fell over.
La chaise a basculé.

I can't get over the fact that he got through.
Je n'en reviens pas qu'il ait réussi.

He took over the shop from his father.
Il a repris le magasin de son père.

Expressions idiomatiques

They think you're all over the hill if you are 40.
Ils pensent qu'on est fichu après 40 ans.

She came over giddy.
Elle se sentit mal.

He's falling over himself to help.
Il se met en quatre.

Let's get it over!
Finissons-en !

Notons enfin que *over* entre dans la composition de nombreux mots, dont beaucoup de verbes : *overwork* (surmener), *overcook* (trop cuire), *overtime* (heures supplémentaires), etc.

7. WITH

● *With* ne peut être qu'une particule prépositionnelle. Elle est très utilisée, à cause de la diversité de ses sens.

● Initialement, elle indique l'accompagnement, la relation, et jusqu'à l'harmonie entre personnes et choses.

> *Who(m) do you live with?*
> Avec qui vivez-vous ?
> *I'm with you in what you say.*
> Je suis d'accord avec vous.

> *What kind of petrol do you fill it with?*
> Avec quel genre d'essence faites-vous le plein ?

● Mais le sens peut s'étendre jusqu'à exprimer, entre autres :
  • La manière :   *He did it with great care* (avec grand soin).
  • Le moyen :   *I saw it with my own eyes* (de mes propres yeux).
  • La cause :   *He cried with joy* (de joie).
  • Le temps :   *With the years he's getting wiser* (les années passant...).

Les associations

With est employée avec pratiquement tous les verbes les plus prolifiques, et très souvent à la suite d'une autre particule.

> *Come on, don't be old-fashioned, get with it.*
> Allons, ne sois pas vieux jeu, sois dans le coup.
> *Try to get on well with him.*
> Essaie de te mettre bien avec lui.

> *Have you got enough work to be getting on with?*
> Avez-vous assez de travail pour vous occuper ?

Expressions idiomatiques

> *Oh, get away with you!*
> Allons ! Je ne vous crois pas !
> *Are you with me?*
> Vous me suivez ? / Vous me comprenez ?
> *Get with it! He's lying to you!*
> Ouvre les yeux ! Il te ment !

> *Yesterday I fell in with a party of climbers.*
> Hier, j'ai rencontré un groupe de grimpeurs.
> *Couldn't you put up with him?*
> Ne pourriez-vous pas vous entendre avec lui ?

Remarquez enfin les verbes *withdraw* (retirer), *withstand* (supporter) et les noms dérivés : *withdrawal* (retrait)...

8. TO

Sens de base

To illustre, au propre comme au figuré, la direction d'un mouvement et éventuellement son aboutissement.

You should go to the dentist's.
Vous devriez aller chez le dentiste.

He's our ambassador to Belgium.
Il est notre ambassadeur en Belgique.

On voit qu'un Anglais imagine plus précisément ce mouvement qu'un Français. De même dans les exemples suivants.

It is a quarter to four.
Il est quatre heures moins le quart.

One person to a room.
Une personne par pièce.

Remarquez que *to* est traduit en français par des formulations utilisant des prépositions différentes.

Les associations

go   come   take   get   put   run   set   stand   be

I have come to the last chapter.
J'en suis au dernier chapitre.

Trains running to London have been delayed.
Les trains à destination de Londres ont du retard.

She has taken to drinking.
Elle s'est mise à boire.

The soldiers stood to attention.
Les soldats se mirent au garde-à-vous.

How can I get it to him?
Comment le lui faire parvenir ?

Have you been to London?
Êtes-vous allé à Londres ?

I'll put / set him to work. Je vais le mettre au travail.

Expressions idiomatiques

What would you say to a beer?
Que diriez-vous d'une bière ?

Here's to you!
À la vôtre !

There's nothing to it.
Rien de plus facile.

He's gone to the dogs.
Il va être ruiné.

The Prime Minister has decided to go to the country.
Le Premier Ministre a décidé de lancer des élections générales.

They really went to town on it.
Ils y ont vraiment mis le paquet.

He's just come to.
Il vient de reprendre connaissance.

9. *FROM*

● *From* ne peut être que préposition.

● Au sens propre, il marque un point de départ, souvent associé à *to*, qui peut désigner un point d'arrivée. Il est alors souvent traduit par « de », « depuis ».

From next week on...
À compter de la semaine prochaine...

Judging from appearances...
Apparemment...

A portrait painted from life. Un portrait d'après nature.

Where are you from?
D'où êtes-vous ?

From what I have heard...
D'après ce que j'ai entendu dire...

Il précède d'autres prépositions comme *behind, above, over there.*

Les associations

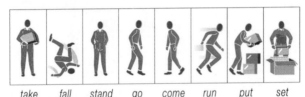

take   fall   stand   go   come   run   put   set

The vicar took his text from St Mark's Gospel.
Le curé a extrait son texte de l'Évangile selon St Marc.

He has stolen $10 from his mother.
Il a volé dix dollars à sa mère.

Let's shelter from the rain here.
Abritons-nous de la pluie ici.

Tell him this from me.
Dis-lui ceci de ma part.

Expressions idiomatiques

Don't drink from the bottle, please.
Ne buvez pas à la bouteille.

Keep him from talking to her.
Empêchez-le de lui parler.

He does not know good from evil.
Il ne fait pas la distinction entre le bien et le mal.

Can you tell pudding from porridge?
Tu sais faire la différence entre du pudding et du porridge?

10. *ABOUT / AROUND / ROUND*

Ces particules apportent à peu près le même sens à la majorité des verbes de notre liste : « non loin », « autour », « aux alentours ».

She is somewhere about.   *He walked about the lake.*
Elle n'est pas loin.   Il a fait le tour du lac.

Ce qui justifie le sens de *about* associé souvent à *be* :
She was about to call the police. Elle était sur le point d'appeler la police.

Les associations

go   come   get   run   fall   take   be   stand   put   set

I always go about by bus.
Je circule toujours en bus.

Your birthday will soon come around.
Ce sera bientôt ton anniversaire.

Stories have been getting round about him.
Des rumeurs ont couru à son sujet.

Who's been putting about these stories?
Qui a fait courir ces bruits ?

What about me?
Et moi, alors ?

No, it's the other way around.
Non, c'est dans l'autre sens.

While you're about it, will you fix me a cup of tea?
Pendant que tu y es, tu peux me faire une tasse de thé ?

Expressions idiomatiques

How do you go about getting permission?
Comment s'y prend-on pour avoir l'autorisation ?

She fainted but soon came round.
Elle s'évanouit mais reprit vite conscience.

There's something about that girl!
Cette fille a un je ne sais quoi...

They often argue but it does not take them long to come around.
Ils se disputent souvent mais ils ne mettent pas longtemps avant de se réconcilier.

He was greatly put out about this event, and yet he's been around!
L'événement l'a beaucoup troublé, et pourtant il n'est pas né d'hier !

Un mot composé intéressant : *I don't know his whereabouts.* (Je ne sais où il est exactement.)

11. VINGT AUTRES PARTICULES

Elles peuvent être adverbe ou préposition. Elles sont ici données dans l'ordre alphabétique, accompagnées de leur sens de base, d'un exemple et d'une expression idiomatique.

- *Above* : au-dessus, en haut (plus haut qu'avec *over*).
  It will cost above £100.   *This is above me.*
  Ça coûtera plus de 100 livres.   C'est trop compliqué pour moi.

- *Across* : de l'autre côté d'une ligne ou d'une surface.
  She lived across the street.   *He couldn't get it across to me.*
  Elle vivait de l'autre côté de la rue.   Il n'a pas pu me le faire comprendre.

- *Against* : contre ; contraire de *with*.
  Against all logic, she agreed.   *He put money by against his retirement.*
  Contre toute logique,   Il a mis de l'argent de côté en prévision
  elle a été d'accord.   de la retraite.

- *Along* : mouvement le long d'une ligne.
  There were trees along the road.   *Come along, children!*
  Des arbres longeaient la route.   Venez, les enfants !

- *Apart* : à côté, à l'écart.
  It came apart in my hands.   *You can't tell them apart.*
  Ça s'est démonté tout seul.   On ne peut pas les distinguer l'un de l'autre.

- *At* : indique une position et, éventuellement, une idée d'hostilité.
  He feels at home here.   *He threw stones at passers-by.*
  Il se sent chez lui ici.   Il jetait des pierres sur les passants.

- *Away* : éloignement, absence.
  Did you take my book away?   *Right away.*
  Tu as emporté mon livre ?   Immédiatement, tout de suite.

- *Back* : en arrière.
  He is just back from holiday.   *It was as far back as 1800.*
  Il vient de rentrer de vacances.   Ça remontait à l'année 1800.

- *Before* : en avant dans le temps, dans le lieu, dans l'ordre ; contraire de *after*.
  You should have told me before.   *He appeared before the court.*
  Tu aurais dû me le dire avant.   Il comparut devant un tribunal.

- *By* : position ou mouvement à côté d'un repère.
  He rushed by me.   *It's difficult but we'll get by.*
  Il est passé à côté de moi en courant.   C'est difficile mais nous y arriverons.

- *For* : vers une destination, un but, un désir, une certitude.
  I took something for the flu.   *We're in for it!*
  J'ai pris quelque chose contre la grippe.   Ça va barder !

- *Forth* : mouvement vers l'avant (proche de *forward*).
  He was walking back and forth.   *He brought forth many ideas.*
  Il marchait de long en large.   Il a proposé des idées intéressantes.

- *Into* : mouvement vers l'intérieur, changement d'état.
  The car crashed into a wall.   *I'm not into it.*
  La voiture s'est écrasée contre un mur.   Ça n'est pas mon truc.

- *Like* : comparaison entre deux états ou mouvements.
  It smells like petrol.   *What's she like?*
  Ça sent l'essence.   De quoi a-t-elle l'air ?

- *Of* : marque des rapports comme l'origine, la possession, la cause.
  What do you think of him?   *What do you think of this?*
  Que pensez-vous de lui ?   Qu'en dis-tu ?

- *Off* : interruption, éloignement, contraste avec *on*.
  The farm is off the road.   *Good bye, I'm off.*
  La ferme est à l'écart de la route.   Au revoir, je m'en vais.

- *Past* : mouvement près de ou au-delà.
  He ran past me.   *He is past caring.*
  Il est passé près de moi en courant.   Il n'en a plus rien à faire.

- *Through* : traversée par l'intérieur, à travers.
  I saw him through the window.   *He got through all his exams.*
  Je l'ai vu par la fenêtre.   Il a été reçu à tous ses examens.

- *Under* : sous, au-dessous.
  He is under 40.   *Look under "plumbers".*
  Il a moins de 40 ans.   Cherche dans la rubrique « plombiers ».

- *Within / Without* : à l'intérieur / à l'extérieur.
  I'll do it within the week.   *I can't do without this book.*
  Je le ferai dans la semaine.   Je ne peux me passer de ce livre.

F O R M A T I O N   D E S   V E R B E S

●●●

Comme les noms ou les adjectifs, les verbes sont souvent des « hybrides ». Tantôt ils se sont formés à partir de mots appartenant à une autre catégorie par simple **conversion** ; tantôt ils sont le résultat de l'addition de deux mots, c'est une **composition** ; tantôt ils sont créés à l'aide d'un préfixe ou d'un suffixe, et l'on parle de **dérivation**.

Par conversion

● C'est encore un caractère de l'anglais que d'avoir, par exemple, la possibilité de passer du nom *bottle*, au verbe *to bottle* (mettre en bouteille) et même au verbe à particule *to bottle up* qui, au figuré, signifie « contenir », « refouler ».

> *He bottled up his anger.* Il a ravalé sa colère.

He's coated the cake with sugar.	*He is keen on being sirred.*
Il a enrobé le gâteau de sucre.	Il tient à se faire appeler Monsieur.
The wound had skinned over.	*He was knifed by some madman.*
La blessure s'était cicatrisée.	Il a été poignardé par un fou.

● L'anglais peut passer, de même, de l'adjectif au verbe.

Calm down.	*They emptied all the bottles.*
Calme-toi.	Ils ont vidé toutes les bouteilles.

Notez qu'il y a parfois cependant un changement d'orthographe comme dans *advice* (des conseils) qui devient *to advise*, ou un déplacement de l'accent, comme dans a *'pre*sent qui devient *to pre'sent*.

Par composition

Les exemples en sont plus rares, mais un Anglais peut toujours en créer, du moment qu'il se fait comprendre.

The car backfired.	*He sleepwalks.*
Le voiture pétaradait.	Il est somnambule.
The plan backfired.	*He spends his time daydreaming.*
Le projet a échoué.	Il ne cesse de rêvasser.

Par dérivation

● **Suffixes**

Certains sont d'origine française, comme *-ise* (*-ize* en américain) : *nationalise*, « nationaliser ».

Un grand nombre, en -*en*, ont un sens réfléchi ou passif, et sont construits à partir d'adjectifs. Ils appartiennent au langage concret des couleurs, des dimensions, des formes, très riche en anglais.

The sky darkened.
Le ciel s'assombrit.

They have broadened the street.
On a élargi la route.

Her loving words softened him.
Ses paroles aimantes l'ont apaisé.

This will quieten him.
Cela le tranquillisera.

• Préfixes

• *Dis-*, dont le sens est négatif.
I disagree with you: you are distorting the meaning of my words.
Je ne suis pas d'accord avec vous, vous dénaturez mes paroles.

• *Re-*, qui, comme en français, marque la répétition ou le retour.
He reappeared in the meetings as soon as he was reappointed.
Il a reparu dans les réunions dès qu'il a été réintégré.

• *Mis-*, qui souligne une erreur.
I don't know if I was misled or misunderstood.
Je ne sais pas si on m'a envoyé dans la mauvaise direction ou si on m'a mal compris.

• *Over-*, qui marque un excès.
"I am overworked." "Oh, come on! Don't overdo it."
« Je suis surmené. » « Oh, ça va ! N'en fais pas trop ! »

• *Un-* (défaire).
They unearthed the body and uncovered the truth about the murder.
Ils déterrèrent le corps et découvrirent la vérité sur le meurtre.

• *Under-* (contraire de *over-*).
They underestimated his strength and so underwent a crushing defeat.
Ils ont sous-estimé sa force et donc subi une cinglante défaite.

• *In-* (ou *en-*) et *inter-*.
We'll have to inquire about why he does not interact with his environment.
Il faudra chercher pourquoi il n'y a pas d'interaction entre lui et ce qui l'entoure.

• *Sub-*.
The storm subsided. La tempête se calma.

• *Trans-*.
He was transfixed with fear. Il fut pétrifié de peur.

• *For-* a le sens de *away* dans, par exemple, *forbid*.
They forbid him to see anyone. Ils lui interdisent de voir qui que ce soit.

• *Fore-* a le sens de *in front of*, en avant.
You should have foreseen it: you had been forewarned about it.
Vous auriez dû le prévoir : on vous avait prévenu.

• *Counter-*.
They counteracted by throwing stones. Ils ont riposté en jetant des pierres.

À SAVOIR

Qu'ils soient groupe nominal ou groupe verbal, les compléments du verbe forment un système aussi diversifié et étendu que le système des particules.

Verbes transitifs et verbes intransitifs

● **Verbes transitifs**
> *Tell me, have you read this book ?*
> Dites-moi, est-ce que vous avez lu ce livre ?

Est transitif tout verbe qui, comme *read* ici, peut être suivi d'un complément d'objet direct.

● **Verbes intransitifs**
> *Come in and sit down.* Entrez et asseyez-vous.

Les verbes *come in* et *sit down* sont intransitifs car ils ne peuvent jamais avoir de complément d'objet direct.

● **De nombreux verbes peuvent être transitifs et intransitifs.**
> *He has adapted his book for the stage.*
> Il a adapté son livre pour la scène.
> *She refused to adapt.*
> Elle a refusé de s'adapter.

Verbes transitifs avec un complément

● **Le complément est un groupe nominal.**
Très nombreux sont les verbes simples complétés directement par un groupe nominal ou par un pronom. La syntaxe, dans ce cas, ne pose pas de problème.
> *Have you read all these books? Yes, I have read them all.*
> Avez-vous lu tous ces livres ? Oui, je les ai tous lus.

La construction est plus complexe en ce qui concerne la place du complément quand il s'agit de verbes à particules (cf. p. 59).

● **Le complément est un groupe verbal.**
Il existe plusieurs types de complémentation, chacune apportant sa nuance particulière.
  • Infinitif avec *to*.
> *I want him to come at once.*
> Je veux qu'il vienne tout de suite.

- Infinitif sans *to*.
    I heard him open the door.
    Je l'ai entendu ouvrir la porte.
- Forme en *-ing*.
    I can't resist asking the question.
    Je ne résiste pas à l'envie de poser la question.
- Préposition suivie d'une forme en *-ing*.
    We agreed about talking it over later.
    Nous sommes tombés d'accord pour en reparler plus tard.
- Complétive introduite par *that*, en particulier au style indirect.
    He said that he was delighted by the idea.
    Il a dit qu'il était ravi de cette idée.
- Interrogative indirecte.
    He wondered why she looked so angry.
    Il se demanda pourquoi elle avait l'air tellement fâchée.
- Verbe au prétérit modal (cf. p. 19).
    I wish you were here.
    Je regrette que tu ne sois pas ici.

Verbes transitifs avec deux compléments

- **Complément d'objet + complément d'attribution.**
    You gave your friend a strange answer.
    You gave a strange answer to your friend.
    Vous avez donné à votre ami une étrange réponse.

    Remarquez la place du complément d'attribution *your friend* selon que l'on emploie la préposition *to* ou non.

    Autres verbes de cette catégorie utilisant :
    - *to* : bring, offer, play, promote, read, sell, send, teach, write.
    - *for* : look, bring, buy, catch, choose, find, get, pay, reach.
    - *from* : buy, steal.

- *Attribut du complément d'objet.*
    Reading makes me happy.
    La lecture me rend heureux.
    Love makes me another man.
    L'amour fait de moi un autre homme.

    L'attribut du complément d'objet peut être un adjectif *(happy)* ou un groupe nominal *(another man)*.

    Trois de ces constructions font l'objet des pages qui suivent : **la forme en *-ing*, l'infinitif** et **le style indirect.**

1. LA FORME EN -*ING*

Sens

Avec la forme en -*ing*, l'action est souvent vue de manière **concrète**. Dans beaucoup de cas, cette forme exprime une **attitude personnelle** envers l'action concernée :

• Soit plutôt favorable.
  I enjoy going to the cinema...
  J'aime beaucoup aller au cinéma...

• Soit plutôt défavorable.
  ...but I avoid watching horror films.
  ...mais j'évite de voir des films d'horreur.

• Soit neutre.
  Have you ever considered spending some time in England?
  Avez-vous jamais envisagé de passer quelque temps en Angleterre ?

Structures

● **Construction directe**
  I wouldn't fancy being in her shoes.
  Je n'aimerais pas être à sa place.

Cette construction est adoptée par de très nombreux verbes comme *enjoy, appreciate, avoid, detest, dread* (craindre), *consider*, etc.

● **Après une préposition**
  He would benefit from spending some time in an English-speaking country.
  Cela lui ferait du bien de passer quelque temps dans un pays anglophone.

Parmi les verbes de ce type, les plus fréquents sont *consent to* (consentir à), *congratulate on* (féliciter de), *reproach for / with* (reprocher de), *think of* (envisager), *agree about* (être d'accord pour), etc.

● **Avec un complément interposé ou, plus souvent, un génitif**
  I enjoy John / him coming to talk with me.
  I enjoy John's / his coming to talk with me.
  J'aime quand John / il vient bavarder avec moi.

Notez quelques expressions courantes bâties sur ces structures :
I don't mind, I'm keen on, I can't bear, I can't stand, it's no use, it's no good, it is(n't) worth, etc.
  I can't bear his talking all the time.
  Je ne supporte pas son bavardage permanent.
  It's no use buying another book than this one.
  Cela ne sert à rien d'acheter un autre livre que celui-ci.

- **Après des verbes exprimant une perception**

  I can smell something burning.
  Je sens qu'il y a quelque chose qui brûle.

  Can you hear that bird singing in the distance?
  Entends-tu cet oiseau qui chante au loin ?

  He felt a spider creeping up his leg.
  Il sentit qu'une araignée grimpait le long de sa jambe.

  Look at that horse running in the meadow.
  Regarde ce cheval qui court dans le pré.

Remarquez l'emploi bien particulier de la forme en *-ing* associée aux particules *into* et *out of* après certains verbes exprimant la manière dont on peut influencer quelqu'un (*into* pour persuader et *out of* pour dissuader) :
coax (câliner), *pressure* (faire pression), *reason* (faire entendre raison), *shock, badger* (importuner), etc.

  We'll talk him into accepting your offer.
  Nous allons lui parler pour le persuader d'accepter votre offre.

  He laughed her out of applying for the job.
  À force de moquerie, il l'a dissuadée de se présenter pour cet emploi.

  The news of the earthquake shocked me out of spending my holiday in Los Angeles.
  La nouvelle du tremblement de terre a été un tel choc que j'ai renoncé à passer mes vacances à Los Angeles.

  She coaxed me into offering her a new ring.
  À force de câlineries, elle a obtenu que je lui offre une nouvelle bague.

  He badgered her out of learning to drive.
  Il l'a importunée jusqu'à ce qu'elle renonce à apprendre à conduire.

Notez qu'une fois encore le verbe indique le moyen, et la particule le résultat (cf. p. 60).

2. L'INFINITIF

Avec l'infinitif, l'action est vue le plus souvent d'une manière plus **abstraite**. L'action est achevée, considérée plutôt dans son résultat. Bon nombre de ces verbes expriment, grâce à l'infinitif, le **désir** de voir l'action achevée, le but atteint.

Structures

- **Sans *to***
  - Après des verbes de perception.
    Did you hear / see him open the door?
    Vous l'avez entendu / vu ouvrir la porte ?
  - Après *make*, exprimant la notion de « faire faire ».
    He made her do all the housework.
    Il lui faisait faire toutes les tâches ménagères.

- **Avec *to***
  - Construction directe.
    I can't afford to go to the cinema every evening.
    Je n'ai pas les moyens d'aller au cinéma tous les soirs.
    I want / wish / hope to buy a new car.
    Je veux / je souhaite / j'espère m'acheter une voiture neuve.
  - Avec un complément interposé, après des verbes comme *allow, order, beg, want,* etc.
    I want them to be ready at one o'clock.
    Je veux qu'ils soient prêts à une heure.

Yes, but...

- **Infinitif ou forme en -*ing* ?**
  Vous avez sans doute remarqué que certains verbes se construisaient tantôt avec une forme en -*ing*, tantôt avec un infinitif. Le choix se fera selon que vous considérez l'action d'une manière concrète, dans sa réalisation (employez alors la forme en -*ing*) ou d'une manière abstraite, en considérant l'action achevée, dans son résultat (avec l'infinitif).

Comparez par exemple :
Have we taken off? I didn't feel the plane move.
On a décollé ? Je n'ai pas senti l'avion bouger.
The plane is about to take off. I can feel it shuddering.
L'avion va décoller. Je le sens vibrer.

Dans le premier exemple, seul le résultat de l'action, terminée, compte (l'avion a décollé et je ne l'ai pas senti) tandis que dans le deuxième, c'est la vibration, en ce moment, de l'avion, qui m'avertit.
De même pour d'autres verbes exprimant la perception, comme *listen, see, watch, feel, notice,* etc.

● On peut aussi considérer qu'avec la forme en *-ing,* on se tourne plutôt vers le passé tandis qu'avec l'infinitif on se tourne plutôt vers l'avenir, par exemple dans l'expression d'une intention. Comparez :
Last time I met her I remember asking her about her grandmother's health.
La dernière fois que je l'ai rencontrée, je me rappelle lui avoir demandé comment allait sa grand-mère.
Next time I meet her I must remember to ask her about her grandmother's health.
La prochaine fois que je la rencontrerai, il faut que je pense à lui demander comment va sa grand-mère.

Dans le premier cas, je me souviens d'une action passée, tandis que dans le deuxième, je fais référence à une action que je dois accomplir, et qui appartient donc à l'avenir.

Cette remarque concerne aussi :

• Des verbes comme *advise, intend, propose, suggest, recommend,* etc.
I advise arriving early.
Je conseille d'arriver tôt. (sous-entendu : j'ai toujours, jusqu'à présent, été de cet avis)
I advise you to arrive early.
Je vous conseille d'arriver tôt. (sous-entendu : à la séance où vous comptez aller)

• Des verbes exprimant une opinion.
I hate missing the beginning of a film.
Je déteste rater le début d'un film. (sous-entendu : et il en a toujours été ainsi)
I would hate to miss the beginning of this film.
Je détesterais manquer le début du film. (... que je compte aller voir)

3. LE STYLE INDIRECT

Le style indirect permet de rapporter les paroles d'autrui. Deux constructions sont possibles.

Complétive introduite par *that*

- La construction est simple, similaire au français, si vous rapportez, au présent grammatical, des paroles qui viennent d'être prononcées.
  He says that he is delighted with your offer.
  Il dit qu'il est ravi de votre proposition.
  He admits that he has not finished yet.
  Il admet ne pas avoir encore fini.

- Mais si vous introduisez votre phrase par un **verbe au passé**, un certain nombre de **transformations** s'imposent. Observez le passage du style direct au style indirect quand les paroles que l'on rapporte sont :

  - Au présent.
    "I am delighted with her offer."
    He said that he was delighted with her offer.
    Il a dit qu'il était ravi de sa proposition.

  - Au *present perfect*.
    "I haven't finished yet."
    He added that he hadn't finished yet.
    Il ajouta qu'il n'avait pas encore fini.

  - Au prétérit.
    " I met him twenty years ago. "
    He announced that he had met him twenty years before.
    Il annonça qu'il l'avait rencontré vingt ans auparavant.

  - Au *pluperfect*.
    "I had just finished when the bell rang."
    He mentioned that he had just finished when the bell had rung.
    Il signala qu'il venait de finir quand la cloche avait sonné.

  - Au futur.
    "I'll phone you as soon as I know the answer."
    He said that he'd phone me as soon as he knew the answer.
    Il a dit qu'il me téléphonerait dès qu'il connaîtrait la réponse.

Remarquez l'emploi du prétérit après l'expression de temps *as soon as*, « parallèle » à l'emploi du présent après un verbe au futur (cf. p. 15).

• Accompagnées d'un auxiliaire modal.
"I may decide to come later," he said.
He said that he might decide to come later.
Il a dit qu'il pourrait décider de venir plus tard.

"You must do as I like," he said.
He reminded me that I had to do as he liked.
Il me rappela que je devais faire ce qu'il voulait.

Interrogative indirecte

Vous retrouverez là les mêmes règles, tout en faisant attention au passage de la forme interrogative à la forme affirmative.
"Why did you decide not to speak to her?"
I asked him why he had decided not to speak to her.
Je lui ai demandé pourquoi il avait décidé de ne pas lui parler.

"Will you bring the pudding you have made?"
She asked him if he would bring the pudding he had made.
Elle lui demanda s'il apporterait le pudding qu'il avait préparé.

Yes, but...

En anglais courant, vous pourrez utiliser indifféremment :
She said that John lived in New York.
She said that John lives in New York.

La deuxième phrase, où le présent grammatical n'a pas été transformé en prétérit, insiste plus sur le fait que les paroles que l'on rapporte correspondent toujours à une réalité au moment où l'on parle. Il est implicite que John vit encore à New York au moment où on parle. Dans le cas contraire, seule la première phrase est possible.

L E   P A S S I F

●●●

Cette forme est plus importante et plus fréquente en anglais qu'en français. Elle permet de donner la première place à qui subit l'action chaque fois qu'on le désire. **Le choix entre la voix active et la voix passive est**, ici encore, de **la responsabilité de celui qui parle.**

Structure de base

- La structure de base est : **sujet + auxiliaire be + participe passé** (+ *by* + complément).
  I was engaged by Smith in 1995. J'ai été embauché par Smith en 1995.

- Cette tournure peut s'utiliser à tous les temps : passé, présent, futur.
  I will be engaged if he is satisfied with the job interview.
  Je serai embauché s'il est satisfait de mon entretien.

- Elle n'est pas incompatible avec la forme en *-ing*.
  I am being tested on my proficiency. On est en train de vérifier ma compétence.

- Elle peut aussi s'accompagner de modaux.
  I might be engaged as early as next month.
  Il se pourrait qu'on m'engage dès le mois prochain.

- Elle peut s'associer aux divers types de complémentation vus précédemment.
  I couldn't stand waiting longer.
  Je ne supporterais pas d'attendre plus longtemps.

- Dans le cas d'un verbe à particule, celle-ci reste accolée à son verbe de base.
  I think my credentials will be accounted for.
  Je pense qu'on tiendra compte de mes références.
  In my previous job I was never taken care of.
  Dans mon emploi précédent, on ne s'est jamais occupé de moi.

- Dans tous les cas, c'est l'auxiliaire *be* qui prend la marque du temps ou de la modalité.

- Le complément d'agent introduit par *by* n'est utilisé que si l'on tient à identifier l'auteur de l'action.

Sens : traduction du français « on »

Le passif permet d'attirer l'attention sur qui subit l'action plutôt que sur son auteur. Il est donc normal de préférer le passif quand la phrase à la voix active aurait pour sujet :
- Un pronom personnel indéterminé : *they* (ils, les gens).
  He has been fired.
  Il a été renvoyé. Il s'est fait renvoyer. On l'a renvoyé.

- Un pronom indéfini *(someone, somebody...)*.
  His job has been taken over. On l'a remplacé sur son poste.
- Un nom avec un sens général.
  Inefficient employees are not thought much of.
  On n'apprécie pas beaucoup les employés incompétents.

Autres emplois

● **Construction de *say* et des verbes de sens voisin** *(think, believe, report*, etc.)
  À la tournure :
  People say that he has been fired for incompetence.
  il faudra, à moins de vouloir insister sur *people*, préférer l'une des deux formules suivantes :
  It is said that Smith has fired him for lack of proficiency.
  On dit que Smith l'a renvoyé pour incompétence.
  Smith is said to have fired him for lack of proficiency.
  On dit de Smith qu'il l'a renvoyé pour incompétence.
  La première tournure permet de rendre la cause encore plus vague, la seconde met le sujet en pleine lumière. Il y a, dans les deux cas, une nuance d'incertitude que l'on peut traduire en français par un conditionnel :
  Smith l'aurait renvoyé pour incompétence.

● **Le passif avec *get***
  Get, avec son sens lexical « devenir », exprime plus fortement le changement d'état que *be*.
  He got fired when they saw he was not fit for the job.
  Il a été renvoyé dès qu'ils ont vu qu'il ne convenait pas pour le poste.

● **Le double passif**
  Comparez :
  My job has been given to Mr Johnson. / Mr Johnson has been given my job.
  On a donné mon poste à Mr Johnson.
  Cette seconde tournure est très souvent employée car c'est la personne qui devient à nouveau le centre de la phrase. Elle est propre à des verbes exprimant un rapport d'un individu à un autre : *give, offer, bring, buy, tell, ask, teach*, etc.

Yes, but...

Au passif, les verbes suivis, à la voix active, de l'infinitif sans *to*, récupèrent leur préposition.
Comparez :
  They made him do my work. He was made to do my work.
  They saw her leave the manager's office. She was seen to leave the manager's office.
On pourra dire aussi : *She was seen leaving the manager's office.*

Tableaux de conjugaison

---

1. Remarque :
– Les formes interro-négatives s'utilisent de préférence contractées.
– Les voix passives du futur, du futur antérieur et du conditionnel en
  -*ing* sont « mécaniquement possibles » mais inusitées.

PRÉSENT

VOIX ACTIVE

Présent simple

forme affirmative

I ask
he / she / it asks
we / you / they ask

forme interrogative

do I ask?
does he / she / it ask?
do we / you / they ask?

forme négative

I do not ask
he / she / it does not ask
we / you / they do not ask

forme interro-négative

do I not ask?
does he / she / it not ask?
do we / you / they not ask?

Présent continu

forme affirmative

I am asking
he / she / it is asking
we / you / they are asking

forme interrogative

am I asking?
is he / she / it asking?
are we / you / they asking?

forme négative

I am not asking
he / she / it is not asking
we / you / they are not asking

forme interro-négative

am I not asking?
is he / she / it not asking?
are we / you / they not asking?

VOIX PASSIVE

Présent simple

forme affirmative

I am asked
he / she / it is asked
we / you / they are asked

forme interrogative

am I asked?
is he / she / it asked?
are we / you / they asked?

forme négative

I am not asked
he / she / it is not asked
we / you / they are not asked

forme interro-négative

am I not asked?
is he / she / it not asked?
are we / you / they not asked?

Présent continu

forme affirmative

I am being asked
he / she / it is being asked
we / you / they are being asked

forme interrogative

am I being asked?
is he / she / it being asked?
are we / you / they being asked?

forme négative

I am not being asked
he / she / it is not being asked
we / you / they are not being asked

forme interro-négative

am I not being asked?
is he / she / it not being asked?
are we / you / they not being asked?

PRÉTÉRIT

VOIX ACTIVE

Prétérit simple	Prétérit continu

forme affirmative

I asked
he / she / it asked
we / you / they asked

forme affirmative

I was asking
he / she / it was aksing
we / you / they were asking

forme interrogative

did I ask?
did he / she / it ask?
did we / you / they ask?

forme interrogative

was I asking?
was he / she / it asking?
were we / you / they asking?

forme négative

I did not ask
he / she / it did not ask
we / you / they did not ask

forme négative

I was not asking
he / she / it was not asking
we / you / they were not asking

forme interro-négative

did I not ask?
did he / she / it not ask?
did we / you / they not ask?

forme interro-négative

was I not asking?
was he / she / it not asking?
were we / you / they not asking?

VOIX PASSIVE

Prétérit simple	Prétérit continu

forme affirmative

I was asked
he / she / it was asked
we / you / they were asked

forme affirmative

I was being asked
he / she / it was being asked
we / you / they were being asked

forme interrogative

was I asked ?
was he / she / it asked?
were we / you / they asked?

forme interrogative

was I being asked?
was he / she / it being asked?
were we / you / they being asked?

forme négative

I was not asked
he / she / it was not asked
we / you / they were not asked

forme négative

I was not being asked
he / she / it was not being asked
we / you / they were not being asked

forme interro-négative

was I not asked?
was he / she / it not asked?
were we / you / they not asked?

forme interro-négative

was I not being asked?
was he / she / it not being asked?
were we / you / they not being asked?

PRESENT PERFECT

VOIX ACTIVE

Present perfect simple	Present perfect continu
forme affirmative	**forme affirmative**
I have asked he / she / it has asked we / you / they have asked	I have been asking he / she / it has been asking we / you / they have been asking
forme interrogative	**forme interrogative**
have I asked? has he / she / it asked? have we / you / they asked?	have I been asking? has he / she / it been asking? have we / you / they been asking?
forme négative	**forme négative**
I have not asked he / she / it has not asked we / you / they have not asked	I have not been asking he / she / it has not been asking we / you / they have not been asking
forme interro-négative	**forme interro-négative**
have I not asked? has he / she / it not asked? have we / you / they not asked?	have I not been asking? has he / she / it not been asking? have we / you / they not been asking?

VOIX PASSIVE

Present perfect simple	Present perfect continu
forme affirmative	**forme affirmative**
I have been asked he / she / it has been asked we / you / they have been asked	I have been being asked he / she / it has been being asked we / you / they have been being asked
forme interrogative	**forme interrogative**
have I been asked? has he / she / it been asked? have we / you / they been asked?	have I been being asked? has he / she / it been being asked? have we / you / they been being asked?
forme négative	**forme négative**
I have not been asked he / she / it has not been asked we / you / they have not been asked	I have not been being asked he / she / it has not been being asked we / you / they have not been being asked
forme interro-négative	**forme interro-négative**
have I not been asked? has he / she / it not been asked? have we / you / they not been asked?	have I not been being asked? has he / she / it not been being asked? have we / you / they not been being asked?

PLUPERFECT

VOIX ACTIVE

Pluperfect simple	Pluperfect continu

forme affirmative

I had asked
he / she / it had asked
we / you / they had asked

forme affirmative

I had been asking
he / she / it had been asking
we / you / they had been asking

forme interrogative

had I asked?
had he / she / it asked?
had we / you / they asked?

forme interrogative

had I been asking?
had he / she / it been asking?
had we / you / they been asking?

forme négative

I had not asked
he / she / it had not asked
we / you / they had not asked

forme négative

I had not been asking
he / she / it had not been asking
we / you / they had not been asking

forme interro-négative

had I not asked?
had he / she / it not asked?
had we / you / they not asked?

forme interro-négative

had I not been asking?
had he / she / it not been asking?
had we / you / they not been asking?

VOIX PASSIVE

Pluperfect simple	Pluperfect continu

forme affirmative

I had been asked
he / she / it had been asked
we / you / they had been asked

forme affirmative

I had been being asked
he / she / it had been being asked
we / you / they had been being asked

forme interrogative

had I been asked?
had he / she / it been asked?
had we / you / they been asked?

forme interrogative

had I been being asked?
had he / she / it been being asked?
had we / you / they been being asked?

forme négative

I had not been asked
he / she / it had not been asked
we / you / they had not been asked

forme négative

I had not been being asked
he / she / it had not been being asked
we / you / they had not been being asked

forme interro-négative

had I not been asked?
had he / she / it not been asked?
had we / you / they not been asked?

forme interro-négative

had I not been being asked?
had he / she / it not been being asked?
had we / you / they not been being asked?

FUTUR

VOIX ACTIVE

Futur simple	Futur continu
forme affirmative	**forme affirmative**
I / we shall ask he / she / it will ask you / they will ask	I / we shall be asking he / she / it will be asking you / they will be asking
forme interrogative	**forme interrogative**
shall I / we ask? will he / she / it ask? will you / they ask?	shall I / we be asking? will he / she / it be asking? will you / they be asking?
forme négative	**forme négative**
I / we shall not ask he / she / it will not ask you / they will not ask	I / we shall not be asking he / she / it will not be asking you / they will not be asking
forme interro-négative	**forme interro-négative**
shall I / we not ask? will he / she / it not ask? will you / they not ask?	shall I / we not be asking? will he / she / it not be asking? will you / they not be asking?

VOIX PASSIVE

Futur simple	Futur continu
forme affirmative	**forme affirmative**
I / we shall be asked he / she / it will be asked you / they will be asked	I / we shall be being asked he / she / it will be being asked you / they will be being asked
forme interrogative	**forme interrogative**
shall I / we be asked? will he / she / it be asked? will you / they be asked?	shall I / we be being asked? will he / she / it be being asked? will you / they be being asked?
forme négative	**forme négative**
I / we shall not be asked he / she / it will not be asked you / they will not be asked	I / we shall not be being asked he / she / it will not be being asked you / they will not be being asked
forme interro-négative	**forme interro-négative**
shall I / we not be asked? will he / she / it not be asked? will you / they not be asked?	shall I / we not be being asked? will he / she / it not be being asked? will you / they not be being asked?

VOIX ACTIVE

Futur antérieur simple

forme affirmative

I / we shall have asked
he / she / it will have asked
you / they will have asked

forme interrogative

shall I / we have asked?
will he / she / it have asked?
will you / they have asked?

forme négative

I / we shall not have asked
he / she / it will not have asked
you / they will not have asked

forme interro-négative

shall I / we not have asked?
will he / she / it not have asked?
will you / they not have asked?

Futur antérieur continu

forme affirmative

I / we shall have been asking
he / she / it will have been asking
you / they will have been asking

forme interrogative

shall I / we have been asking?
will he / she / it have been asking?
will you / they have been asking?

forme négative

I / we shall not have been asking
he / she / it will not have been asking
you / they will not have been asking

forme interro-négative

shall I / we not have been asking?
will he / she / it not have been asking?
will you / they not have been asking?

VOIX PASSIVE

Futur antérieur simple

forme affirmative

I / we shall have been asked
he / she / it will have been asked
you / they will have been asked

forme interrogative

shall I / we have been asked?
will he / she / it have been asked?
will you / they have been asked?

forme négative

I / we shall not have been asked
he / she / it will not have been asked
you / they will not have been asked

forme interro-négative

shall I / we not have been asked?
will he / she / it not have been asked?
will you / they not have been asked?

Futur antérieur continu

forme affirmative

I / we shall have been being asked
he / she / it will have been being asked
you / they will have been being asked

forme interrogative

shall I / we have been being asked?
will he / she / it have been being asked?
will you / they have been being asked?

forme négative

I / we shall not have been being asked
he / she / it will not have been being asked
you / they will not have been being asked

forme interro-négative

shall I / we not have been being asked?
will he / she / it not have been being asked?
will you / they not have been being asked?

CONDITIONNEL PRÉSENT

VOIX ACTIVE

Conditionnel présent simple

forme affirmative

I / we should ask
he / she / it would ask
you / they would ask

forme interrogative

should I / we ask?
would he / she / it ask?
would you / they ask?

forme négative

I / we should not ask
he / she / it would not ask
you / they would not ask

forme interro-négative

should I / we not ask?
would he / she / it not ask?
would you / they not ask?

Conditionnel présent continu

forme affirmative

I / we should be asking
he / she / it would be asking
you / they would be asking

forme interrogative

should I / we be asking?
would he / she / it be asking?
would you / they be asking?

forme négative

I / we should not be asking
he / she / it would not be asking
you / they would not be asking

forme interro-négative

should I / we not be asking?
would he / she / it not be asking?
would you / they not be asking?

VOIX PASSIVE

Conditionnel présent simple

forme affirmative

I / we should be asked
he / she / it would be asked
you / they would be asked

forme interrogative

should I / we be asked?
would he / she / it be asked?
would you / they be asked?

forme négative

I / we should not be asked
he / she / it would not be asked
you / they would not be asked

forme interro-négative

should I / we not be asked?
would he / she / it not be asked?
would you / they not be asked?

Conditionnel présent continu

forme affirmative

I / we should be being asked
he / she / it would be being asked
you / they would be being asked

forme interrogative

should I / we be being asked?
would he / she / it be being asked?
would you / they be being asked?

forme négative

I / we should not be being asked
he / she / it would not be being asked
you / they would not be being asked

forme interro-négative

should I / we not be being asked?
would he / she / it not be being asked?
would you / they not be being asked?

CONDITIONNEL PASSÉ

VOIX ACTIVE

Conditionnel passé simple

forme affirmative

I / we should have asked
he / she / it would have asked
you / they would have asked

forme interrogative

should I / we have asked?
would he / she / it have asked?
would you / they have asked?

forme négative

I / we should not have asked
he / she / it would not have asked
you / they would not have asked

forme interro-négative

should I / we not have asked?
would he / she / it not have asked?
would you / they not have asked?

Conditionnel passé continu

forme affirmative

I / we should have been asking
he / she / it would have been asking
you / they would have been asking

forme interrogative

should I / we have been asking?
would he / she / it have been asking?
would you / they have been asking?

forme négative

I / we should not have been asking
he / she / it would not have been asking
you / they would not have been asking

forme interro-négative

should I / we not have been asking?
would he / she / it not have been asking?
would you / they not have been asking?

VOIX PASSIVE

Conditionnel passé simple

forme affirmative

I / we should have been asked
he / she / it would have been asked
you / they would have been asked

forme interrogative

should I / we have been asked?
would he / she / it have been asked?
would you / they have been asked?

forme négative

I / we should not have been asked
he / she / it would not have been asked
you / they would not have been asked

forme interro-négative

should I / we not have been asked?
would he / she / it not have been asked?
would you / they not have been asked?

Conditionnel passé continu

forme affirmative

I / we should have been being asked
he / she / it would have been being asked
you / they would have been being asked

forme interrogative

should I / we have been being asked?
would he / she / it have been being asked?
would you / they have been being asked?

forme négative

I / we should not have been being asked
he / she / it would not have been being asked
you / they would not have been being asked

forme interro-négative

should I / we not have been being asked?
would he / she / it not have been being asked?
would you / they not have been being asked?

PRONONCIATION

Terminaison du présent (troisième personne du singulier)

- Elle se prononce [s] :
  après les consonnes [f] *(laughs)*, [k] *(blinks)*, [p] *(grasps)*, [t] *(lifts)* et [θ] *(smooths)*.

- Elle se prononce [z] :
  – après les consonnes [v] *(loves)*, [g] *(bangs)*, [b] *(disturbs)*, [d] *(bings)*, [l] *(travels)*, [m] *(seems)*, [n] *(abandons)*, [ð] *(bathes)* ;
  – après une voyelle, le plus souvent [i], *(carries)* ;
  – après les diphtongues [ei] *(plays)*, [ai] *(sighs)*, [əu] *(bows)*, [ɔi] *(annoys)*.

- Après les consonnes [s], [z], [ʒ], [ʃ], il serait difficile de prononcer immédiatement le son [s]. Les Anglais prononcent donc [iz], comme dans *convinces, advises, changes, washes*.

  Dans certains cas, cela impliquera une **modification orthographique**.

Terminaison du passé des verbes réguliers *(ed)*

- Elle se prononce le plus souvent [d] :
  loved, banged, disturbed, travelled, seemed, abandonned, bathed, carried, played, sighed, bowed, annoyed...

- Mais elle se prononce :
  – **[id]** après [t] *(lifted)* et [d] *(handed)* ;
  – **[t]** après [f] *(laughed)*, [k] *(blinked)*, [p] *(grasped)*, [s] *(convinced)*, [ʃ] *(washed)*.

MODIFICATIONS ORTHOGRAPHIQUES

Terminaison de la troisième personne du singulier

- La terminaison *-y* devient *-ies* : *carry → carries*.

- La prononciation **[iz]** se manifeste par l'ajout d'un *e* de soutien devant le *s* final :
  pass → passes, watch → watches, buzz → buzzes.

Terminaison des verbes réguliers *(ed)*

- La terminaison *-y* devient *-ied* : *carry → carried*.

- On n'ajoute que le *-d* après les verbes se terminant en *-e* : *love → loved*.

Terminaison en *-ing*

- La terminaison *-e* est remplacée par *-ing* : *love → loving*.

- La terminaison *-ie* devient *-ying* : *lie → lying*.

Redoublement de la consonne finale

Le redoublement a lieu :
- quand le verbe ne comporte qu'une seule syllabe et que la consonne finale est précédée d'une seule voyelle courte :
  beg → begged, begging

- quand le verbe a plusieurs syllabes dont la dernière est accentuée et que la consonne est immédiatement précédée d'une seule voyelle courte :
  admit → admitted, admitting

Toutes ces modifications sont indiquées dans l'**Index général**, p. 115.

TABLEAU DES CONTRACTIONS

Forme affirmative		Forme
auxiliaire *be*		
I am he is we are	I'm he's we're	I am not he is not we are not
		I was not we were not
auxiliaire *have*		
I have he has we have	I've he's we've	I have not he has not we have not
I had	I'd	I had not
auxiliaire *do*		
		I do not he does not
		he did not
auxiliaires *shall / will*		
I shall he will	I'll he'll	I shall not he will not
auxiliaires *should / would*		
I should he would	I'd he'd	I should not he would not
I should have he would have	I should've he would've	I should not have he would not have
auxiliaire *can*		I cannot
auxiliaire *could*		I could not
auxiliaire *must*		I must not
auxiliaire *might*		I might not
auxiliaire *ought to*		I ought not to

négative	Forme interro-négative	
I'm not	am I not?	aren't I? (fam.) / ain't I? (fam.)
he isn't / he's not	is he not?	isn't he?
we aren't / we're not	are we not?	aren't we?
I wasn't	was I not?	wasn't I?
we weren't	were we not?	weren't we?
I haven't	have I not?	haven't I?
he hasn't	has he not?	hasn't he?
we haven't	have we not?	haven't we?
I hadn't	had I not?	hadn't I?
I don't	do I not?	don't I?
he doesn't	does he not?	doesn't he?
he didn't	did he not?	didn't he?
I shan't	shall I not?	shan't I?
he won't	will he not?	won't he?
I shouldn't	should I not?	shouldn't I?
he wouldn't	would he not?	wouldn't he?
I shouldn't have	should I not have?	shouldn't I have?
he wouldn't have	would he not have?	wouldn't he have?
I can't	can I not?	can't I?
I couldn't	could I not?	couldn't I?
I mustn't	must I not?	mustn't I?
I mightn't	might I not?	mightn't I?
I oughtn't to	ought I not to?	oughtn't I to?

COMMENT POSER UNE QUESTION ?

Il vous faudra faire la différence entre deux types de questions : les questions fermées, pour lesquelles on attend une réponse par *yes* ou *no* et les questions ouvertes, qui suggèrent de répondre de façon circonstanciée.

Questions fermées

- Dans le cas d'un verbe ordinaire au présent ou au prétérit, l'ajout de l'auxiliaire *do* ou *did*, en début de question, est indispensable.

  Do you go out with him?
  Est-ce que tu sors avec lui ?
  Does she like this book?
  Est-ce qu'elle aime ce livre ?
  Did they write to him?
  Lui ont-ils écrit ?

- Inutile d'ajouter un auxiliaire si la phrase en contient déjà un, qu'il s'agisse de *be*, de *have* ou d'un modal : une simple inversion suffit.

  Are you going with him?
  Allez-vous avec lui ?
  Has she read this book?
  A-t-elle lu ce livre ?
  Must you really go now?
  Vous devez vraiment partir maintenant ?

Dans le cas de plusieurs auxiliaires, l'inversion ne porte qu'entre le premier d'entre eux et le sujet.

  Could they have missed their train?
  Se pourrait-il qu'ils aient raté leur train ?

- Si vous attendez plutôt une réponse positive, utilisez la forme interro-négative, en accolant *n't* à l'auxiliaire.

  Don't you like him?
  Tu ne l'apprécies pas ?
  Hasn't she bought a new dress?
  N'a-t-elle pas acheté une nouvelle robe ?
  Shouldn't they be here now?
  Ne devraient-ils pas être arrivés ?

Attention toutefois à la place de la négation, juste avant le verbe, si la forme n'est pas contractée (cf. tableau p. 98).

  Does he not like tea?
  N'aime-t-il pas le thé ?

Questions ouvertes

- Elles requièrent toujours un mot interrogatif, qui peut être :
  - **un adverbe ou une expression adverbiale :**

    When do you go to London?
    Quand allez-vous à Londres ?

    Why didn't you tell him about it?
    Pourquoi ne lui as-tu pas dit ?

    How did you like the film?
    Qu'as-tu pensé du film ?

How peut aussi être placé devant un adjectif ou un adverbe.

    How far can she run?
    Jusqu'où peut-elle courir ?

    How long have they been reading?
    Depuis combien de temps lisent-ils ?

    How good are you at English?
    Quel est votre niveau en anglais ?

    How well can he swim?
    Quel est son niveau en natation ?

  - **un pronom interrogatif complément :**

    Who(m) did you meet in London?
    Qui as-tu rencontré à Londres ?

    What does he have to do in London?
    Que doit-il faire à Londres ?

  - **un pronom interrogatif sujet** (il n'y a alors ni inversion du sujet, ni emploi de *do / does / did*) :

    Who will go to London with me?
    Qui ira à Londres avec moi ?

    What happened?
    Que s'est-il passé ?

- Si la question comporte un **verbe à particules**, celle-ci se place :
  - en début de question :

    To whom will you offer this book?
    À qui offriras-tu ce livre ?

  - ou, **de préférence**, en fin de question :

    Who will you offer this book to?

- Enfin, si la question porte sur un **choix** entre deux choses ou deux personnes, c'est le pronom *which* qui s'impose.

    Which would you rather have dinner with, Jack or Jim?
    Avec lequel préférerais-tu dîner, Jack ou Jim ?

LES TAGS

Pour éviter de répéter inutilement un verbe, l'anglais possède une série de structures qui, toutes construites à partir d'auxiliaires, permettent aussi bien de répondre brièvement à une question que d'exprimer des réactions.

Elles se placent à la fin d'une question ou d'une phrase affirmative, d'où leur nom de *tag* qui désigne en anglais l'extrémité de quelque chose (par exemple *the tag line* : le dernier vers d'un poème).

Réponses courtes

Do you know the Joneses? Yes, I do. / No, I don't.
Vous connaissez les Jones ? Oui. / Non.

Haven't you already met them? Yes, I have. / No, I haven't.
Ne les avez-vous pas déjà rencontrés ? Oui. / Non.

Can you see that tree in the distance? Yes, I can. / No, I can't.
Vous voyez cet arbre au loin ? Oui. / Non.

Reprises interrogatives

C'est l'équivalent du français « n'est-ce pas ? » ou, dans une langue moins soutenue, « hein ? ».

- Phrase **affirmative** → *tag* **interro-négatif.**
  Sheila knows them, doesn't she?
  Sheila les connaît, n'est-ce pas ?
  You went with him, didn't you?
  Tu es allé avec lui, n'est-ce pas ?
  You can hear me, can't you?
  Vous m'entendez, n'est-ce pas ?

- Phase **négative** → *tag* **interrogatif.**
  You won't leave me, will you?
  Tu ne me quitteras pas, hein ?
  David shouldn't be here, should he?
  David ne devrait pas être là, n'est-ce pas ?

L'intonation varie selon qu'il s'agit d'une simple demande de confirmation (intonation descendante) ou d'une demande de renseignement (intonation ascendante).

- Phrase à **l'impératif** → *tag* **interrogatif.**
  Open the door, will you?
  Ouvre la porte, veux-tu ?
  Let's have dinner, shall we?
  Et si nous dînions ?

Une intonation descendante insistera sur le caractère impérieux de l'ordre donné.

Réactions

- **Étonnement**

    Le *tag* traduit des expressions comme « Tiens ? », « Vraiment ? », « Vous croyez ? », « Ah oui ? »...

    – Phrase **affirmative** → *tag* **interrogatif**.
    "He can swim very fast." "Can he ?"
    « Il nage très vite. » « Ah bon ? »

    – Phrase **négative** → *tag* **interro-négatif**.
    "He didn't know this." "Didn't he?"
    « Il ne savait pas ça. » « Vraiment ? »

    L'auxiliaire du *tag* est accentué. L'intonation sera montante pour exprimer la surprise, descendante pour exprimer le doute ou l'indifférence.

- **Constatation**

    Le *tag* traduit des expressions comme « Eh oui ! », « C'est bien vrai », « Bien sûr ! »
    "He adores tea." "So he does."
    « Il adore le thé. » « Ça, tu peux le dire ! »

    À ne pas confondre avec le *tag* suivant : (*so* + auxiliaire + sujet).

- **« Moi aussi... » « Moi non plus... »**

    – Phrase **affirmative** → *so* + auxiliaire + sujet.
    "I'd like a nice cup of tea." "So would I."
    « J'aimerais une bonne tasse de thé. » « Moi aussi. »
    "He reads a lot." "So does Ann."
    « Il lit beaucoup. » « Anne aussi. »

    – Phrase **négative** → *neither* + auxiliaire + sujet.
    "I can't see them." "Neither can I."
    « Je ne les vois pas. » « Moi non plus. »

- **Contradiction**

    – Phrase **affirmative** → *tag* **négatif**.
    "I'll go with them." "I won't."
    « J'irai avec eux. » « Pas moi. »

    – Phrase **négative** → *tag* **affirmatif**.
    "I don't like this film." "I do."
    « Je n'aime pas ce film. » « Moi, si. »

    Attention à *never*, *hardly*, qui ont un sens négatif.
    "I have never read such a good book." "Neither have I."
    « Je n'ai jamais lu un aussi bon livre. » « Moi non plus. »
    "I can hardly imagine anything better." "Neither can I."
    « Je ne peux rien imaginer de mieux. » « Moi non plus. »

TABLEAUX DES VERBES IRRÉGULIERS

Définition

- La majorité des verbes anglais ont très régulièrement quatre formes : *like, likes, liked, liking.*

- Moins de deux cents verbes sont dit « irréguliers » parce qu'ils ont des formes spéciales pour le prétérit et le participe passé : *begin, begins, began, begun, beginning.*
La voyelle centrale marque le changement essentiel : elle peut rester la même aux trois temps ; elle peut aussi changer une ou deux fois.

Classement

- C'est ce fait qui détermine notre classement et pourra aider à la mémorisation. On distinguera trois catégories, en symbolisant la voyelle (ou diphtongue) centrale du présent par A, celle du prétérit par B et celle du participe passé par C :

1. Trois voyelles semblables :	*hit,*	*hit,*	*hit*	atteindre, frapper
2. Deux voyelles semblables :	*cling*	*clung*	*clung*	s'accrocher
	run	*ran*	*run*	courir
3. Trois voyelles différentes :	*begin*	*began*	*begun*	commencer

- Secondairement, la terminaison peut également varier.
Le *d* de l'infinitif peut se changer en *t* : *build, built, built* (construire).
Ou encore on peut observer l'addition d'un *n* : *break, broke, broken* (casser).

Mémorisation

Vous pourrez ainsi vous servir de ces groupements par ressemblance. Vous trouverez la liste complète page 213.

- Il peut vous être utile de savoir que les verbes irréguliers concernent généralement :
  - des activités vitales et quotidiennes, liées à la survie : *eat, drink, sleep, build, dwell...*
  - des mouvements et activités du corps : *see, smell, lie, run, swim, make...*
  - des relations humaines de communication : *say, speak, tell, teach, learn...*
  - des relations humaines de lutte pour la vie : *beat, fight, hit, strike...*
  - des relations humaines commerciales : *bid, buy, sell...*

- Sachez d'autre part que :
  - plusieurs de ces verbes sont rares ;
  - dans d'assez nombreux cas, une forme faible en *ed* est possible ;
  - tous les verbes nouveaux – il en naît chaque année – rejoignent la forme rassurante des verbes réguliers en *ed*.

TROIS VOYELLES SEMBLABLES : AAA

A	**A**	**A**	
[i]	**[i]**	**[i]**	
hit	*hit*	*hit*	atteindre, frapper
knit	*knit (knitted)*	*knit (knitted)*	tricoter [1]
quit	*quit*	*quit*	quitter
slit	*slit*	*slit*	fendre, inciser
split	*split*	*split*	fendre
rid	*rid (ridded)*	*rid (ridded)*	débarrasser [2]
bid	*bid (bade)*	*bid (bidden)*	offrir (prix), ordonner
build	*built*	*built*	bâtir
gild	*gilt (gilded)*	*gilt (gilded)*	dorer [3] (rare)
spill	*spilt (spilled)*	*spilt (spilled)*	répandre (liquide)
[e]	**[e]**	**[e]**	
bet	*bet*	*bet*	parier
let	*let*	*let*	laisser, permettre, louer
set	*set*	*set*	placer
shed	*shed*	*shed*	verser (larmes, sang)
spread	*spread*	*spread*	étendre, répandre
bend	*bent*	*bent*	courber
lend	*lent*	*lent*	prêter
rend	*rent*	*rent*	déchirer (rare)
send	*sent*	*sent*	envoyer
spend	*spent*	*spent*	dépenser, passer (temps)
dwell	*dwelt*	*dwelt*	habiter
smell	*smelt (smelled)*	*smelt (smelled)*	sentir (nez)
spell	*spelt (spelled)*	*spelt (spelled)*	épeler
[ʌ]	**[ʌ]**	**[ʌ]**	
cut	*cut*	*cut*	couper
shut	*shut*	*shut*	fermer
thrust	*thrust*	*thrust*	enfoncer
[u]	**[u]**	**[u]**	
put	*put*	*put*	mettre
[ɔ]	**[ɔ]**	**[ɔ]**	
cost	*cost*	*cost*	coûter

---

1. **knit** : régulier au sens propre *(a knitted sweater)*, irrégulier au sens figuré *(a well-knit plot* : une conspiration bien ourdie).
2. **rid** : surtout employé au participe passé : *to get rid of* (se débarrasser de).
3. **gild** : le plus souvent faible.

TROIS VOYELLES SEMBLABLES : AAA

A	A	A	
[iː]	[iː]	[iː]	
beat	*beat*	*beaten*	battre [1]
[əː]	[əː]	[əː]	
burst	*burst*	*burst*	éclater
hurt	*hurt*	*hurt*	faire mal
burn	*burnt (burned)*	*burnt (burned)*	brûler
gird	*girt (girded)*	*girt (girded)*	ceindre (rare)
learn	*learnt (learned)*	*learnt (learned)*	apprendre
[aː]	[aː]	[aː]	
broadcast	*broadcast*	*broadcast*	diffuser
cast	*cast*	*cast*	lancer [2]
forecast	*forecast*	*forecast*	prévoir
[ɔi]	[ɔi]	[ɔi]	
spoil	*spoilt (spoiled)*	*spoilt (spoiled)*	gâter, gâcher
[æ]	[æ]	[æ]	
have	*had*	*had*	avoir
[ei]	[ei]	[ei]	
grave	*graved*	*graven (graved)*	graver
lade	*laded*	*laden (laded)*	charger
make	*made*	*made*	fabriquer
lay	*laid*	*laid*	poser à plat
pay	*paid*	*paid*	payer

---

1. **beat** : le participe passé est *beat* dans *dead-beat* (crevé de fatigue) (fam.)
2. **cast** : surtout au sens figuré.

A	A	A	
[ɔː]	[ɔː]	[ɔː]	
saw	sawed	sawn (sawed)	scier
[uː]	[uː]	[uː]	
strew	strewed	strewn (strewed)	joncher
[juː]	[juː]	[juː]	
hew	hewed	hewn (hewed)	tailler à la hache
[ou]	[ou]	[ou]	
mow	mowed	mown (mowed)	faucher
show	showed	shown (showed)	montrer
sow	sowed	sown (sowed)	semer
sew	sewed	sewn (sewed)	coudre

Dans cette catégorie, le participe passé est le plus souvent devenu aussi régulier. La forme irrégulière est quelquefois conservée pour l'adjectif.

On peut y ajouter des formes isolées comme :
- **wrought** (de *to work* : œuvrer) dans *wrought iron* : le fer forgé,
- **shaven** dans *a clean-shaven face* : un visage bien rasé,
- **molten** (de *to melt* : fondre) dans *molten lead* : plomb fondu,
- **rotten** (de *to rot* : pourrir) dans *rotten eggs*,
  alors que les participes passés à valeur verbale sont réguliers.

DEUX VOYELLES SEMBLABLES : ABB

A	B	B	
[i]	[ʌ]	[ʌ]	
cling	clung	clung	s'accrocher
dig	dug	dug	creuser
fling	flung	flung	lancer, jeter
sling	slung	slung	lancer (fronde)
slink	slunk	slunk	aller furtivement
spin	spun	spun	tournoyer
stick	stuck	stuck	coller
sting	stung	stung	piquer (insecte)
string	strung	strung	enfiler [1]
swing	swung	swung	(se) balancer
wring	wrung	wrung	tordre
win	won	won	gagner
[æ]	[ʌ]	[ʌ]	
hang	hung (hanged)	hung (hanged)	pendre [2]
[ai]	[ʌ]	[ʌ]	
strike	struck	struck	frapper [3]
[ai]	[i]	[i]	
bite	bit	bitten / bit	mordre
chide	chid	chidden	gronder
hide	hid	hidden / hid	cacher
light	lit	lit	allumer [4]
slide	slid	slid	glisser
[ai]	[ɔ]	[ɔ]	
shine	shone	shone	briller [5]
[ei]	[e]	[e]	
say	said	said	dire [6]

---

1. **string** : on utilise le participe passé régulier dans *stringed instruments* (instruments à cordes).
2. **hang** : le verbe est régulier dans le sens de : exécuter par pendaison.
3. **strike** : au sens figuré, le participe passé peut être *stricken*.
4. **light** : le participe régulier est employé comme une épithète : *a lighted candle*. Le participe passé irrégulier s'emploie après *be (the candle is lit)* et dans les composés (*floodlit* : illuminé).
5. **shine** : le verbe est régulier dans : *to shine shoes* (cirer des chaussures).
6. **say** : la voyelle est courte [sed] au prétérit et au participe passé, alors qu'elle est longue dans *gain-say* (contredire).

DEUX VOYELLES SEMBLABLES : ABB

A	B	B	
[iː]	**[e]**	**[e]**	
lead	led	led	mener
read	read	read	lire
bleed	bled	bled	saigner
breed	bred	bred	élever (bêtes) [1]
feed	fed	fed	nourrir
flee	fled	fled	fuir [2]
speed	sped (speeded)	sped (speeded)	(se) hâter
berèave	bereft (bereaded)	bereft (bereaved)	dépouiller (rare)
cleave	cleft (cleaved)	cleft (cleaved)	fendre [3]
leave	left	left	laisser, quitter
deal	dealt	dealt	distribuer
dream	dreamt (dreamed)	dreamt (dreamed)	rêver
lean	leant (leaned)	leant (leaned)	s'appuyer
leap	leapt (leaped)	leapt (leaped)	sauter
mean	meant	meant	signifier
creep	crept	crept	ramper
feel	felt	felt	ressentir
keep	kept	kept	garder
kneel	knelt	knelt	s'agenouiller
meet	met	met	(se) rencontrer
sleep	slept	slept	dormir
sweep	swept	swept	balayer
weep	wept	wept	pleurer
[æ]	**[u]**	**[u]**	
stand	stood	stood	être debout
understand	understood	understood	comprendre
[e]	**[ou]**	**[ou]**	
sell	sold	sold	vendre
tell	told	told	raconter
[uː]	**[ɔ]**	**[ɔ]**	
shoe	shod	shod	ferrer [4]
lose	lost	lost	perdre
shoot	shot	shot	tirer (armes)

---

1. **breed** : quand il s'agit d'enfants : *bring up*.
2. **flee** : à l'infinitif, on emploie plutôt *fly away*.
3. **cleave** : emplois courants du participe passé *cloven*, dans *cloven hoof* (sabot / pied fourchu), de *cleft* dans *to be in a cleft stick* (être dans une impasse).
4. **shoe** : pour les personnes, s'emploie surtout au participe passé (*well shod* : bien chaussé).

DEUX VOYELLES SEMBLABLES : ABB

A	B	B	
[ai]	[au]	[au]	
bind	bound	bound	lier
find	found	found	trouver
grind	ground	ground	moudre
wind	wound	wound	enrouler
[ou]	[æ]	[æ]	
clothe	clad (clothed)	clad (clothed)	vêtir (rare)
[ou]	[e]	[e]	
hold	held	held	tenir
[iə]	[əː]	[əː]	
hear	heard	heard	entendre
[iː]	[ɔː]	[ɔː]	
beseech	besought (beseeched)	besought (beseeched)	implorer
seek	sought	sought	chercher
teach	taught	taught	enseigner
[i]	[ɔː]	[ɔː]	
bring	brought	brought	apporter
think	thought	thought	penser
[ai]	[ɔː]	[ɔː]	
buy	bought	bought	acheter
fight	fought	fought	combattre
[æ]	[ɔː]	[ɔː]	
catch	caught	caught	attraper
[i]	[æ]	[æ]	
sit	sat	sat	être assis
spit	spat	spat	cracher
[e]	[ɔ]	[ɔ]	
forget	forgot	forgot (forgotten)	oublier
get	got	got	obtenir [1]
tread	trod	trodden	piétiner

---

1. **get** : gotten = obtained, become (américain). Dans les composés : forget → forgotten (britannique),
beget → begotten.

A	B	B	
[iː]	[ou]	[ou]	
cleave	clove / cleft (cleaved)	cloven / cleft (cleaved)	fendre
heave	hove (heaved)	hove (heaved)	soulever [1]
speak	spoke	spoken	parler
steal	stole	stolen	dérober
weave	wove	woven	tisser
freeze	froze	frozen	geler
[uː]	[ou]	[ou]	
choose	chose	chosen	choisir
[ei]	[ou]	[ou]	
awake	awoke	awoken	éveiller
break	broke	broken	casser [2]
wake	woke (waked)	woken (waked)	réveiller [3]
[ai]	[ei]	[ei]	
lie	lay	lain	être couché [4]
[ɛə]	[ɔː]	[ɔː]	
bear	bore	born / borne	(sup)porter [5]
tear	tore	torn	déchirer
swear	swore	sworn	jurer
wear	wore	worn	porter, user (vêtements)

A	A	B	
[e]	[e]	[ou]	
swell	swelled	swollen (swelled)	enfler
[ai]	[ai]	[i]	
shrive	shrived	shriven (shrived)	confesser
[iə]	[iə]	[ɔː]	
shear	sheared	shorn (sheared)	tondre

---

1. **heave** : le verbe n'est irrégulier que dans la langue des marins (to heave the anchor : lever l'ancre).
2. **break** : le participe passé broke est employé dans un sens familier : fauché.
3. **wake** : régulier parfois en américain.
4. **lie** : régulier dans le sens de mentir.
5. **bear** : to be born = naître (verbe passif).

DEUX VOYELLES SEMBLABLES : ABA

A	B	A	
[ʌ]	[æ]	[ʌ]	
run	*ran*	*run*	courir
[ʌ]	[ei]	[ʌ]	
become	*became*	*become*	devenir
come	*came*	*come*	venir
[i]	[ei]	[i]	
forgive	*forgave*	*forgiven*	pardonner
give	*gave*	*given*	donner
[iː]	[e]	[iː]	
eat	*ate*	*eaten*	manger [1]
[iː]	[ɔː]	[iː]	
see	*saw*	*seen*	voir
[iː]	[ɔ]	[iː]	
be	*was (were)*	*been*	être
[ɔː]	[e]	[ɔː]	
fall	*fell*	*fallen*	tomber
[ɔː]	[uː]	[ɔː]	
draw	*drew*	*drawn*	tirer
withdraw	*withdrew*	*withdrawn*	(se) retirer
[ei]	[u]	[ei]	
mistake	*mistook*	*mistaken*	se tromper
shake	*shook*	*shaken*	secouer
take	*took*	*taken*	prendre
undertake	*undertook*	*undertaken*	entreprendre
[ei]	[uː]	[ei]	
slay	*slew (slayed)*	*slain*	assassiner
[ou]	[uː]	[ou]	
blow	*blew*	*blown*	souffler
grow	*grew*	*grown*	croître
throw	*threw*	*thrown*	jeter
[əu]	[juː]	[əu]	
know	*knew*	*known*	savoir

---

1. ***eat*** : *ate* est prononcé [et] en Grande-Bretagne et [eit] aux Etats-Unis.

TROIS VOYELLES DIFFÉRENTES : ABC

A	B	C	
[i]	**[æ]**	**[ʌ]**	
begin	began	begun	commencer
swim	swam	swum	nager
ring	rang	rung	sonner [1]
sing	sang	sung	chanter
spring	sprang	sprung	bondir
drink	drank	drunk	boire [2]
shrink	shrank	shrunk	se rétrécir [3]
sink	sank	sunk	sombrer [4]
stink	stank	stunk	puer
[ai]	**[ou]**	**[i]**	
arise	arose	arisen	survenir
drive	drove	driven	conduire
strive	strove	striven	s'efforcer
thrive	throve (thrived)	thriven (thrived)	prospérer
ride	rode	ridden	chevaucher
stride	strode	stridden	enjamber
smite	smote	smitten	frapper
write	wrote	written	écrire
rise	rose	risen	se lever
[uː]	**[i]**	**[ʌ]**	
do	did	done	faire
[ou]	**[e]**	**[ɔ]**	
go	went	gone	aller
[ai]	**[uː]**	**[ou]**	
fly	flew	flown	voler (air)

---

1. **ring** : régulier dans le sens de : encercler.
2. **drink** : le participe passé *drunken* est utilisé comme épithète *(a drunken man)* mais on dit : *he is drunk.*
3. **shrink** : de même *shrunken* : ratatiné.
4. **sink** : de même *sunken* : creux (joues, yeux).

Index général

	Abréviations utilisées

T   transitif
I   intransitif
A   auxiliaire
C   verbe à complémentation (voir liste des verbes à
    complémentation p. 169)
◊   verbe pouvant s'associer avec 1 à 10 particules
◊◊ verbe pouvant s'associer avec 11 à 20 particules
◊◊◊ verbe pouvant s'associer avec plus de 20 particules
    (voir liste des verbes à particules p. 177)

Les verbes irréguliers sont en couleur (voir liste des verbes
irréguliers p. 213).
Entre parenthèses, sont indiquées les modifications
orthographiques.

- **bb**, **gg**, **ll**, **rr**, **tt**... = redoublement de la consonne finale :
  beg → begged / begged / begging

- **ie** = **y** final remplacé par **ie** au présent (3e pers. du sing.)
  et au passé :
  carry → carries / carried

- **es** = **e** ajouté au présent (3e pers. du sing.) :
  harrass → harrasses

- **yi** = **ie** devient **y** devant **ing** :
  die → dying

abandon, ◊, T, C
abase, T
abash (es), ◊, T
abate, T/I
abbreviate, ◊, T
abdicate, T/I
abduct, T
abet (tt), ◊, T
abhor (rr), T, C
abide, ◊, T/I
abjure, T
abnegate, T
abolish (es), T
abominate, T, C
abort, T/I
abound, ◊, I
abrade, T
abridge, T
abrogate, T
abseil, I
absent, ◊, T
absolve, ◊, T
absorb, ◊, T, C
abstain, ◊, I, C
abstract, ◊, T
abuse, T
abut (tt), ◊, I
accede, ◊, I
accelerate, T/I
accent, T
accentuate, T
accept, ◊, T, C
access (es), ◊, I
acclaim, T
acclimatise (am. -ize), ◊, T/I

accommodate, ◊, T
accompany (ie), T
accomplish (es), T
accord, ◊, T/I
accost, T
account, ◊, T, C
accredit, ◊, T
accrue, ◊, I
accumulate, T/I
accuse, ◊, T, C
accustom, ◊, T, C
ache, ◊, I, C
achieve, T
acidify (ie), T
acidulate, T
acknowledge, ◊, T, C
acquaint, ◊, T
acquiesce, ◊, I
acquire, T
acquit (tt), ◊, T
act, ◊, T/I
activate, T
actuate, T
adapt, ◊, T/I
add, ◊, T/I, C
addict, ◊, T, C
addle, T/I
address (es), ◊, T
adduce, T
adhere, ◊, I
adjoin, T/I
adjourn, ◊, T/I
adjudge, T
adjudicate, ◊, T/I
adjure, T, C
adjust, ◊, T/I
ad-lib, T/I
administer, ◊, T/I
administrate, T
admire, ◊, T
admit (tt), ◊, T, C

admix (es), T/I
admonish (es), T, C
adopt, ◊, T
adore, T, C
adorn, ◊, T
adulate, T
adulterate, T
adumbrate, T
advance, ◊, T/I
advantage, T
adventure, T/I
advert, ◊, I
advertise, ◊, T/I, C
advise, ◊, T/I, C
advocate, T, C
aerate, T
affect, ◊, T
affiliate, ◊, T
affirm, ◊, T, C
affix (es), ◊, T
afflict, ◊, T
afford, T, C
afforest, T
affront, T
age, T/I
agglomerate, T/I
agglutinate, ◊, T/I
aggrandise (am. -ize), T
aggravate, T
aggregate, T/I
aggrieve, T
agitate, ◊, T/I
agonise (am. -ize), T/I
agree, ◊, T/I, C
aid, T, C
ail, T/I
aim, ◊, T/I, C
air, T
airmail, ◊, T
alarm, ◊, T
alcoholise (am. -ize), T

alert, ◊, T

alienate, ◊, T

alight, ◊, I

align, ◊, T/I

allay, T

allege, T, C

allegorise (am. -ize), T/I

alleviate, T

alliterate, T/I

allocate, ◊, T, C

allot (tt), ◊, T, C

allow, ◊, T, C

alloy, T

allude, ◊, I

allure, ◊, T

ally (ie), ◊, T/I

alphabetise (am. -ize), T

alter, T/I

alternate, ◊, T/I

amalgamate, ◊, T/I

amass, T

amaze, ◊, T

amble, ◊◊◊, I

ambush (es), T/I

ameliorate, T/I

amend, T/I

americanize, T

amortise (am. -ize), T

amount, ◊, I, C

amplify (ies), T

amputate, T

amuse, ◊, T, C

anæsthetise / anesthetise
  (am. -ize), T

analyse, T

anathematise (am. -ize), T

anatomise (am. -ize), T

anchor, T/I

anforise (am. -ize), T

anger, T

angle, ◊, T/I

anglicise (am. -ize), T

animadvert, ◊, T

animalise (am. -ize), T

animate, T

annex (es), ◊, T

annihilate, T

annotate, T

announce, ◊, T, C

annoy, ◊, T

annul (ll), T

annunciate, T, C

anoint, ◊, T

answer, ◊, T/I, C

antagonise (am. -ize), T

antedate, T

anticipate, T, C

ape, T

apologise (am. -ize), ◊, I, C

apparel, T

appalatise (am. -ize), ◊, T/I

appeal, ◊, I, C

appear, ◊, I

appease, T

append, ◊, T

appertain, ◊, I

applaud, T

apply (ie), ◊, T/I, C

appoint, ◊, T, C

apportion, ◊, T

appose, ◊, T

appraise, T

appreciate, T/I, C

apprehend, T

apprentice, ◊, T

apprise, ◊, T

approach (es), ◊, T/I

approbate, ◊, T

appropriate, ◊, T

approve, ◊, T, C

approximate, ◊, T/I

arbitrate, ◊, T/I

arc, ◊, I

arch (es), ◊, T/I

argue, ◊, T/I, C

arise, ◊, I

arm, ◊, T/I

armour (am. -or), T

arouse, ◊, T

arraign, ◊, T, C

arrange, ◊, T/I, C

array, T

arrest, T

arrive, ◊, I

arrogate, ◊, T

arrow, T/I

article, T

articulate, T/I

ascend, T/I

ascertain, T

ascribe, ◊, T

ask, ◊, T/I, C

aspirate, T

aspire, ◊, I, C

assail, ◊, T

assassinate, T

assault, T

assemble, T/I

assent, ◊, I

assert, T, C

assess (es), ◊, T

asseverate, T, C

assign, ◊, T

assimilate, ◊, T/I

assist, ◊, T/I, C

associate, ◊, T/I, C

assort, ◊, T/I

assuage, T

assume, T, C

assure, ◊, T, C

asterisk, T

astonish (es), ◊, T, C

astound, T

atomise (am. -ize), T
atone, ◊, T, C
atrophy, (ies), I
attach (es), ◊, T/I
attack, T
attain, ◊, T/I
attempt, T, C
attend, ◊, T/I
attenuate, T/I
attest, ◊, T/I, C
attire, ◊, T
attitudinise (am. -ize), I
attract, ◊, T
attribute, ◊, T
attune, ◊, T
auction, ◊, T
audit, T
audition, ◊, T/I
augment, T/I
augur, T/I, C
auscultate, T
authenticate, T
author, T
authorise (am. -ize), T, C
autodecrement, T
autograph, T
autoincrement, T
auto-index (es), T
automate, T
automatise (am. -ize), T
avail, ◊, T/I
avalanche, I
avenge, ◊, T
aver (rr), T/I, C
average, ◊, T/I
avert, ◊, T
avoid, T, C
await, T
awake, ◊, T/I
awaken, ◊, T/I
award, ◊, T

awe, ◊, T
axe, T

b

baa, I
babble, ◊, T/I
baby (ie), T
baby-sit (tt), T/I
back, ◊, T/I
back-comb, T
backdate, ◊, T
backfire, I
back-order, T
backslide, I
backspace, I
backtab (bb), I
backtrack, I
badger, ◊, T, C
baffle, T
bag (gg), ◊, T/I
bail, ◊, T
bait, ◊, T, C
bake, T/I
balance, ◊, T/I
bale, ◊, T
balk, ◊, T/I
ball, ◊, T/I
ballast, T
balloon, I
ballot, ◊, I
bamboozle, ◊, T, C
ban (nn), T
band, ◊, T/I
bandage, ◊, T
bandy (ie), ◊, T

bang, ◊, T/I
banish (es), ◊, T
bank, ◊, T/I
bankroll, T
bankrupt, T
banquet, T/I
bant, I
banter, T/I
baptise (am. -ize), T
bar (rr), ◊, T, C
barb, T
barbarise (am. -ize), T/I
barbecue, T
barber, T
bard, T
bare, ◊, T
bargain, ◊, I
barge, ◊◊◊, T/I
bark, ◊, T/I, C
barrack, T
barrel, T/I
barricade, ◊, T
barter, ◊, T/I
base, ◊, T
bash (es), ◊, T
bask, ◊, I
bastardise (am. -ize), T
baste, T
bat (tt), ◊, T/I
batch (es), I
bath, T/I
bathe, ◊, T/I
batten, ◊, T/I
batter, ◊, T/I
battle, ◊, I
bawl, ◊, T/I
bay, ◊, I
bayonet, T
be, ◊◊◊, I/A
beach (es), T/I
beacon, T

bead, T / I

beagle, I

beam, ◊, T / I

bear, ◊◊, T / I, C

beard, T

beat, ◊◊, T / I, C

beatify (ie), T

beautify (ie), T

beckon, ◊, T / I

become, ◊, T / I

bed (dd), ◊, T / I

bedaub, ◊, T

bedeck, ◊, T

bedevil (ll), T

bedew, ◊, T

bedizen, T

beef, ◊, T / I

beep, T / I

beetle, ◊, I

befall, T / I

befit (tt), T

befoul, ◊, T

befriend, T

befuddle, ◊, T

beg (gg), ◊, T / I, C

beget (tt), T

begin (nn), ◊, T / I, C

begrime, ◊, T

begrudge, T

beguile, ◊, T, C

behave, ◊, I

behead, T

behold, T

behove, T, C

belay, T / I

belch, ◊, T / I

belie (yi), T

believe, ◊, T / I, C

belittle, T

bell, T

bellow, ◊, T / I

belly (ie), ◊, T / I

belong, ◊, I

belt, ◊, T / I

bemoan, T

bemuse, T

bench (es), T

benchmark, T

bend, ◊, T / I

benefit, ◊, T / I, C

benumb, ◊, T

bequeath, ◊, T

berate, T

bereave, ◊, T

berry (ie), I

berth, T / I

beseech (es), T, C

beseem, T / I, C

beset (tt), ◊, T

besiege, ◊, T

beslobber, T

besmear, ◊, T

besmirch (es), T

besot (tt), ◊, T

bespangle, T

bespatter, ◊, T

bespeak, T

besprinkle, ◊, T

best, ◊, T

bestir (rr), T

bestow, ◊, T

bestraddle, T

bestrew, ◊, T

bestride, T

bet (tt), ◊, T / I, C

betake, T

bethink, ◊, T, C

betide*, T / I

betray, ◊, T

betroth, ◊, T

better, T / I

bevel (ll), T / I

bewail, T

beware, ◊, T / I

bewilder, T

bewitch (es), T

bias (es), ◊, T

bicker, ◊, I

bicycle, ◊◊◊, I

bid (dd), ◊, T / I, C

bide, T / I

biff, T

bifurcate, T / I

bike, ◊◊◊, I

bilk, ◊, T, C

bill, T

billet, ◊, T

billow, ◊, I

bind, ◊, T / I, C

birch (es), T

bisect, T / I

bitch (es), ◊, I

bite, ◊, T/I

bivouac, T

blab (bb), ◊, T / I, C

blabber, ◊, T

black, ◊, T / I

blackball, T

blacken, ◊, T / I

blacklist, T

blackmail, ◊, T, C

blame, ◊, T

blanch (es), T / I

blank, ◊, T

blanket, ◊, T

blare, ◊, T / I, C

blaspheme, ◊, T / I

---

* *Betide* n'existe qu'à l'impératif (3e personne du singulier) : *Woe betide those who*... Malheur à ceux qui...

blast, ◊, T, C

blather, T/I

blaze, ◊, T/I

blazon, ◊, T

bleach (es), ◊, T/I

blear, T

bleat, ◊, T/I, C

bleed, ◊, T/I

bleep, T/I

blemish (es), T

blench (es), T

blend, ◊, T/I

bless (es), ◊, T

blether, T/I

blight, T

blind, ◊, T

blindfold, T

blink, ◊, T/I

blister, T/I

blitz (es), T

bloat, T/I

block, ◊, T/I

blockade, T

blood, T

bloom, ◊, I

blossom, ◊, I

blot (tt), ◊, T/I

blotch (es), T/I

blow, ◊◊, T/I

blubber, ◊, T/I, C

bludgeon, T

blue, T

bluff, ◊, T/I, C

blunder, ◊, T/I

blunt, T

blur (rr), ◊, T

blurt, ◊, T, C

blush (es), ◊, I, C

bluster, ◊, I

board, ◊, T/I

boast, ◊, T/I, C

boat, T/I

bob (bb), ◊, T/I

bode, T/I

bodge, T

bog (gg), ◊, T/I

boggle, ◊, I

boil, ◊, T/I

bolster, ◊, T

bolt, ◊, T/I

bomb, ◊, T/I

bombard, ◊, T

bond, T

bone, T

boo, T/I

boob, I

book, ◊, T/I

boom, T/I

boomerang, I

boost, ◊, T

boot, ◊, T

bootleg (gg), T/I

bootstrap (pp), T

booze, I

border, ◊, T/I

bore, ◊, T/I

borrow, ◊, T

boss (es), ◊, T

botanise (am. -ize), I

botch (es), ◊, T

bother, ◊, T/I, C

bottle, ◊, T

bottle-feed, T

bottom, ◊, T/I

bounce, ◊◊◊, T/I

bound, ◊, T/I

bouse / bowse, ◊, T

bow, ◊, T/I

bowdlerise (am. -ize), T

bowl, ◊, T/I

box (es), ◊, T/I

brace, ◊, T/I

bracket, T

brag (gg), ◊, T/I, C

braid, T/I

brain, T

brake, I

branch (es), ◊, T/I

brand, ◊, T

brandish (es), T

brave, T

brawl, I

bray, I

braze, T

brazen, ◊, T

breach (es), T/I

bread, T

break, ◊◊, T/I

breakfast, ◊, I

breast, T

breast-feed, T

breathalyze, T

breathe, ◊, T/I

breech (es), T

breed, ◊, T/I

breeze, ◊, I

brew, ◊, T/I

bribe, ◊, T, C

brick, ◊, T

bridge, ◊, T

bridle, ◊, T/I

brief, T

brigade, T

brighten, ◊, T/I

brim (mm), ◊, T/I

bring, ◊◊, T, C

brisk, ◊, T/I

bristle, ◊, T/I

broach (es), ◊, T

broadcast, T/I, C

broaden, ◊, T/I

brocade, T

broil, T/I

bronze, T / I
brood, ◊, I
brook, T
browbeat, ◊, T, C
brown, ◊, T / I
browse, ◊, T / I
bruise, T / I
brush (es), ◊, T / I
brutalise (am. -ize), ◊, T
bubble, ◊, I
buck, ◊, T / I
buckle, ◊, T / I
bud (dd), T / I
budge, T / I
budget, ◊, T
buffer, T
buffet,◊, T / I
bug (gg), ◊, T
bugger, ◊, T
build, ◊, T / I
bulge, ◊,T / I
bulk, ◊, I
bull, T
bulldoze, ◊, T, C
bullshit (tt), T
bully (ie), ◊, T / I, C
bum (mm), ◊, T / I
bump, ◊, T / I
bunch (es), ◊, T / I
bundle, ◊, T / I
bung, ◊, T
bungle, T / I
bunk, ◊, I
bunker, T
buoy, ◊, T
burble, I
burden, ◊, T
burgeon, I
burglarise (am. -ize), T

burgle, T / I
burke, T
burn, ◊, T / I, C
burnish (es), T / I
burp, ◊, T
burr, T / I
burrow, ◊, T / I
burst, ◊, T / I, C
bury (ie), ◊, T
bus (ss / es), T / I
busk, T
bust, ◊, T / I, C
bustle, ◊, T / I
busy (ie) ◊, T / I, C
butcher, T
butt, ◊, T / I
butter, ◊, T
button, ◊, T
buttonhole, T
buttress (es), ◊, T
buy, ◊, T / I
buzz (es), ◊, T / I
bypass (es), T

C

cable, ◊, T, C
cache, T
cackle, I
cadge, ◊, T / I
cage, ◊, T
cajole, ◊, T, C
cake, ◊, T / I
calcify (ie), T / I
calcine, T / I

calculate, ◊, T / I, C
calibrate, T
calk, T
call, ◊◊, T / I
calm, ◊, T / I
calve, I
camber, T / I
camouflage, T
camp, ◊, T / I
campaign, ◊, I
can* (nn), T
can, A
canalize, ◊, T
cancel (ll), ◊, T
cane, T
canker, T
cannibalise (am. -ize), T
cannon, ◊, I
canonise (am. -ize), T
canoodle, T / I
canopy (ie), T
cant, T / I
canter, T / I
canvass (es), ◊, T / I
cap (pp), ◊, T
capacitate, T
caper, I
capitalise (am. -ize), ◊, T / I
capitulate, I
capsise (am. -ize), T / I
captain, T
caption, T
captivate, T
capture, ◊, T
caramelise (am. -ize), T / I
carbolise (am. -ize), T
carbonise (am. -ize), T
carburise (am. -ize), T
card, T

---

* Ne pas confondre l'auxiliaire *can* avec le verbe ordinaire *to can* : mettre en conserve.

care, ◊, I, C

careen, T/I

career, ◊◊◊, I

caretake, T

carol (ll), T/I

carom, I

carouse, I

carp, ◊, I

carpenter, I

carpet, ◊, T

carry (ie), ◊◊, T/I

cart, T

cartoon, T

carve, ◊, T

cascade, ◊◊, T/I

case, T

cash (es), ◊, T

cashier, T

casserole, T

cast, ◊◊, T/I

castigate, T

castrate, T

catapult, T

catch (es), ◊, T/I

categorise (am. -ize), T

cater, ◊, I

caterwaul, I

catnap (pp), I

caulk, T

cause, T, C

cauterise (am. -ize), T

caution, ◊, T, C

cave, ◊, T/I

cavil (ll), ◊, I

cavort, I

caw, I

cease, ◊, T/I, C

cede, ◊, T

celebrate, T/I

cellar, T

cement, T

censor, T

censure, ◊, T

center, ◊, T/I

centralise (am. -ize), T/I

centre, ◊, T/I

centuple, T

centuplicate, T

certificate, T

certify (ie), ◊, T, C

chafe, ◊, T/I

chaff, T

chaffer, ◊, T/I

chagrin, ◊, T, C

chain, ◊, T

chain-smoke, T/I

chair, T

chalk, ◊, T

challenge, T, C

chamfer, T

champ, ◊, T/I

champion, T, C

chance, ◊, T/I, C

change, ◊◊, T/I

channel (ll), ◊, T

channelise (am. -ize), T

chant, T/I

chap (pp), T/I

chaperon, T

char (rr), T/I

characterise (am. -ize), T

charge, ◊, T/I, C

charm, ◊, T/I

chart, ◊, T

charter, T

chase, ◊, T

chasten, T

chastise, ◊, T, C

chat (tt), ◊, I

chatter, I

chauffeur, T

cheapen, T/I

cheat, ◊, T/I, C

check, ◊, T/I

checkmate, T

checkpoint, T

checksum, T

cheek, ◊, T

cheep, T/I

cheer, ◊, T/I, C

cheese, ◊, T

chequer, T

cherish (es), T

chew, ◊, T/I

chide, ◊, T, C

chill, T/I

chime, ◊, T/I

chink, T/I

chip (pp), ◊, T/I

chirp, I

chirr, I

chisel (ll), ◊, T

chitter, I

chivvy (ie), ◊, T, C

chlorinate, T

chloroform, T

chock, T

choir, T/I

choke, ◊, T/I

chomp, T

choose, ◊, T/I, C

chop (pp), ◊, T/I

choreograph, T

chortle, I

chorus (es), T/I

christen, ◊, T

christianise (am. -ize), T

chronicle, T

chuck, ◊, T

chuckle, ◊, I

chug (gg), ◊◊◊, I

chum (mm), I

churn, ◊, T/I

cicatrise (am. -ize), T / I

cipher, T / I

circle, ◊, T / I

circularise (am. -ize), T

circulate, ◊, T / I

circumcise, T

circumnavigate, T

circumscribe, ◊, T

circumvent, T

cite, ◊, T

civilise (am. -ize), T

clack, T / I

claim, ◊, T, C

clamber, ◊, I

clamour (am. -or), ◊, I

clamp, ◊, T / I

clank, T / I

clap (pp), ◊, T / I

clarify (ies), T

clash (es), ◊, T / I

clasp, ◊, T

class (es), ◊, T

classify (ie), T

clatter, ◊, T / I

claw, ◊, T / I

clean, ◊, T / I

cleanse, T

clear, ◊, T / I

cleave, ◊, T / I

clench (es), T

clerk, I

click, ◊, T / I

climb, ◊, T / I

clinch (es), T / I

cling, ◊, I

clink, T / I

clip (pp), ◊, T

cloak, T

clobber, T

clock, ◊, T

clog (gg), ◊, T / I

cloister, T

clone, T

clop, ◊◊◊, I

close, ◊◊, T / I

closet, ◊, T

clot (tt), T / I

clothe, ◊, T

cloud, ◊, T / I

clout, T

clown, ◊, I

cloy, T / I

club (bb), ◊, T / I

cluck, ◊, T

clue, ◊, T

clump, T / I

cluster, ◊, T / I

clutch (es), ◊, T / I

clutter, ◊, T / I

coach (es), ◊, T / I

coagulate, T / I

coal, T / I

coalesce, I

coarsen, I

coast, ◊, T / I

coat, ◊, T

coax (es), ◊, T, C

cobble, T

cock, ◊, T

cockle, T / I

cocoon, T / I

coddle, T

code, T

codify (ie), T

coerce, ◊, T, C

coexist, ◊, I

cogitate, ◊, T / I, C

cohabit, ◊, I

cohere, I

coil, ◊, T / I

coin, ◊, T

coincide, ◊, I

cold-shoulder, T

collaborate, ◊, I

collapse, T / I

collar, T

collate, ◊, T

collect, ◊, T / I

collectivise (am. -ize), T

collide, ◊, I

collocate, ◊, T

colonise (am. -ize), T

colour (am. -or), ◊, T / I

comb, ◊, T / I

combat, ◊, T / I

combine, ◊, T / I

come, ◊◊◊, I, C

comfort, T

command, T / I, C

commandeer, T

commemorate, T

commence, ◊, T / I, C

commend, ◊, T

comment, ◊, T / I

commentate, ◊, T / I

commercialise (am. -ize), T

commingle, T / I

comminute, T

commiserate, ◊, T / I

commission, ◊, T, C

commit (tt), ◊, T, C

commune, ◊, I

communicate, ◊, T / I

communise (am. -ize), T

commutate, T

commute, ◊, T / I

compact, ◊, T

compare, ◊, T / I

compartmentalise (am. -ize), T

compass (es), ◊, T

compel (ll), ◊, T, C

compensate, ◊, T / I

compere, T / I

compete, ◊, I

compile, T

complain, ◊, I, C

complement, T

complete, T

complicate, ◊, T

compliment, ◊, T

comply (ie), ◊, I

comport, ◊, T/I

compose, ◊, T

compost, T

compound, ◊, T/I

comprehend, T

compress (es), ◊, T

comprise, ◊, T

compromise, ◊, T/I

compute, T, C

computerise (am. -ize), T

con (nn), ◊, T, C

concatenate, ◊, T

conceal, ◊, T

concede, ◊, T/I, C

conceive, ◊, T/I

concentrate, ◊, T/I

concentre, T/I

concern, ◊, T

concert, ◊, T/I

conciliate, T

conclude, ◊, T/I, C

concoct, T

concrete, T/I

concur (rr), ◊, I, C

concuss (es), T

condemn, ◊, T, C

condense, T/I

condescend, ◊, I, C

condition, ◊, T, C

condole, ◊, I

condone, T

conduce, ◊, I, C

conduct, ◊, T

cone, T

confabulate, I

confect, T

confederate, ◊, T/I

confer (rr), ◊, T/I

confess (es), ◊, T/I, C

confide, ◊, T/I, C

configure, T

confine, ◊, T, C

confirm, ◊, T, C

confiscate, ◊, T

conflate, T

conflict, ◊, I

conform, ◊, T/I

confound, ◊, T

confront, ◊, T

confuse, ◊, T, C

confute, T

congeal, T/I

congest, T/I

conglomerate, T/I

congratulate, ◊, T, C

congregate, T/I

conjecture, T/I, C

conjoin, T/I

conjugate, T/I

conjure, ◊, T/I, C

conk, ◊, T/I

connect, ◊, T/I

connive, ◊, I

connote, T

conquer, T

conscript, ◊, T

consecrate, ◊, T, C

consent, ◊, I, C

conserve, T

consider, ◊, T, C

consign, ◊, T

consist, ◊, I, C

console, ◊, T

consolidate, T/I

consort, ◊, I

conspire, ◊, T/I, C

constipate, T

constitute, T

constrain, ◊, T, C

constrict, T

construct, ◊, T

construe, ◊, T/I

consult, ◊, T/I

consume, ◊, T

consummate, T

contact, T

contain, ◊, T

containerise (am. -ize), T

contaminate, T

contemplate, T, C

contend, ◊, T/I, C

content ◊, T, C

contest, ◊, T/I

continue, ◊, T/I, C

contort, T

contour, T

contract, ◊, T/I, C

contradict, T

contrast, ◊, T/I

contravene, T

contribute, ◊, T/I, C

contrive, T, C

control (ll), T

controvert, T

convalesce, ◊, I

convene, T/I

conventionalise (am. -ize), T

converge, ◊, T/I

converse, ◊, I

convert, ◊, T

convey, ◊, T, C

convict, ◊, T, C

convince, ◊, T, C

convoke, T

convoy, T

convulse, ◊, T

coo, T/I

cook, ◊, T/I

cool, ◊, T/I

coop, ◊, T

cooperate, ◊, I

co-opt, ◊, T

co-ordinate, T

cop (pp), ◊, T

cope, ◊, I, C

copper, T

copulate, ◊, I

copy (ie), ◊, T

copyright, T

cord, T

cordon, ◊, T

core, T

cork, ◊, T

corner, T/I

corral, T

correct, T

correlate, ◊, T/I

correspond, ◊, I

corroborate, T

corrode, T/I

corrugate, T

corrupt, T/I

coruscate, I

cosh, T

cosher, ◊, T

cosset, ◊, T, C

cost, ◊, T/I

co-star (rr), ◊, T/I

cotton, ◊, T/I

couch (es), ◊, T/I

cough, ◊, T/I

could, A

counsel (ll), T/I, C

count, ◊◊, T/I, C

counter, ◊, T/I

counteract, T

counterbalance, T

countercheck, T

counterfeit, T

countermand, T

countermine, T

countermure, T

counterpierce, T

counterplot (tt), T/I

counterpoise, T

countersign, T

countersink, T

countervail, T/I

counterweigh, T/I

counterwork, T/I

couple, ◊, T/I

course, ◊, T/I

court, ◊, T/I, C

court-martial (ll), T

covenant, ◊, T/I, C

cover, ◊, T/I

covet, T

cow, ◊, T, C

cower, ◊, I

cox (es), T/I

crab (bb), ◊◊, T/I

crack, ◊, T/I

crackle, T/I

cradle, T

cram (mm), ◊, T/I

cramp, T

crane, ◊, T/I

crank, ◊, T

crash (es), ◊, T/I

crate, T

crave, ◊, T/I

crawl, ◊, I

crayon, T

craze, T/I

creak, I

cream, ◊, T

crease, ◊, T/I

create, T

credit, ◊, T, C

creep, ◊◊, I

cremate, T

creosote, T

crepitate, I

crest, T

crew, T/I

crib (bb), ◊, T/I

crick, T

criminate, T

crimp, T

cringe, ◊, I

crinkle, T/I

cripple, ◊, T

crisp, ◊, T/I

crisscross (es), T/I

criticise (am. -ize), ◊, T, C

croak, T/I

crock, ◊, T/I

crook, T

croon, T/I

crop (pp), ◊, T/I

cross (es), ◊, T/I

crossbrace, T

crossbreed, T/I

cross-check, T

cross-connect, T

crosscut (tt), T

cross-examine, T

crosshatch (es), T

cross-perforate, T

cross-question, T

cross-reference, T/I

cross-rule, T

cross-talk, I

cross-thread, T

crouch (es), ◊, I

crow, ◊, I

crowd, ◊, T/I

crown, ◊, T

crucify (ie), T
cruise, I
crumble, ◊, T/I
crumple, ◊, T/I
crunch (es), ◊, T/I
crusade, ◊, I
crush (es), ◊, T/I
crust, ◊, T/I
cry (ie), ◊, T/I
crystallise (am. -ize), T/I
cube, T
cuddle, ◊, T/I
cudgel (ll), T
cue, ◊, T
cuff, T
cull, ◊, T
culminate, ◊, I, C
cultivate, T
cup (pp), ◊, T
curb, ◊, T
curdle, T/I
cure, ◊, T
curl, ◊, T/I
curry (ie), T
curse, ◊, T/I
curtail, ◊, T
curtain, ◊, T
curve, T/I
cushion, T
customise (am. -ize), T
cut (tt), ◊◊, T/I
cycle, ◊◊◊, I

dab (bb), ◊, T
dabble, ◊, T/I
dally (ie), ◊, I
dam (mm), ◊, T
damage, T
damn, T
damp, ◊, T
dampen, ◊, T/I
dance, ◊◊◊, T/I
dandle, T
dangle, ◊, T/I
dapple, T/I
dare*, T/A, C
darken, T/I
darn, T
dart, ◊◊◊, T/I
dash (es), ◊◊, T/I
date, ◊, T/I
daub, ◊, T
daunt, T
dawdle, ◊, T/I
dawn, ◊, I, C
daydream, ◊, I
daze, T
dazzle, T
deactivate, T
deaden, ◊, T
deafen, T
deal, ◊, T/I
de-allocate, T
de-archive, T
de-assign, T
debar (rr), ◊, T, C
debark, T/I

debase, T
debate, ◊, T/I, C
debauch (es), T
debilitate, T
debit, ◊, T
deblock, T
debouch (es), I
debrief, T
debug (gg), T
debunk, T
decaffeinate, T
decalcify (ie), T
decamp, ◊, I
decant, T
decapitate, T
decapsulate, T
decarbonise (am. -ize), T
decay, T/I
decease, I
deceive, ◊, T/I, C
decelerate, T/I
decentralise (am. -ize), T/I
decide, ◊, T/I, C
decimalise (am. -ize), T,
decimate, T
decipher, T
deck, ◊, T
declaim, ◊, T/I
declare, ◊, T/I, C
declassify (ie), T
decline, T/I, C
declutch (es), I
decode, T
decoke, T
decolonize, T
decolourise (am. -orize), T
decompose, T/I
decompress (es), T
deconfigure, T

---

* *Dare* se comporte ou bien comme auxiliaire, ou bien comme verbe à part entière (voir p. 43).

126

deconsecrate, T

decontaminate, T

decontrol (ll), T

decorate, ◊, T, C

decorticate, T

decoy, ◊, T, C

decrease, ◊, T/I

decree, T, C

decrement, T

decript, T

decry (ie), T

decuple, T/I

dedicate, ◊, T, C

deduce, ◊, T, C

deduct, ◊, T

deed, ◊, T

deem, T, C

de-emphasise (am. -ize), T

de-energise (am. -ize), T

deepen, T/I

deep-fry, (ie), T

de-expedite, T

deface, ◊, T

defalcate, I

defame, T

default, ◊, T/I

defeat, T

defecate, I

defect, ◊, I

defend, ◊, T, C

defer (rr), T/I, C

defile, I

define, ◊, T

deflagrate, T/I

deflate, T

deflect, ◊, T/I

deflower, T

defoliate, T

deforest, T

deform, T

defraud, ◊, T

defray, T

defreeze, T

defrock, T

defrost, T

defuse, T

defy (ie), T, C

degauss (es), T

degenerate, ◊, I, C

degrade, T

dehumanise (am. -ize), T

dehumidify (ie), T

dehydrate, T

de-ice, T

deify (ie), T

deign, T, C

deinstall, T

deject, T

delay, ◊, T/I, C

delegate, ◊, T

delete, ◊, T

deliberate, ◊, T/I, C

delight, ◊, T/I, C

delimit, T

delineate, T

deliver, ◊, T

delouse, T

delude, ◊, T, C

deluge, ◊, T

delve, ◊, I

demagnetise (am. -ize), T

demand, ◊, T, C

demarcate, T

demean, T/I

demilitarise (am. -ize), T

demise, ◊, T

demist, T

demobilise (am. -ize), T

democratise (am. -ize), T/I

demolish (es), T

demonetise (am. -ize), T

demonstrate, ◊, T/I, C

demoralise (am. -ize), T

demote, ◊, T

demount, T

demultiplex (es), T

demur (rr), ◊, I

denationalise (am. -ize), T

denature, T

denazify (ie), T

denicotinise (am. -ize), T

denigrate, T

denominate, T

denormalise (am. -ize), T

denote, T

denounce, ◊, T

dent, T

denude, ◊, T

deny (ie), ◊, T, C

deodorise (am. -ize), T

deoxidise (am. -ize), T

deoxygenate, T

depart, ◊, T/I

depend, ◊, I, C

depersonalise (am. -ize), T

depict, T

depilate, T

deplenish (es), T

deplete, ◊, T

deplore, T, C

deploy, T/I

depolarise (am. -ize), T

depopulate, T

deport, T

depose, ◊, T/I, C

deposit, ◊, T

deprave, T

deprecate, T

depreciate, T/I

depress (es), T

deprive, ◊, T

depute, ◊, T, C

deputise (am. -ize), ◊, T/I

derail, T

derange, T

derate, T

derestrict, T

deride, T

derive, ◊, T/I

derogate, ◊, I

desalinate, T

descale, T

descant, ◊, I

descend, ◊, T/I, C

describe, ◊, T

descry (ie), T

desecrate, T

desegregate, T

desensitise (am. -ize), T

desert, T/I

deserve, T/I, C

design, ◊, T

designate, ◊, T

desire, T, C

desist, ◊, I, C

deskew, T

deskill, T

desolate, T

despair, ◊, I, C

despatch (es), ◊, T

despise, ◊, T, C

despoil, ◊, T

despond, I

desquamate, T/I

destine, ◊, T

destroy, T

destruct, T/I

desulfurise (am. -ize), T

detach (es), ◊, T/I

detail, ◊, T

detain, T

detect, T

deter (rr), ◊, T, C

deteriorate, T/I

determine, ◊, T/I, C

detest, T, C

dethread, T

dethrone, T

detonate, T/I

detour, I

detract, ◊, T/I

detrain, T/I

detune, T

de-underscore, T

de-update, T

devaluate, T

devalue, T

devastate, T

develop, ◊, T/I

deviate, ◊, I

devil (ll), ◊, T/I

devise, T

devitalise (am. -ize), T

devolve, ◊, T/I

devote, ◊, T, C

devour, ◊, T

dew, T

dewater, T

diagnose, T

dial (ll), T

dice, ◊, T/I

dictate, ◊, T/I

diddle, ◊, T

die (yi), ◊◊, I

diet, T/I

differ, ◊, I

differentiate, ◊, T/I

diffract, T

diffuse, T/I

dig (gg), ◊, T/I

digest, T/I

digitalise (am. -ize), T

digitise (am. -ize), T

dignify (ie), T

digress (es), ◊, I

dilate, ◊, T/I

dilly-dally (ie), I

dilute, ◊, T

dim (mm), ◊, T/I

diminish (es), T/I

dimple, T/I

din (nn), ◊, T/I

dine, ◊, T/I

dip (pp), ◊, T/I

diphthongise (am. -ize), T/I

direct, ◊, T

dirty (ie), ◊, T/I

disable, T

disabuse, ◊, T

disadvantage, T

disagree, ◊, I, C

disallow, T

disappear, ◊, I

disappoint, ◊, T, C

disappropriate, T

disapprove, ◊, T/I, C

disarm, T/I

disarrange, T

disassemble, T

disavow, T

disband, T/I

disbar (rr), ◊, T

disbelieve, ◊, T/I

disbud (dd), T

disburden, ◊, T

disburse, T

discard, T/I

discern, ◊, T

discharge, ◊, T/I

discipline, T

disclaim, T

disclose, T

discolour (am. -or), T/I

discomfit, T

discommode, T

discompose, T

disconcert, T

disconnect, ◊, T

discontinue, T / I

discord, ◊, I

discount, T

discourage, ◊, T, C

discourse, ◊, I

discover, T, C

discredit, T

discriminate, ◊, T / I

discuss (es), ◊, T

disdain, T, C

disembark, ◊, T / I

disembarrass (es), ◊, T

disembowel, T

disenable, T

disenchant, T

disencumber, ◊, T

disenfranchise, T

disengage, ◊, T / I

disentail, T

disentangle, ◊, T / I

disestablish (es), T

disfigure, T

disfranchise, T

disgorge, T / I

disgrace, T

disguise, ◊, T

disgust, ◊, T, C

dish (es), ◊, T

dishonour (am. -or), T

disillusion, T

disincline, T / I

disinfect, T

disinherit, T

disinstall, T

disintegrate, T / I

disinter (rr), T

disjoint, T / I

dislike, T, C

dislocate, T

dislodge, ◊, T

dismantle, ◊, T

dismast, T

dismay, ◊, T, C

dismember, T

dismiss (es), ◊, T, C

dismount, ◊, T / I

disobey, T

disorder, T

disorganise (am. -ize), T

disorientate, T

disown, T

disparage, T

dispatch (es), ◊, T

dispel (ll), T

dispense, ◊, T / I, C

disperse, T / I

dispirit, T

displace, T

display, T

displease, ◊, T

disport, T

dispose, ◊, T / I

dispossess (es), ◊, T

disprove, T

dispute, ◊, T / I, C

disqualify (ie), ◊, T, C

disquiet, T

disquieten, T

disregard, T

disremember, T, C

disrobe, T / I

disrupt, T

dissatisfy (ie), ◊, T, C

dissect, T

dissemble, T / I

disseminate, T

dissent, ◊, I, C

dissimulate, T / I

dissipate, T / I

dissociate, ◊, T

dissolve, ◊, T / I

dissuade, ◊, T, C

distance, T

distemper, T

distend, T / I

distill (am. distil [ll]), T / I

distinguish (es) ◊, T / I

distort, T

distract, ◊, T, C

distrain, ◊, I

distress (es), T

distribute, ◊, T

distrust, T

disturb, T

disunite, T

ditch (es), T / I

dither, I

divagate, ◊, I

dive, ◊, I

diverge, ◊, I

diversify (ie), T

divert, ◊, T

divest, ◊, T

divide, ◊, T / I

divine, T

divorce, ◊, T

divulge, ◊, T

dizzy, (ie), T

do (es), ◊◊, T / A, C

dock, ◊, T / I

docket, T

doctor, T

document, T

dodder, ◊, I

dodge, T / I

doff, T

dog (gg), T

dogmatise (am. -ize), I

dole, ◊, T

doll, ◊, T

dolly (ie), ◊, T

domesticate, T
domicile, T
dominate, ◊, T/I
domineer, ◊, I
don (nn), T
donate, ◊, T
doodle, I
doom, ◊, T
dope, ◊, T
dose, ◊, T
doss (es), ◊, I
dot (tt), ◊, T
dote, ◊, I
double, ◊, T/I
double-check, T/I
double-glaze, T
double-park, T/I
doubt, ◊, T/I, C
douse, T/I
dovetail, ◊, T/I
dowel (ll), T
down, T
downgrade, T
download, T
downshift, T
dowse, I
doze, ◊, I
draft, ◊, T
drag (gg), ◊, T/I
draggle, T/I
dragoon, ◊, T, C
drain, ◊, T/I
dramatise (am. -ize), T
drape, ◊, T
draw, ◊◊, T/I
drawl, ◊, T/I
dread, T, C
dream, ◊, T/I, C
dredge, ◊, T/I
drench (es), ◊, T
dress (es), ◊, T/I

dribble, T/I
drift, ◊, I
drill, ◊, T/I, C
drink, ◊, T/I
drip (pp), T/I
drive, ◊◊◊, T/I
drivel (ll), ◊, I
drizzle, ◊, I
drone, ◊, T/I
drool, ◊, I
droop, ◊, T/I
drop (pp), ◊◊, T/I
drown, ◊, T/I
drowse, ◊, T/I
drub (bb), T
drudge, I
drug (gg), T
drum (mm), ◊, T/I
dry (ie), ◊, T/I
dry-clean, T
dub (bb), ◊, T
duck, ◊, T/I
duel (ll), I
duff, T
dull, ◊, T/I
dumbfound, T
dummy (ie), T/I
dump, ◊, T
dun (nn), ◊, T
dung, T/I
dunk, ◊, T/I
dupe, T
duplicate, T
dust, ◊, T
dwarf, T
dwell, ◊, I
dwindle, ◊, I
dye, T/I
dyke, T
dynamite, T

e

earmark, ◊, T
earn, T
earth, ◊, T/I
ease, ◊, T/I
eat, ◊, T/I
eavesdrop (pp), ◊, I
ebb, ◊, I
echo (es), ◊, T/I
eclipse, T
economise (am. -ize), ◊, T/I
eddy (ie), I
edge, ◊, T/I
edify (ie), T
edit, ◊, T
editorialize, I
educate, ◊, T
educe, ◊, T
efface, T
effect, T
effervesce, I
egg, ◊, T, C
ejaculate, T
eject, ◊, T
eke, ◊, T
elaborate, ◊, T/I
elapse, I
elate, ◊, T
elbow, ◊, T/I
elect, ◊, T
electrify (ie), T
electrocute, T
electrolyse, T
electroplate, T
electrotype, T
elevate, ◊, T
elicit, T
elide, T

eliminate, ◊, T

elongate, T/I

elope, ◊, I

elucidate, T

elude, T

emaciate, T

emanate, ◊, I

emancipate, ◊, T

emasculate, T

embalm, T

embank, T

embargo (es), T

embark, ◊, T/I

embarrass (es), T

embattle, T

embed (dd), ◊, T

embellish (es), ◊, T

embezzle, T

embitter, T

emblazon, ◊, T

embody (ie), ◊, T

embolden, T, C

embosom, ◊, T

emboss (es), T

embower, T/I

embrace, ◊, T/I

embroider, T

embroil, ◊, T

embus (ss), T/I

emcee, T

emend, T

emerge, ◊, I

emigrate, ◊, I

emit (tt), ◊, T

emote, I

empanel (ll), T

empathize, I

emphasise (am. -ize), T

employ, ◊, T, C

empower, T, C

empty (ie), ◊, T/I

emulate, T

emulsify (ie), T

enable, T, C

enact, T

enamel (ll), T

enamour (am. -or), ◊, T

encage, T

encamp, T/I

encapsulate, T

encase, ◊, T

encash (es), T

enchain, T

enchant, ◊, T

encipher, T

encircle, T

enclave, T

enclose, ◊, T

encode, T

encompass (es), ◊, T

encore, T

encounter, T

encourage, ◊, T, C

encroach (es), ◊, I

encrust, ◊, T

encumber, ◊, T

end, ◊, T/I, C

endanger, T

endear, ◊, T

endeavour, I, C

endorse, ◊, T

endow, ◊, T

endue, ◊, T

endure, T/I, C

energise (am. -ize), T

enervate, T

enfeeble, T

enfilade, T

enfold, ◊, T

enforce, ◊, T

enfranchise, T

engage, ◊, T/I, C

engender, T

engineer, T

engorge, ◊, T/I

engraft, ◊, T

engrave, ◊, T

engross (es), ◊, T

engulf, ◊, T

enhance, T

enjoin, ◊, T

enjoy, T, C

enlarge, ◊, T/I

enlighten, ◊, T

enlist, ◊, T/I

enliven, T

enmesh (es), ◊, T

ennoble, T

enquire, ◊, T/I

enrage, T

enrapture, T

enrich (es), ◊, T

enrol (ll), ◊, T/I

ensconce, ◊, T

enshrine, ◊, T

enshroud, T

enslave, T

ensnare, ◊, T, C

ensue, ◊, I

ensure, ◊, T

entail, ◊, T

entangle, ◊, T

enter, ◊, T/I

entertain, ◊, T

enthral (ll), ◊, T, C

enthrone, ◊, T

enthuse, ◊, I

entice, ◊, T, C

entitle, ◊, T, C

entomb, ◊, T

entrain, T/I

entrance, T

entrap (pp), ◊, T, C

entreat, ◊, T, C

entrench (es), T

entrust, ◊, T

entwine, ◊, T/I

enucleate, T

enumerate, T

enunciate, T

envelop, ◊, T

envenom, T

envisage, T

envy (ie), T

epitomise (am. -ize), T

equal (ll), ◊, T

equalise (am. -ize), T

equate, ◊, T

equilibrate, T/I

equip (pp), ◊, T

equivocate, I

eradicate, T

erase, ◊, T

erect, T

erode, T

err, ◊, I

error, I

eructate, I

erupt, ◊, I

escalate, T

escape, ◊, T/I, C

eschew, T

escort, ◊, T

espouse, T

espy (ie), T

essay, T, C

establish (es), ◊, T

esteem, T

estimate, ◊, T

estrange, ◊, T

etch (es), ◊, T/I

eternise (am. -ize), T

etherise (am. -ize), T

eulogise (am. -ize), T

evacuate, ◊, T

evade, T

evaluate, ◊, T

evanesce, I

evangelise (am. -ize), T

evaporate, ◊, T/I

even, ◊, T

evict, ◊, T

evince, T

eviscerate, T

evoke, T

evolve, ◊, T/I

exacerbate, T

exact, ◊, T

exaggerate, T/I

exalt, T

examine, ◊, T

exasperate, ◊, T

excavate, T

exceed, ◊, T/I

excel (ll), ◊, T/I, C

except, ◊, T

excerpt, ◊, T

exchange, ◊, T

excise, T

excite, ◊, T

exclaim, ◊, T/I, C

exclude, ◊, T

excogitate, T

excommunicate, T

excoriate, T

excrete, T

excruciate, T

exculpate, T

excuse, ◊, T, C

execrate, T

execute, T

exemplify (ie), T

exempt, ◊, T, C

exercise, ◊, T/I, C

exert, T, C

exfoliate, T

exhale, T/I

exhaust, T

exhibit, T

exhilarate, T

exhort, T, C

exhume, T

exile, ◊, T

exist, ◊, I

exit*, I

exonerate, ◊, T

exorcise, ◊, T

expand, ◊, T/I

expatiate, ◊, I

expatriate, ◊, T

expect, ◊, T, C

expectorate, T/I

expedite, T

expel (ll), ◊, T

expend, ◊, T, C

experience, T

experiment, ◊, I

expiate, T

expire, T/I

explain, ◊, T, C

explicate, T

explode, ◊, T/I

exploit, T

explore, T

export, ◊, T

expose, ◊, T

expostulate, ◊, I

expound, ◊, T

express (es), ◊, T

expropriate, ◊, T

---

* *Exit* ne s'emploie qu'à la troisième personne du singulier du présent, au théâtre : *Exit Hamlet.* Hamlet sort.

expunge, ◊, T

expurgate, ◊, T

extemporise (am. -ize), T/I

extend, ◊, T/I, C

extenuate, T

exteriorise (am. -ize), T

exterminate, T

externalise (am. -ize), T

extinguish (es), ◊, T

extirpate, T

extol (ll), T

extort, ◊, T

extract, ◊, T

extradite, ◊, T

extrapolate, T

extravasate, I

extricate, ◊, T

extrude, ◊, T

exude, T/I

exult, ◊, I, C

eye, ◊, T

fabricate, T

face, ◊, T/I

facet, T

facilitate, T

factorise (am. -ize), T

fade, ◊, T/I

fag (gg), ◊, T/I

fail, ◊, T/I, C

faint, ◊, I

fake, ◊, T/I

fall, ◊◊, I

falsify (ie), T

falter, ◊, T/I

familiarise (am. -ize), ◊, T, C

fan (nn), ◊, T

fancy (ie), T, C

fantasise (am. -ize), ◊, I

fare, ◊, I

farm, ◊, T/I

farrow, T/I

fart, I

fascinate, T

fashion, ◊, T

fast, ◊, I

fasten, ◊, T/I

father, ◊, T

fathom, ◊, T, C

fatigue, T

fatten, ◊, T/I

fault, T

favour (am. -or), ◊, T

fawn, ◊, T/I

fax, ◊, T, C

fear, ◊, T/I, C

feast, T/I

feather, ◊, T/I

feature, ◊, T

federate, T/I

feed, ◊, T/I

feel, ◊, T/I, C

feign, T/I

feint, I

felicitate, T

fell, T

fence, ◊, T/I

fend, ◊, T/I

ferment, T/I

ferret, ◊, T/I

ferry (ie), ◊, T/I

fertilise (am. -ize), T

fester, T/I

festoon, ◊, T

fetch (es), ◊, T

fete, T

fetter, T

feud, ◊, I

fib (bb), I

fictionalize, T

fiddle, ◊, I

fiddle-faddle, I

fidget, ◊, I

field, T/I

field-test, T

fig, ◊, T

fight, ◊◊, T/I

figure, ◊, T/I

filch (es), ◊, T

file, ◊, T

filibuster, I

fill, ◊, T/I

fillet, T

fillip, T

film, ◊, T/I

filter, ◊, T/I

finalise (am. -ize), T

finance, T

find, ◊, T, C

fine, ◊, T

finesse, T/I

fine-tune, T

finger, T/I

finish (es), ◊, T/I, C

fire, ◊, T/I

firm, ◊, T/I

fish (es), ◊, T/I

fissure, T/I

fit (tt), ◊, T/I

fix (es), ◊, T/I

fizz (es), ◊, I

fizzle, ◊, I

flabbergast, ◊, T

flag (gg), ◊, T/I

flagellate, ◊, T

flail, T/I

flake, ◊, T/I

flambé, T

flame, ◊, I

flank, ◊, T

flap (pp), ◊, T/I

flare, ◊, T/I

flash (es), ◊, T/I

flatten, ◊, T/I

flatter, ◊, T, C

flaunt, T/I

flavour (am. -or), ◊, T

flay, T

fleck, ◊, T

flee, ◊, T/I

fleece, T

fleet, I

flesh (es), ◊, T/I

flex (es), T/I

flick, ◊, T/I

flicker, ◊, I

flinch (es), I

fling, ◊◊, T/I

flip (pp), ◊, T/I

flirt, ◊, T/I

flit (tt), ◊, I

float, ◊, T/I

flock, ◊, I

flog (gg), ◊, T

flood, ◊, T/I

floor, T

flop (pp), ◊, I

flounce, ◊, I

flounder, ◊, I

flour, T

flourish (es), T/I

flout, T

flow, ◊, I

flowchart, T

flower, I

fluctuate, I

fluff, ◊, T

flummox, T

flunk, ◊, T/I

fluoresce, I

flurry (ie), T

flush (es), ◊, T/I

fluster, ◊, T/I

flute, T

flutter, ◊◊◊, T/I

fly (ie), ◊◊◊, T/I

foal, T/I

foam, ◊, I

fob (bb), ◊, T

focus (es), ◊, T/I

fodder, T

fog (gg), T/I

foil, T

foist, ◊, T

fold, ◊, T/I

follow, ◊, T/I

foment, T

fondle, T

fool, ◊, T/I, C

foot, T

footle, ◊, I

forage, T/I

foray, I

forbear, ◊, T/I, C

forbid (dd), T, C

force, ◊, T, C

force-feed, T

ford, T

forebode, T

forecast, T

foreclose, ◊, T/I

foregather, ◊, I

forego, T

foreordain, T

foresee, T, C

foreshadow, T

foreshorten, T

forespace, I

forestall, T

foretell, T, C

forewarm, T

forfeit, T

forgather, ◊, I

forge, T/I

forget (tt), ◊, T/I, C

forgive, ◊, T, C

forgo (es), T

fork, ◊, T/I

form, ◊, T/I

formalise (am. -ize), T

format, T

formulate, T

fornicate, I

forsake, T

forswear, T

fortify (ie), ◊, T

forward, ◊, T

fossilise (am. -ize), T/I

foster, T

foul, ◊, T/I

found, ◊, T

founder, I

fox (es), T/I

fracture, T/I

fragment, T/I

frame, ◊, T/I

frank, T

fraternise (am. -ize), I

fray, T/I

frazzle, T

freak, ◊, I

freckle, T/I

free, ◊, T

freeze ◊, T/I

freight, T

frenchify (ie), T/I

frequent, T

freshen, ◊, T/I

fret (tt), ◊, T/I

frig (gg), ◊, T

frighten, ◊, T, C

frill, T

fringe, ◊, T

frisk, ◊, T/I

fritter, ◊, T

frivol (ll), T/I

frizz (es), T/I

frizzle, ◊, T/I

frog-march, (es), ◊, T

frolic, ◊, I

front, ◊, T/I

frost, ◊, T

froth, ◊, I

frown, ◊, T/I

fructify (ie), I

fruit, I

frustrate, T

fry (ie), ◊, T/I

fuck ◊, T/I

fuddle, T

fudge, ◊, T/I

fuel (ll), T/I

fulfil (ll), T

fulminate, ◊, T/I

fumble, ◊, T/I

fume, ◊, T/I, C

function, I

fund, T

funk, ◊, T/I, C

funnel, ◊, T

fur (rr), ◊, T/I

furbish (es), ◊, T

furl, T

furnish (es), ◊, T

furrow, T

further, T

fuse, ◊, T/I

fuss (es), ◊, T/I

fustigate, T

fuzz (es), ◊, T/I

g

gab (bb), I

gabble, ◊, T/I

gad (dd), ◊, I

gaff, T/I

gag (gg), T/I

gage, T

gaggle, I

gain, ◊, T/I

gainsay, T

gall, T

gallivant, ◊, I

gallop, ◊◊◊, T/I

galumph, ◊◊, I

galvanise (am. -ize), ◊, T

gamble, ◊, T/I

gambol, ◊◊◊, I

game, ◊, T/I

gang, ◊, I

gangrene, T/I

gaol, T

gape, ◊, I

garage, T

garb, ◊, T

garble, T

garden, I

gargle, T/I

garland, T

garner, ◊, T

garnish (es), ◊, T

garrison, T

garrotte, T

gas (ss), ◊, T/I

gash (es), T

gasify (ie), T/I

gasp, ◊, T/I

gate, T

gatecrach, (es), T/I

gather, ◊, T/I

gauge, T

gawk, ◊, I

gawp, I

gaze, ◊, I

gazette, T

gazump, I

gear, ◊, T/I

gel (ll), I

geld, T

gen (nn), ◊, T/I

generalise (am. -ize), ◊, T/I

generate, ◊, T

genuflect, I

germinate, T/I

gesticulate, T/I

get (tt), ◊◊◊, T/I, C

ghost, T

ghost-write, T

gibber, I

gibe, ◊, T/I

giggle, ◊, I

gild, T

ginger, ◊, T

gird, ◊, T

girdle, ◊, T

give, ◊◊, T/I, C

gladden, T

glamorise (am. -ize), T

glance, ◊, I

glare, ◊, I

glass (es), ◊, T

glaze, ◊, T/I

gleam, ◊, I

glean, ◊, T/I

glide, ◊◊◊, T/I

glimmer, I

glimpse, T

glint, I

glissade, I

glisten, ◊, I
glitter, ◊, I
gloat, ◊, I
glorify (ie), T
glory (ie), ◊, I, C
gloss (es), ◊, T
glove, T
glow, ◊, I
glower, ◊, I
glue, ◊, T
glut (tt), ◊, T
gnash (es), T
gnaw, ◊, T/I
go (es), ◊◊◊, I, C
goad, ◊, T, C
gobble, ◊, T/I
goggle, ◊, I
golf, I
gong, T
goof, ◊, I
goose, ◊, T
gore, ◊, T
gorge, ◊, T/I
gormandise (am. -ize), T/I
gossip, ◊, I
gouge, ◊, T
govern, T/I
gown, T/I
grab (bb), ◊, T/I
grace, ◊, T
gradate, T/I
grade, ◊, T
graduate, ◊, T/I
graft, ◊, T/I
grain, T
grant, ◊, T, C
granulate, T
graph, ◊, T
grapple, ◊, T/I
grasp, ◊, T/I
grass (es), ◊, T

grate, ◊, T/I
gratify (ie), T
grave, T
gravel (ll), T
gravitate, ◊, I
graze, ◊, T/I
grease, T
greet, ◊, T
grey, I
grieve, ◊, T/I
grill, T
grimace, I
grin (nn), ◊, T/I
grind, ◊, T/I
grip (pp), T/I
gripe, ◊, T/I
grit (tt), T/I
grizzle, T/I
groan, ◊, I
groom, ◊, T
groove, T
grope, ◊, I
grouch (es), I
ground, ◊, T/I
group, ◊, T/I
grouse, ◊, I
grout, ◊, T
grovel (ll), ◊, I
grow, ◊◊, T/I
growl, ◊, T/I
grub (bb), ◊, T/I
grudge, T
grumble, ◊, T/I
grunt, T/I
guarantee, ◊, T
guard, ◊, T/I
guess (es), ◊, T/I, C
guffaw, T/I
guide, T
guillotine, T
gull, ◊, T, C

gully (ie), T/I
gulp, ◊, T/I
gum (mm), ◊, T/I
gun (nn), ◊, T/I
gurgle, ◊, T/I
gush (es), ◊, I
gussy (ie), ◊, T
gut (tt), T
gutter, T/I
guy, T
guzzle, ◊, T/I
gyp (pp), T
gyrate, I

habituate, ◊, T, C
hack, ◊, T/I
hackle, T/I
haemorrage, I
haft, T
haggle, ◊, I
hail, ◊, T/I
hallmark, T
hallo (es), ◊, I
hallucinate, T/I
halo (es), T
halt, T/I
halve, T
ham (mm), ◊, T/I
hammer, ◊, T/I
hamper, T
hand, ◊, T
handicap (pp), T
handle, T/I
hang, ◊◊, T/I

hanker, ◊, I

happen, ◊, I, C

harangue, T/I

harass (es), T

harbour (am. -or), T

harden, ◊, T/I

hare, ◊, I

hark, ◊, I

harm, T

harmonise (am. -ize), ◊, T/I

harness (es), ◊, T

harp, ◊, I

harpoon, T

harrow, T

harry (ie), T

harvest, T/I

hash (es), ◊, T

hasten, T/I, C

hatch (es), ◊, T/I

hate, T, C

haul, ◊, T/I

haunt, T

have, ◊◊, T/A

hawk, ◊, T/I

hazard, T

haze, ◊, T

head, ◊, T/I

headline, T

heal, ◊, T/I

heap, ◊, T

hear, ◊, T/I, C

hearten, ◊, T/I

heat, ◊, T/I

heave, ◊, T/I

heckle, T

hector, T, C

hedge, ◊, T/I

heed, T

hee-haw, I

heel, ◊, T/I

heighten, T

hellenise (am. -ize), T/I

help, ◊◊, T/I, C

hem (mm), ◊, T

henna, T

herald, T

herd, ◊, T/I

hesitate, ◊, I, C

hew, ◊, T

hex (es), T

hibernate, I

hiccup (pp), I

hide, ◊, T/I

higgle, I

highlight, T

hijack, T

hike, T/I

hinder, ◊, T, C

hinge, ◊, T/I

hink, T

hint, ◊, T/I, C

hire, ◊, T

hiss (es), ◊, T/I

hit (tt), ◊, T/I

hitch (es), ◊, T/I

hitch-hike, ◊◊, T/I

hive, ◊, T/I

hoard, ◊, T

hoax (es), ◊, T, C

hobble, ◊◊, T/I

hobnob (bb), ◊, I

hock, T

hocus (ss), T

hocus-pocus (ss), T/I

hoe, T

hog (gg), T/I

hoick, T

hoist, ◊, T

hoke, ◊, T

hold, ◊◊, T/I

hole, ◊, T/I

holiday, I

hollow, ◊, T/I

home, ◊, T

homogenise (am. -ize), T

hone, T

honeymoon, I

honour (am. -or), ◊, T, C

hoodwink, ◊, T, C

hoof, ◊, T/I

hook, ◊, T/I

hoop, T

hoot, ◊, T/I

hoover, T

hop (pp), ◊◊◊, T/I

hope, ◊, T/I, C

horn, ◊, I

horrify (ie), T

horse, ◊, I

horsewhip (pp), T

hose, ◊, T

hospitalise (am. -ize), T

hound, ◊, T

house, ◊, T

housetrain, T

hover, ◊, I

howl, ◊, T/I

huckster, T/I

huddle, ◊, T/I

huff, T/I

hug (gg), T

hulk, I

hull, T

hum (mm), ◊, T/I

humanise (am. -ize), T

humble, T

humbug (gg), ◊, T, C

humidify, T

humiliate, ◊, T, C

humour (am. -or), T

hump, ◊, T

hunch (es), ◊, T

hunger, ◊, I

hunker, ◊, I
hunt, ◊, T / I
hurdle, T / I
hurl, ◊, T
hurrah, T / I
hurry (ie), ◊◊, T / I
hurt, T / I
hurtle, ◊, T / I
husband, T
hush (es), ◊, T / I
husk, T
hustle, ◊, T / I, C
hybridise (am. -ize), T
hydrate, T
hydrogenate, T
hydrogenise (am. -ize), T
hydroplane, I
hype, ◊, T
hyphen, T
hyphenate, T
hypnotise (am. -ize), ◊, T, C
hypothesise (am. -ize), T / I

i

ice, ◊, T
ice-skate, I
idealise (am. -ize), T
identify (ie), ◊, T
idle, ◊, I
idolise (am. -ize), T
ignite, T / I
ignore, T
illuminate, ◊, T
illumine, T
illustrate, ◊, T

imagine, T, C
imbibe, T / I
imbricate, T / I
imbue, ◊, T
imitate, T
immaterialise (am. -ize), T
immerse, ◊, T
immigrate, ◊, I
immobilise (am. -ize), T
immolate, T
immortalise (am. -ize), T
immunise (am. -ize), ◊, T
immure, T
impair, T
impale, ◊, T
impanel (ll), T
impart, ◊, T
impeach (es), ◊, T, C
impede, T
impel (ll), ◊, T, C
impend, ◊, I
imperil (ll), T
impersonate, T
impinge, ◊, I
implant, ◊, T
implement, T
implicate, ◊, T
implode, T / I
implore, T, C
imply (ie), T, C
import, ◊, T, C
importune, T / I
impose, ◊, T / I
impound, T
impoverish (es), T
imprecate, ◊, T / I, C
impregnate, ◊, T
impress (es), ◊, T, C
imprint, ◊, T
imprison, ◊, T
improve, ◊, T / I

improvise, T / I
impugn, T
impute, ◊, T
inaugurate, T
incapacitate, ◊, T, C
incarcerate, ◊, T
incarnate, T
incense, T
inch (es), T
incinerate, T
incise, T
incite, ◊, T
incline, ◊, T / I
include, ◊, T, C
incommode, T
inconvenience, T
incorporate, ◊, T / I
increase, ◊, T / I
increment, T
incubate, T / I
inculcate, ◊, T
inculpate, T / I
incur (rr), T
indemnify (ie), ◊, T
indent, ◊, T / I
index (es), T
indicate, T
indict, ◊, T, C
indispose, ◊, T, C
individualise (am. -ize), T
indoctrinate, ◊, T
indorse, T
induce, ◊, T, C
induct, T
indulge, ◊, T / I, C
industrialise (am. -ize), T
inebriate, T
infatuate, ◊, T
infect, ◊, T
infer (rr), ◊, T, C
infest, ◊, T

infile, T

infiltrate, ◊, T/I

inflame, T/I

inflate, ◊, T

inflect, T

inflict, ◊, T

influence, T

inform, ◊, T/I, C

infringe, ◊, T/I

infuriate, T

infuse, ◊, T

ingest, T

ingraft, ◊, T

ingratiate, ◊, T

ingurgitate, T

inhabit, T

inhale, T/I

inhere, ◊, I

inherit, ◊, T

inhibit, ◊, T, C

inhume, T

initial, T

initialise (am. -ize), T

initiate, ◊, T

inject, ◊, T

injure, T

ink, ◊, T

inlay, ◊, T

innovate, ◊, T/I

inoculate, ◊, T

input, T, ◊◊

inquire, ◊, T/I, C

inscribe, ◊, T

inseminate, T

insert, ◊, T

inset (tt), ◊, T

insinuate, ◊, T, C

insist, ◊, I, C

inspect, T

inspire, ◊, T, C

install, ◊, T

instantiate, T

instigate, T, C

instil (ll), ◊, T

institute, ◊, T

institutionalize, T

instruct, ◊, T, C

instrument, T

insufflate, T

insulate, ◊, T

insult, T

insure, ◊, T

integrate, ◊, T/I

intend, ◊, T, C

intensify (ie), T/I

inter (rr), T

interact, ◊, I

interbreed, ◊, T/I

intercalate, T

intercede ◊, I

intercept, T

interchange, ◊, T

intercommunicate, I

interconnect, T/I

interdepend, I

interdict, ◊, T, C

interest, ◊, T, C

interfere, ◊, I

interfile, T

interfold, T

interject, T

interlace, ◊, T/I

interlard, ◊, T

interleave, ◊, T

interline, T

interlink, ◊, T/I

interlock, T/I

interlope, I

intermarry (ie), ◊, I

intermediate, ◊, I

intermingle, ◊, T/I

intermit (tt), T/I

intermix (es), T

intern, ◊, T

internalize, T

internationalise (am. -ize), T

interpenetrate, T

interpolate, T

interpose, ◊, T/I

interpret, ◊, T/I

interrelate, T

interrogate, ◊, T

interrupt, T

intersect, ◊, T/I

intersperse, ◊, T

intertwine, T/I

intervene, ◊, I

interview, ◊, T

interweave, ◊, T/I

intimate, ◊, T, C

intimidate, ◊, T

intone, T

intoxicate, ◊, T

intrigue, ◊, T/I

introduce, ◊, T

intrude, ◊, T/I

intrust, ◊, T

inundate, ◊, T

inure, ◊, T

invade, T

invalid, ◊, T

invalidate, T

inveigh, ◊, I

inveigle, ◊, T, C

invent, T

invert, T

invest, ◊, T/I

investigate, T

invigilate, I

invigorate, T

invite, ◊, T, C

invoice, T

invoke, ◊, T

involve, ◊, T, C
iodise (am. -ize), T
ionise (am. -ize), T
irk, T, C
iron, ◊, T / I
irradiate, T / I
irrigate, ◊, T
irritate, T
isolate, ◊, T
issue, ◊, T / I
italicise (am. -ize), T
itch (es), ◊, I, C
itemise (am. -ize), T
itinerate, I

j

jab (bb), ◊, T / I
jabber, T / I
jack, ◊, T
jacket, T
jacknife, T / I
jag (gg), T
jam (mm), ◊, T / I
jangle, ◊, T / I
japan (nn), T
jar (rr), ◊, T / I
jaunt, ◊, T
jaw, ◊, T / I
jazz (es), ◊, T / I
jeer, ◊, T / I
jell, I
jelly (ie), T / I
jeopardise (am. -ize), T
jerk, ◊, T / I

jest, ◊, I
jet (tt), T / I
jettison, T
jib (bb), ◊, I, C
jibe, I
jig (gg), T / I
jigger, ◊, T
jiggle, T
jilt, T
jingle, T / I
jink , ◊◊◊, I
jitter, I
job (bb), ◊, T / I
jockey, ◊, T / I, C
jog (gg), ◊◊◊, T / I
joggle, T / I
join, ◊, T / I, C
joint, T
joke, ◊, I
jolly (ie), ◊, T
jolt, T/I
josh (es), T / I
jostle, ◊, T / I
jot (tt), ◊, T
journalise (am. -ize), T / I
journey, I
joust, I
jubilate, I
judder, I
judge, ◊, T / I
jug (gg), T
juggle, ◊, T / I
jumble, ◊, T
jump, ◊, T / I
junk, T
justify (ie), ◊, T, C
jut (tt), ◊, I
juxtapose, T

k

k.o., T
kart, I
kedge, T
keel, ◊, T / I
keep, ◊◊, T / I, C
key, T
keyboard, T
keypunch, T
keystroke, T
kick, ◊◊, T / I
kid (dd), ◊, T / I
kidnap (pp), T
kill, ◊, T
kindle, ◊, T / I
kink, T/I
kip (pp), ◊, I
kiss (es), ◊, T / I
kit (tt), ◊, T
knead, T
kneecap (pp), T
kneel, ◊, I
knife, T
knight, T
knit (tt), ◊, T / I
knock, ◊◊, T / I
knot (tt), ◊, T / I
know, ◊, T / I, C
knuckle, ◊, I
kowtow, ◊, I

l

laager, I
label (ll), ◊, T
labour (am. -or), ◊, T / I, C
lace, ◊, T / I
lacerate, T
lack, ◊, T / I
lacquer, T
lactate, I
ladder, T / I
lade, ◊, T
ladle, ◊, T
lag (gg), ◊, T / I
laicise (am. -ize), T
lallylag, (gg), I
lam, (mm), ◊, T / I
lamb, I
lambast/e, T
lame, T
lament, ◊, T / I
laminate, T / I
lampoon, T
lance, T
land, ◊, T / I
languish (es), ◊, I
lap (pp), ◊, T / I
lapidate, T
lapse, ◊, I
lard, ◊, T
lark, ◊, I
lash (es), ◊, T / I
lasso (es), T
last, ◊, T / I
latch (es), ◊, T / I
lath, T
lather, ◊, T / I
latinise (am. -ize), T

lattice, T
laud, T
laugh, ◊, T / I, C
launch (es), ◊, T / I
launder, T / I
lavish (es), ◊, T
lay, ◊◊, T / I, C
layer, T
laze, ◊, T / I
leach (es), ◊, T / I
lead, ◊◊, T / I, C
leaf, ◊, T / I
league, ◊, T / I
leak, ◊, T / I
lean, ◊, T / I
leap, ◊, T / I
learn, ◊, T / I, C
lease, ◊, T
leash (es), T
leather, T
leave, ◊◊, T / I, C
leaven, ◊, T
lecture, ◊, T / I
leech (es), T / I
leer, ◊, I
left-justify (ie), T / I
legalise (am. -ize), T
legislate, ◊, I
legitimate, T
lend, ◊, T, C
lengthen, ◊, T / I
lessen, T / I
let (tt), ◊, T / A, C
letter, T
level (ll), ◊, T / I
lever, ◊, T
levigate, T
levitate, T / I
levy (ie), ◊, T
liaise, ◊, I
libel (ll), T

liberate, ◊, T
license, ◊, T, C
lick, ◊, T
lie (yi), ◊◊, T / I
lie (yi), ◊, I
lift, ◊, T / I
ligature, T
light, ◊, T / I
lighten, T / I
like, T, C
liken, ◊, T
lilt, T / I
limber, ◊, T / I
lime, T
limit, ◊, T, C
limp, ◊, I
line, ◊, T / I
linearise (am. -ize), T
linger, ◊, I
link, ◊, T / I
lionise (am. -ize), T
liquefy (ie), T / I
liquidate, T
liquidise (am. -ize), T
lisp, ◊, T / I
list, T / I
listen, ◊, T / I, C
litigate, T / I
litter, ◊, T / I
live, ◊◊, T / I
liven, ◊, T / I
load, ◊, T / I
loaf, ◊, I
loan, ◊, T
loathe, T, C
lob (bb), ◊, T / I
lobby (ie), ◊, T / I
localise (am. -ize), T
locate, T / I
lock, ◊, T / I
lodge, ◊, T / I

loft, T
log (gg), ◊, T / I
loiter, ◊, I
loll, ◊, T / I
long, ◊, I, C
look, ◊◊, T / I, C
loom, ◊, I
loop, T / I
loose, ◊, T / I
loosen, ◊, T / I
loot, T / I
lop (pp), ◊, T / I
lope, ◊◊◊, I
lord, T
lose, ◊, T / I
lot (tt), T / I
louden, T
lounge, ◊, I
lour, ◊, T / I
louse, ◊, T
love, T, C
low, T / I
lower, ◊, T / I
lubricate, T
luff, ◊, I
lug (gg), ◊◊◊, T
lull, ◊, T / I, C
lumber, ◊, T
lump, ◊, T / I
lunch (es), ◊, T / I
lunge, ◊, T / I
lurch (es), I
lure, ◊, T, C
lurk, ◊, I
lust, ◊, I
lustre, T / I
lute, T / I
luxuriate, ◊, I
lynch (es), T

m

macadamise (am. -ize), T
mace, T
macerate, T / I
machinate, T / I
machine, T
madden, ◊, T
maffick, I
magnetise (am. -ize), T
magnify (ie), T
mail, ◊, T
maim, T
maintain, ◊, T, C
major, ◊, I
make, ◊◊, T / I, C
malign, T
malinger, I
maltreat, T
man (nn), ◊, T
manacle, T
manage, ◊, T / I, C
mandate, T
manducate, I
mangle, ◊, T
manhandle, T
manicure, T
manifest, T
manifold, T
manipulate, T
manœuvre, ◊, T / I
mantle, ◊, T
manufacture, T
manumit (tt), T
manure, T
map (pp), ◊, T
mar (rr), T
maraud, T / I
marble, T

march (es), ◊, T / I
margin, T
marinate, T
mark, ◊, T / I, C
market, T / I
maroon, T
marry (ie), ◊, T / I
marshal (ll), ◊, T
martyr, T
martyrise (am. -ize), T
marvel (ll), ◊, I, C
mash (es), ◊, T
mask, ◊, T
masquerade, ◊, I
mass (es), T / I
massacre, T
massage, T
mast, T
master, T
masticate, T / I
masturbate, T / I
mat (tt), T / I
match (es), ◊, T / I
mate, ◊, T / I
materialise (am. -ize), T / I
matriculate, I
matter, ◊, I, C
mature, T / I
maul, ◊, T
maunder, I
maximise (am. -ize), T
may, A
mean, ◊, T, C
meander, I
measure, ◊, T
mechanise (am. -ize), T
meddle, ◊, I
mediate, ◊, T / I
medicate, T
meditate, ◊, T / I, C
meet, ◊, T / I

meld, T/I

mellow, T/I

melt, ◊, T/I

memorialise (am. -ize), T

memorise (am. -ize), T

menace, T

mend, T/I

menstruate, I

mention, ◊, T, C

meow, I

mercerise (am. -ize), T

merchandise, T/I

merge, ◊, T/I

merit, T

mesh (es), ◊, T/I

mesmerise (am. -ize), ◊, T, C

mess (es), ◊, T/I

metabolise (am. -ize), T

metal (ll), T

metallise (am. -ize), T

metamorphose, ◊, T/I

mete, ◊, T

meter, T

metrify, (ie), I

mew, I

miaow, I

microfilm, T

micturate, T/I

midwife, T

miff, T

might, A

migrate, ◊, I

mike, I

mildew, T/I

militarise (am. -ize), T

militate, ◊, I

milk, T/I

mill, ◊, T/I

mime, T/I

mimic, T

mince, ◊, T/I

mind, ◊, T/I, C

mine, ◊, T/I

mingle, ◊, T/I

miniaturise (am. -ize), T

minimise (am. -ize), T

minister, ◊, I

minor, T

mint, T

minute, T

mire, T/I

mirror, T

misapply (ie), T

misapprehend, T

misappropriate, T

misbecome, T

misbehave, I

misbrand, T

miscalculate, ◊, T/I

miscall, T

miscarry (ie), I

miscast, T

misconceive, ◊, T/I

misconduct, T

misconstrue, T

miscopy (ie), T

miscount, T/I

miscue, T

misdate, T

misdeal, T/I

misdeem, T

misdirect, T

misdo, (es), T

misdoubt, T

misesteem, T

misestimate, T

misfeed, T

misfile, T

misfire, I

misfit (tt), T/I

misgive, T

misgovern, T/I

mishandle, T

mishear, T

mishit, (tt), T

misinform, T

misinterpret, T

misjudge, T

misknow, T

mislabel (ll), T

mislay, T

mislead, T

mismanage, T

mismatch (es), T

mismate, T

misname, T

misnumber, T

misplace, T

misplay, T

misprint, T

misprize, T

mispronounce, T

mispunch (es), T

misquote, T

misread, T

misreckon, T

misreport, T

misrepresent, T

misroute, T

misrule, T

miss (es), ◊, T/I, C

missort, T

misspell, T

misspend, T

misstate, T

mist, ◊, T/I

mistake, ◊, T

mistime, T

mistranslate, T

mistreat, T

mistrust, T

mistype, T

misunderstand, T

misuse, T

mitigate, T

mitre, T

mix (es), ◊, T/I

mizzle, I

moan, ◊, T/I

mob (bb), T

mobilise (am. -ize), T/I

mock, ◊, T/I

model (ll), ◊, T

moderate, T/I

modernise (am. -ize), T

modify (ie), T

modularise (am. -ize), T

modulate, ◊, T/I

moil, I

moisten, ◊, T/I

moisturise (am. -ize), T

molest, T

mollify (ie), T

mollycoddle, T

monetise (am. -ize), T

monger, T/I

monitor, T

monkey, ◊, I

monopolise (am. -ize), T

moo, I

mooch (es), ◊◊, I

moon, ◊, T/I

moor, T/I

moot, T

mop (pp), ◊, T

mope, ◊, I

moralise (am. -ize), ◊, T/I

mortar, T

mortgage, T

mortify (ie), T

mortise, T

moss, T

mother, T

motion, ◊, T/I, C

motivate, T

motor, T/I

motorise (am. -ize), T

mottle, T

mould, ◊, T/I

moulder, I

moult, T/I

mount, ◊, T/I

mountaineer, I

mourn, ◊, T/I

mouse, T/I

mouth, T/I

move, ◊◊◊, T/I

mow, ◊, T

muck, ◊, T/I

mud (dd), T

muddle, ◊, T

muddy (ie), ◊, T

muff, T/I

muffle, ◊, T

mug (gg), ◊, T

mulch (es), T

mulct, ◊, T

mull, ◊, T

multiplex (es), T

multiply (ie), ◊, T/I

mumble, T/I

mummify (ie), T

munch (es), T/I

munition, T

murder, T

murmur, ◊, T/I

muscle, ◊, I

muse, ◊, T/I

mushroom, I

muss (es), ◊, T

must, A

muster, ◊, T/I

mutate, T/I

mute, T

mutilate, T

mutiny (ie), ◊, I

mutter, T/I

muzz, ◊◊, T/I

muzzle, T

mystify (ie), T

n

nab (bb), T

nag (gg), ◊, T/I

nail, ◊, T

name, ◊, T

nap (pp), I

narcotise (am. -ize), T

nark, I

narrate, T

narrow, ◊, T/I

nasalise (am. -ize), T

nationalise (am. -ize), T

natter, I

naturalise (am. -ize), T/I

nauseate, T/I

navigate, ◊◊◊, T/I

navvy, (ie), I

nazify (ie), T

neap, T/I

near, T

neaten, T

necessitate, T

neck, T/I

need, T/A, C

needle, T

negate, T

negative, T

neglect, T, C

negotiate, ◊, T/I

neigh, I

neighbour (am. -or), ◊, I

nerve, ◊, T, C
nest, ◊, T/I
nestle, ◊, I
net (tt), T
nettle, ◊, T
neuter, T
neutralise (am. -ize), T
nibble, ◊, T/I
nick, ◊, T
nickel (ll), T
nicker, I
nickname, T
nictitate, I
niggle, ◊, I
nip (pp), ◊, T/I
nitrate, T
nobble, T
nod (dd), ◊, T/I
noise, ◊, T
nominate, ◊, T
nonplus (ss), T
nonsuit, T
noodge, T
noose, T
normalise (am. -ize), T
nose, ◊, T/I
nosh (es), I
notarize, T
notch (es), ◊, T
note, ◊, T, C
notice, T, C
notify (ie), ◊, T
nourish (es), ◊, T
nudge, T
nullify (ie), T
numb, ◊, T
number, ◊, T/I
nurse, ◊, T
nurture, ◊, T
nuzzle, ◊, I

O

oar, I
obey, T/I
obfuscate, T
object, ◊, T/I, C
objectify, (ie), T
objurgate, T
obligate, T, C
oblige, ◊, T, C
oblique, I
obliterate, T
obscure, ◊, T
observe, ◊, T, C
obsess (es), ◊, T
obstruct, T
obtain, ◊, T/I
obtest, T
obtrude, ◊, T/I
obturate, T
obvert, I
obviate, T
occasion, T
occlude, T/I
occupy (ie), ◊, T, C
occur (rr), ◊, I, C
odorize, T
off, T/I
offend, ◊, T/I
offer, ◊, T/I, C
officer, T
officiate, ◊, I
offset (tt), T/I
ogle, ◊, T/I
oil, T
okay, I
omen, T
omit (tt), ◊, T, C
ooze, ◊, T/I

open, ◊, T/I
operate, ◊, T/I
opine, T/I, C
oppose, ◊, T, C
oppress (es), T
opt, ◊, I
orate, I
orbit, T/I
orchestrate, T
ordain, T
order, ◊, T/I, C
organise (am. -ize), T/I
orientate, T/I
originate, ◊, T/I
ornament, T
orphan, T
oscillate, ◊, I
osculate, ◊, T/I
ossify (ie), T/I
ostracise (am. -ize), T
oust, ◊, T
out, T/I
outbid (dd), T
outbrave, T
outbreed, T
outclass (es), T
outcrop (pp), I
outcross (es), T
outdistance, T
outdo (es), T
outface, T
outfight, T
outfit (tt), T
outflank, T
outfoot, T
outfox (es), T
outgas (es), I
outgo (es), T
outgrow, T
outguess (es), T
outgun (nn), T

outjockey, T

outlast, T

outlaw, T

outline, T

outman (nn), T

outmanœuvre, T

outmatch (es), T

outnumber, T

outpace, T

outperform, T

outplay, T

outrace, T

outrage, T

outrange, T

outrank, T

outreach, T

outride, T

outrival, T

outrun (nn), T

outrusk (es), T

outscore, T

outshine, T

outsmart, T

outsoar, I

outspan (nn), T

outspeak, T

outspend, T

outspread, T

outstand, T

outstare, T

outstay, T

outstretch (es), T

outstrip (pp), T

outtalk, T

outthink, T

outvie (yi), T

outvote, T

outwear, T

outweigh, T

outwind, T

outwit (tt), T

outwork, T

over, T

overachieve, T

overact, T/I

overawe, T

overbalance, T/I

overbear, T

overbid (dd), T/I

overbook, T

overbuild, T

overburden, ◊, T

overcall, T

overcast, T

overcharge, T/I

overcloud, T/I

overcome, ◊, T

overcrowd, ◊, T/I

overdo (es), T

overdose, T

overdraw, T

overdress (es), T

overdrive, T

overeat, I

overestimate, T

overexcite, T

overexert, T

overextend, I

overfeed, T/I

overflow, ◊, T/I

overfly (ie), T

overgraze, T

overgrow, T/I

overhand, T

overhang, T/I

overhaul, T

overhear, T

overheat, T/I

overindulge, T

overink, T

overkill, I

overlap (pp), T/I

overlay, ◊, T

overleap, I

overlie (yi), T

overlive, T

overload, T

overlook, T

overmaster, T

overmatch (es), T

overpass (es), ◊, T/I

overpay, T

overpersuade, T

overpitch (es), I

overplay, T

overpower, ◊, T

overpraise, T

overproduce, T

overrate, T

overreach (es), T/I

override, T

overrule, T

overrun (nn), ◊, T/I

overscore, T

oversee, T

oversell, T

overset (tt), T

oversew, T

overshadow, T

overshoot, T

overslaugh, T

oversleep, I

overspend, T

overspill, I

overstate, T

overstay, T

oversteer, I

overstep (pp), T

overstock, ◊, T

overstrain, T

overstress (es), T

overstrew, T

overstuff, T

overtake, T
overtask, T
overtax (es), T
overthrow, T
overtop (pp), T
overtrade, I
overtrump, T
overturn, T / I
overvalue, T
overweary (ie), ◊, T
overweigh, T / I
overweight, T
overwhelm, ◊, T
overwind, T
overwinter, I
overword, I
overwork, T / I
overwrite, T
owe, ◊, T, C
own, ◊, T
oxidise (am. -ize), T / I
oxygenate, T

p

pace, ◊◊◊, T / I
pacify (ie), T
pack, ◊, T / I
package, T
pad (dd), ◊◊◊, T
paddle, T / I
padlock, T
page, ◊, T
paginate, T
pain, T, C
paint, ◊, T / I

pair, ◊, T / I
pal (ll), ◊, I
palatalise (am. -ize), T
palaver, I
pale, ◊, I
palisade, T
pall, ◊, I
palliate, T
palm, ◊, T
palpate, T
palpitate, I
palter, ◊, I
pamper, T
pan (nn), ◊, T / I
pancake, I
pander, ◊, T / I
panel (ll), T
panhandle, T / I
panic, T / I
pant, ◊, T / I
pantomime, T / I
paper, ◊, T
parachute, ◊, T / I
parade, T / I
paraffin, T
paragraph, T
parallel, T
paralyse, T
paraphrase, T
parboil, T
parcel (ll), ◊, T
parch (es), ◊, T / I
pardon, ◊, T, C
pare, ◊, T
parenthesise (am. -ize), T
park, T / I
parlance, I
parley, ◊, I
parody (ie), T
parole, T
parry (ie), T / I

parse, T
part, ◊, T / I
partake, ◊, I
participate, ◊, I
particularise (am. -ize), T / I
partition, ◊, T
partner, ◊, T
pass (es), ◊◊, T / I
paste, ◊, T
pasteurise (am. -ize), T
pasture, T / I
pat (tt), ◊, T
patch (es), ◊, T
patent, T
patrol (ll), T / I
patronise (am. -ize), T
patter, ◊, I
pattern, ◊, T
pauperise (am. -ize), T
pause, ◊, I
pave, ◊, T
paw, ◊, T
pawn, T
pay, ◊◊, T / I, C
peach (es), ◊, T / I
peak, ◊, I
peal, ◊, T / I
pearl, I
pebble, T
peck, ◊, T
peculate, I
pedal (ll), T / I
peddle, T / I
pee, I
peek, ◊, I
peel, ◊, T / I
peep, ◊, I
peer, ◊, I
peeve, T
peg (gg), ◊, T / I
pelt, ◊, T / I

pen (nn), ◊, T

penalise (am. -ize), ◊, T, C

pencil (ll), T

penetrate, ◊, T/I

pension, ◊, T

people, ◊, T

pep (pp), ◊, T

pepper, ◊, T

perambulate, T/I

perceive, T, C

perch (es), ◊, T/I

percolate, ◊, T/I

percuss (es), T/I

perfect, T

perforate, ◊, T/I

perform, ◊, T/I

perfume, T

perish (es), ◊, T/I

perjure, T

perk, ◊, T/I

permeate, ◊, T/I

permit (tt), ◊, T/I, C

permute, T

perorate, I

peroxide, T

perpend, T

perpetrate, T

perpetuate, T

perplex (es), T

persecute, T

persevere, ◊, I, C

persist, ◊, I, C

personalise (am. -ize), T

personate, T

personify (ie), T

perspire, I

persuade, ◊, T, C

pertain, ◊, I

perturb, T

peruse, T

pervade, ◊, T

pervert, T

pester, ◊, T, C

pestle, T/I

pet (tt), T

peter, ◊, I

petition, ◊, T

petrify (ie), T/I

pettifog (gg), I

phase, ◊, T

philander, ◊, I

philosophise (am. -ize), ◊, I

phone, ◊, T/I

photograph, T/I

photoset (tt), T

photostat (tt), T

phrase, T

picaroon, T

pick, ◊, T/I

picket, T/I

pickle, T

picnic, I

picture, ◊, T

piddle, I

piece, ◊, T

pierce, ◊, T/I

pig (gg), ◊, I

pigment, T

pile, ◊, T/I

pilfer, ◊, T/I

pillage, T/I

pillory (ie), T

pillow, ◊, T

pilot, ◊, T

pimp, ◊, I

pin (nn), ◊, T

pinch (es), ◊, T/I

pine, ◊, I

ping, I

pinion, ◊, T

pink, ◊, T

pioneer, T/I

pip (pp), T

pipe, ◊, T/I

pique, ◊, T

pirate, T

pirouette, I

piss (es), ◊, T/I

pit (tt), ◊, T

pitch (es), ◊, T/I

pitchfork, T

pith, T

pity (ie), T

pivot, ◊, T/I

placard, T

placate, T

place, ◊, T

plagiarise (am. -ize), T

plague, ◊, T

plait, T

plan (nn), ◊, T/I, C

plane, ◊, T/I

planish (es), T

plank, ◊, T

plant, ◊, T

plash (es), I

plaster, ◊, T

plasticise (am. -ize), T

plate, ◊, T

platinise (am. -ize), T

platitudinise (am. -ize), I

play, ◊◊◊, T/I, C

pleach (es), T

plead, ◊, T/I

please, T

pleat, T

pledge, ◊, T, C

plight, T

plink, T

plod (dd), ◊◊◊, I

plonk, ◊, T

plop (pp), I

plot (tt), ◊, T/I, C

plotz, ◊, I

plough, ◊, T / I

plow, ◊, T / I

pluck, ◊, T

plug (gg), ◊, T / I

plumb, T

plume, ◊, T / I, C

plummet, T / I

plump, ◊, T / I

plunder, T

plunge, ◊, T / I

plunk, ◊, T

ply (ie), ◊, T / I

poach (es), ◊, T / I

pocket, T

pod (dd), T / I

poeticise (am. -ize), T

point, ◊, T / I, C

poise, ◊, T / I

poison, ◊, T

poke, ◊◊, T / I

polarise (am. -ize), T

pole, T

poleaxe, T

polemise (am. -ize), I

police, T

polish (es), ◊, T

poll, T / I

pollard, T

pollard, T

pollinate, T

pollute, ◊, T

pommel (ll), T

ponce, I

ponder, ◊, T / I

pong, I

pontificate, I

pony (ie), T / I

pooh-pooh, T / I

pool, T

poop, ◊, T

pop (pp), ◊◊, T / I

popularise (am. -ize), T

populate, T

pore, ◊, I

portend, T

portion, ◊, T

portray, T

pose, ◊, T / I

posh (es), ◊, T

position, T

possess (es), ◊, T

post, ◊, T / I

postdate, T

postpone, ◊, T, C

post-synchronise (am. -ize), T

postulate, ◊, T / I

posture, T / I

pot (tt), ◊, T

potter, ◊, I

pouch (es), T

poultice, T

pounce, ◊, I

pound, ◊, T / I

pour, ◊◊, T / I

pout, I

powder, ◊, T

power, ◊, T

powwow, ◊, I

practise, ◊, T / I

praise, ◊, T, C

prance, ◊, I

prang, T

prank, I

prate, ◊, I

prattle, ◊, I

pray, ◊, T / I, C

preach (es), ◊, T / I

prearrange, T

precede, T

precipitate, ◊, T / I

preclude, ◊, T, C

preconceive, T

precondition, T

precool, T

predate, T

predecease, T

predestinate, ◊, T

predestine, ◊, T

predetermine, T

predict, T / I, C

predispose, ◊, T

predominate, ◊, I

pre-empt, T

preen, ◊, T

pre-establish (es), T

pre-exist, I

prefabricate, T

preface, ◊, T

prefer (rr), ◊, T, C

prefigure, T

prefix (es), ◊, T

preheat, T

prejudge, T

prejudice, ◊, T, C

prelude, ◊, T / I

premeditate, T

premiere, T

premise, T, C

preoccupy (ie), T

preordain, T

prepack, T

prepare, ◊, T / I, C

prepay, T

preponderate, ◊, I

prepossess (es), ◊, T

prerecord, T

presage, ◊, T, C

prescribe, ◊, T, C

present, ◊, T

preserve, ◊, T

pre-shrink, T

preside, ◊, I

presort, T
press (es), ◊◊, T/I, C
pressure, ◊, T, C
pressurise (am. -ize), T
prestore, T
prestress (es), I
presume, ◊, T/I, C
presuppose, T, C
pretend, ◊, T/I, C
pretermit, T
pretext, T
prettify (ie), T
prevail, ◊, I
prevaricate, I
prevent, ◊, T, C
prey, ◊, I
price, ◊, T
prick, ◊, T/I
prickle, T/I
pride, ◊, T, C
prim (mm), ◊, T
prime, ◊, T
primp, ◊, T/I
prink, ◊, T/I
print, ◊, T/I, C
prise (am. -ize), ◊, T
prize, ◊, T
privilege, T, C
probate, T
probe, ◊, T
proceed, ◊, I, C
process (es), T
proclaim, T
procrastinate, I
procreate, T
procure, ◊, T
prod (dd), ◊, T, C
produce, ◊, T/I
profane, T
profess (es), T, C
proffer, T

profile, T
profit, ◊, T/I, C
profiteer, I
prognosticate, T
program (mm), T/I
progress (es), ◊, I
prohibit, ◊, T, C
project, ◊, T/I
prolapse, I
proletarianise (am. -ize), T
proliferate, I
prolong, T
promenade, I
promise, ◊, T/I, C
promote, ◊, T
prompt, T, C
promulgate, T
pronounce, ◊, T
proof, T
prop (pp), ◊, T
propagandise (am. -ize), T/I
propagate, T/I
propel (ll), T
prophesy (ie), T/I, C
propitiate, T
proportion, T
propose, ◊, T, C
proposition, T
propound, T
prorate, T
prorogue, T
proscribe, T, C
prosecute, ◊, T, C
proselyte, T/I
proselytise (am. -ize), T/I
prospect, ◊, T/I
prosper, ◊, T/I
prostitute, T
prostrate, ◊, T
protect, ◊, T
protest, ◊, T/I, C

protract, T
protrude, ◊, T/I
prove, ◊, T/I, C
provide, ◊, T/I
provision, ◊, T
provoke, ◊, T, C
prowl, ◊, I
prune, ◊, T/I
pry (ie), ◊, T/I
psalmodise (am. -ize), I
psych, ◊, T/I
psychoanalise, T
publicise (am. -ize), T
publish (es), T
pucker, ◊, T/I
puddle, ◊, T/I
puff, ◊◊◊, T/I
pug (gg), T
puke, T/I
pule, I
pull, ◊◊◊, T
pullulate, I
pulp, T
pulsate, I
pulse, ◊, I
pulverise (am. -ize), T/I
pummel (ll), T
pump, ◊, T/I
pun (nn), I
punch (es), ◊, T
punctuate, ◊, T
puncture, T/I
punish (es), ◊, T, C
punt, T/I
pup (pp), I
pupate, I
purchase, T
purge, ◊, T
purify (ie), ◊, T
purl, T
purloin, T

purport, T, C
purpose, T, C
purr, I
purse, ◊, T
pursue, T
purvey, T
push (es), ◊◊◊, T/I
pussyfoot, ◊◊, I
put (tt), ◊◊◊, T/I, C
putrefy (ie), T/I
putt, T/I
putter, ◊, I
putty (ie), ◊, T
puzzle, ◊, T/I, C

q

quack, I
quadrate, T/I
quadruple, T/I
quaff, T
quail, ◊, I
quake, ◊, I
qualify (ie), ◊, T/I
quantise (am. -ize), T
quarantine, T
quarrel (ll), ◊, I, C
quarry (ie), T
quarter, T
quash (es), T
quaver, I
queen, T/I
queer, T
quell, T
quench (es), T
query (ie), ◊, T, C
question, ◊, T, C

queue, ◊, I
quibble, ◊, I
quicken, ◊, T/I
quicksilver, T
quiesce, I
quiet, ◊, T/I
quieten, ◊, T/I
quilt, T
quintuple, T/I
quip (pp), T/I
quirt, T
quit (tt), ◊, T/I, C
quiver, ◊, T/I
quiz (zz), T
quod, T
quoin, T
quote, ◊, T

r

rabbet, T
rabbit, ◊, I
race, ◊◊◊, T/I
rack, ◊, T
racket, ◊, I
raddle, T
radiate, ◊, T/I
radio, T/I
radiograph, T
raffle, T
raft, ◊, T/I
rag (gg), T
rage, ◊, I
raid, T
rail, ◊, T/I
railroad, ◊, T, C
rain, ◊, T/I
rainproof, T

raise, ◊, T
rake, ◊, T
rally (ie), ◊, T/I
ram (mm), ◊, T
ramble, ◊, I
ramify (ie), T/I
ramp, ◊, I
rampage, ◊, I
ranch (es), I
randomise (am. -ize), T
range, ◊, T/I
rank, ◊, T/I
rankle, ◊, I
ransack, ◊, T
ransom, T
rant, I
rap (pp), ◊, T/I
rape, T
rarefy (ie), T/I
rase, T
rasp, ◊, T/I
rat (tt), ◊, I
rate, ◊, T/I
ratify (ie), T
ratiocinate, I
ration, ◊, T
rationalise (am. -ize), T
rattle, ◊◊◊, T/I
ravage, T
rave, ◊, I
ravel (ll), ◊, T/I
raven, T/I
ravish (es), T
raze, ◊, T
razz (es), T
reabsorb, T
reach (es), ◊, T/I
react, ◊, I
read, ◊◊, T/I, C
readjust, T
ready (ie), T

realise (am. -ize), ◊, T, C

ream, ◊, T

reanimate, T

reap, ◊, T

reappear, I

reapply (ie), ◊, T/I

reappoint, T

reapportion, T

rear, ◊, T/I

rearm, T

rearrange, T

reason, ◊, T/I, C

reassemble, T/I

reassert, T

reassess (es), T

reassign, T

reassume, T

reassure, ◊, T

reawaken, T/I

rebate, I

rebel (ll), ◊, I, C

rebind, T

reboot, T

rebore, T

rebound, ◊, I

rebroadcast, T

rebuff, T

rebuild, T

rebuke, ◊, T, C

recalculate, T

recalibrate, T

recall, ◊, T, C

recant, T/I

recap (pp), T/I

recapitulate, T/I

recapture, T

recast, ◊, T

recede, ◊, I

receipt, T

receive, ◊, T

recess (es), T/I

recharge, T/I

rechristen, T

reciprocate, T/I

recite, ◊, T/I

reck, ◊, I

reckon, ◊, T/I, C

reclaim, ◊, T

recline, ◊, T/I

reclothe, T

recognise (am. -ize), ◊, T

recoil, ◊, I, C

recollect, T/I, C

recommence, T/I

recommend, ◊, T, C

recommission, T

recommit (tt), T

recompense, ◊, T, C

recomplement, T

recompute, T

reconcile, ◊, T

recondition, T

reconfigure, T

reconnect, T

reconnoitre, T/I

reconquer, T

reconsider, T, C

reconsolidate, T

reconstitute, T

reconstruct, ◊, T

reconvene, T

reconvert, T

recopy (ie), T

record, ◊, T

recork, T

recount, ◊, T, C

recoup, ◊, T

recover, ◊, T/I

recreate, T

recriminate, ◊, I

recross (es), T/I

recrudesce, I

recruit, ◊, T

rectify (ie), T

recultivate, T

recuperate, ◊, T/I

recur (rr), ◊, I

recut (tt), T

redact, T

redden, T/I

rede, T

redecorate, T

redeem, ◊, T

redeploy, T

redial (ll), T

redirect, ◊, T

rediscover, T

redistribute, T

redo (es), T

redouble, T/I

redound, ◊, I

redraft, T

redraw, T

redress (es), T

reduce, ◊, T/I, C

reduplicate, T

re-echo (es), T/I

re-edit, T

re-educate, T

reef, ◊, T

reek, ◊, I

reel, ◊, T/I

re-elect, T

re-embark, T/I

re-emerge, I

re-employ, T

re-enable, T

re-enact, T

re-engage, T

re-enlist, T/I

re-enter, T/I

re-equip (pp), ◊, T

re-erect, T

re-establish (es), ◊, T

reeve, ◊, T

re-examine, T

reface, T

refan (nn), T

refashion, T

refasten, T

refeed, T

refer (rr), ◊, T/I

referee, T/I

refile, T

refill, ◊, T

refine, ◊, T/I

refit (tt), T

reflate, T

reflect, ◊, T/I, C

refloat, T

refold, T

reforge, T

reform, T/I

refract, T

refrain, ◊, I, C

reframe, T

refresh (es), ◊, T/I

refrigerate, T

refuel (ll), ◊, I

refund, ◊, T

refurbish (es), T

refurnish (es), T

refuse, ◊, T/I, C

refute, T

regain, ◊, T

regale, ◊, T

regard, ◊, T

regenerate, T/I

regig (gg), T

regigger, T

regild, T

regiment, T

register, ◊, T/I

regorge, T/I

regrade, T

regress (es), ◊, I

regret (tt), T, C

regrind, T

regroup, T/I

regularise (am. -ize), T

regulate, ◊, T

regurgitate, T/I

rehabilitate, T

rehandle, T

reharden, T/I

rehash (es), T

rehear, T

rehearse, T

reheat, T

rehouse, T

reign, ◊, I

reignite, T

reimburse, ◊, T

reimport, T

reimpose, T

rein, ◊, T

reincarnate, T/I

reincorporate, T

reinflate, T

reinforce, ◊, T

reingratiate, ◊, T

reinitialise (am. -ize), T

reinitiate, T

reinsert, T

reinstall, T

reinstate, ◊, T

reinsure, T

reintegrate, ◊, T

reinter (rr), T

reinterrogate, T

reintroduce, T

reinvent, T

reinvest, T/I

reinvigorate, T

reinvite, T

reissue, T

reiterate, T

reject, T

rejoggle, T

rejoice, ◊, T/I, C

rejoin, ◊, T/I

rejoint, T

rejuvenate, T/I

rekey, T

rekindle, T/I

relabel (ll), T

relapse, ◊, I

relate, ◊, T/I, C

relax (es), ◊, T/I

relay, ◊, T

re-lay, T

relearn, T

release, ◊, T

relegate, ◊, T

relent, I

relet (tt), T

relieve, ◊, T

relight, T/I

reline, T

relink, T

relinquish (es), T

relish (es), T, C

relive, T

reload, T

relocate, T

rely (ie), ◊, I

remain, ◊, I, C

remainder, T

remake, T

remand, ◊, T

remark, ◊, T/I, C

remarry (ie), I

rematch, T

remedy (ie), T

remelt, T/I

remember, ◊, T/I, C

remilitarise (am. -ize), T

remind, ◊, T, C

reminisce, ◊, I

remit (tt), ◊, T

remodel (ll), T

remonstrate, ◊, T/I, C

remould, T

remount, T/I

remove, ◊, T/I

remunerate, ◊, T

rename, T

rend, ◊, T

render, ◊, T

rendezvous (es), I

renege, ◊, I

renew, T/I

renounce, T

renovate, T

rent, ◊, T

renumber, T

reoccupy (ie), T

reopen, T/I

reorder, T

reorganise (am. -ize), T/I

repackage, T

repaginate, T

repaint, T

repair, T

repaper, T

repatriate, T

repay, ◊, T

repeal, T

repeat, T/I, C

repel (ll), ◊, T

repent, ◊, T/I, C

repeople, T

rephrase, T

repine, ◊, I

replace, ◊, T

replant, T

replaster, T

replate, ◊, T

replay, T

repleat, T

replenish (es), ◊, T

replicate, T

replot (tt), T

replug (gg), T

reply (ie), ◊, T/I, C

repolish (es), T

report, ◊, T/I, C

repose, ◊, T/I

reposition, T

repossess (es), T

repot (tt), T

reprehend, ◊, T, C

represent, ◊, T, C

repress (es), T

reprieve, T

reprimand, ◊, T, C

reprint, ◊, T

reprise, T

reproach (es), ◊, T, C

reprobate, T

reprocess (es), T

reproduce, ◊, T/I

reprogram (mm), T

reproof, T

reprove, ◊, T, C

republicanise (am. -ize), T

republish (es), T

repudiate, T

repulse, ◊, T

repurchase, T

repute, ◊, T, C

request, ◊, T, C

require, ◊, T, C

requisition, ◊, T

requite, ◊, T

reread, T

reroute, T

rerun (nn), T

resaddle, T

rescale, T

reschedule, T

rescind, T

rescue, ◊, T

research (es), ◊, T/I

reseat, T

resect, T

resell, T

resemble, T

resent, T, C

reserve, ◊, T

reset (tt), T

resettle, ◊, T/I

reshape, T

reship (pp), T

reshoe, T

reshuffle, T

reside, ◊, I

resign, ◊, T/I, C

re-silver, T

resist, T/I, C

resole, T

resolve, ◊, T/I, C

resort, ◊, I, C

resound, ◊, I

respect, ◊, T

respire, T/I

respite, T

respond, ◊, T/I

respool, T

respray, T

ressource, T

rest, ◊, T/I

restack, T

restart, T/I

restate, T

restitch (es), T

restitute, ◊, T

restock, ◊, T

restore, ◊, T

restow, T

restrain, ◊, T, C

restrict, ◊, T, C

restring, T

result, ◊, I, C

resume, T / I, C

resurface, T

resurge, I

resurrect, T

resuscitate, T / I

ret (tt), T

retail, ◊, T

retain, ◊, T

retake, T

retaliate, ◊, I

retard, T

retch (es), I

retell, T

retemper, T

reticulate, T / I

retighten, T

retile, T

retire, ◊, T / I

retool, T

retort, T, C

retouch (es), T

retrace, T

retract, T / I

retrain, T / I

retranslate, T

retransmit (tt), T

re-tread, T / I

retread, T

retreat, ◊, T / I

retrench (es), T

retrieve, ◊, T

retrim (mm), T

retroact, ◊, I

retrocede, T / I

retrograde, I

retrogress (es), I

retry (ie), T

returf, T

return, ◊, T / I

reunite, ◊, T / I

rev (vv), ◊, T / I

revaccinate, T

revalorise (am. -ize), T

revalue, T

revarnish (es), T

reveal, ◊, T, C

revel (ll), ◊, I, C

revenge, ◊, T

reverberate, T / I

revere, T

reverence, T

reverse, T / I

revert, ◊, I, C

review, T

revile, ◊, T / I

revise, T

revisit, T

revitalise (am. -ize), T

revive, T / I

revivify (ie), T

revoke, T / I

revolt, ◊, T / I, C

revolutionise (am. -ize), T

revolve, ◊, T / I

reward, ◊, T, C

reweigh, T

rewind, T

rewire, T

reword, T

rewrite, T

rhapsodise (am. -ize), ◊, I

rhyme, ◊, T / I

rib (bb), T

rice, T

rick, T

ricochet (tt), I

rid (dd), ◊, T

riddle, ◊, T

ride, ◊◊◊, T / I

ridge, T / I

ridicule, T

riffle, T

rifle, ◊, T

rig (gg), ◊, T

right, T

rile, T

rind, T

ring, ◊, T / I

ring, ◊, T / I

rinse, ◊, T

riot, I

rip (pp), ◊, T / I

ripen, T / I

riposte, I

ripple, T / I

rise, ◊, I

risk, ◊, T

rival (ll), T

rivalise (am. -ize), ◊, I

rive, T / I

rivet, ◊, T

roam, ◊, T / I

roar, ◊, T / I

roast, T / I

rob (bb), ◊, T

robe, T / I

rock, ◊, T / I

rocket, ◊, I

roister, I

roll, ◊◊, T / I

rollick, I

romance, I

romanise (am. -ize), T / I

romanticise (am. -ize), T / I

romp, ◊, I

roneo (es), T

roof, ◊, T

rook, T

room, ◊, I
roose, T
roost, I
root, ◊, T/I
rootle, T/I
rope, ◊, T/I
roster, T
rot (tt), ◊, T/I
rotate, T/I
rotavate, T
rototill, T
rouge, T
rough, ◊, T
round, ◊, T/I
rouse, ◊, T/I
rout, ◊, T/I
route, ◊, T
rove, ◊, T/I
row, ◊◊◊, T/I
rub (bb), ◊◊, T/I
rubber, T
rubberise (am. -ize), T
rubberneck, I
ruck, ◊, T/I
ruckle, ◊, T/I
ruddy (ie), T
rue, T
ruff, T/I
ruffle, ◊, T
ruggerdize, T
ruin, T
rule, ◊, T/I
rumble, ◊, I
ruminate, ◊, T/I
rummage, ◊, T/I
rumple, T
run (nn), ◊◊◊, T/I
rupture, T/I
rush (es), ◊◊◊, T/I, C
russianise (am. -ize), T
rust, ◊, T/I

rusticate, T/I
rustle, ◊, T/I
rut (tt), T/I

S

sabotage, T
sack, T
sacrifice, ◊, T
sadden, T/I
saddle, ◊, T
safeguard, ◊, T
sag (gg), ◊, I
sail, ◊◊◊, T/I
sain, T
salaam, T/I
salivate, I
sally (ie), ◊, I
salt, ◊, T
salute, ◊, T
salvage, ◊, T
salve, T
sample, T
sanctify (ie), T
sanction, T
sand, ◊, T
sandbag (gg), T
sandpaper, T
sandwich (es), ◊, T
sanforize, T
sanitize, T
sap (pp), T/I
saponify (ie), T/I
sashay, ◊◊◊, I
sass (es), T
sate, T
satiate, ◊, T
satin, T

satirise (am. -ize), T
satisfy (ie), ◊, T/I
saturate, ◊, T
sauce, T
saunter, ◊, I
sauté, T
savage, T
save, ◊, T/I
savour (am. -or), ◊, T/I
savvy (ie), T
saw, ◊, T/I
say, ◊, T/I, C
scab (bb), ◊, I
scaffold, T
scald, T
scale, ◊, T/I
scallop, T
scalp, T
scam (mm), T/I
scamp, T
scamper, ◊◊◊, I
scan (nn), T/I
scandalise (am. -ize), ◊, T
scant, T/I
scar (rr), ◊, T/I
scare, ◊, T, C
scarf, T
scarify (ie), T
scarper, T
scat (tt), T
scatter, ◊, T/I
scavenge, T/I
scent, ◊, T
s(c)help (pp), T
s(c)hmooze, I
schedule, ◊, T, C
schematise (am. -ize), T/I
scheme, ◊, T/I, C
school, ◊, T, C
scintillate, I
scissor, T

scoff, ◊, I

scold, ◊, T/I, C

scoop, ◊, T

scoot, ◊, I

scope, ◊, T

scorch (es), ◊, T/I

score, ◊, T/I

scorn, T, C

scotch (es), T

scour, ◊, T/I

scourge, T

scout, ◊, T/I

scowl, ◊, I

scrabble, ◊, I

scrag (gg), T

scram (mm), I

scramble, ◊◊◊, T/I

scrap (pp), T

scrape, ◊, T/I

scratch (es), ◊, T/I

scrawl, ◊, T/I

scream, ◊, T/I

screech (es), T/I

screen, ◊, T

screw, ◊, T/I

scribble, ◊, T/I

scribe, T/I

scroll, ◊, T/I

scrounge, ◊, T/I

scrub (bb), ◊, T/I

scrummage, T

scrump, T

scrunch (es), T/I

scruple, I, C

scrutinise (am. -ize), T

scud (dd), ◊◊◊, I

scuff, ◊, T/I

scuffle, ◊, I

scull, T/I

sculpt, T/I

sculpture, ◊, T

scum (mm), T/I

scupper, T

scurry (ie), ◊◊◊, I

scutter, T

scuttle, ◊◊◊, I

scuzz (es) ◊, T

scythe, T

seal, ◊, T

seam, ◊, T

sear, T

search (es), ◊, T/I

season, ◊, T/I

seat, ◊, T

secede ◊, I

seclude, ◊, T

second, ◊, T

second-guess (es), T/I, C

secrete, T/I

section, ◊, T

secularise (am. -ize), T

secure, ◊, T/I

sedate, T

seduce, ◊, T, C

see, ◊◊, T/I, C

seed, T/I

seek, ◊, T/I, C

seem, I, C

seep, ◊, I

seesaw, I

seethe, ◊, I

segment, T/I

segregate, ◊, T/I

seise, ◊, T/I

seize, ◊, T/I

select, ◊, T

sell, ◊, T/I

semaphore, T

send, ◊◊, T/I

sense, T, C

sensitise (am. -ize), T

sentence, ◊, T

sentimentalise (am. -ize), T/I

separate, ◊, T/I

sequester, T

sequestrate, T

serenade, T

serialise (am. -ize), T

sermonise (am. -ize), T/I

serrate, T

serve, ◊, T/I

service, T

set (tt), ◊◊◊, T/I, C

settle, ◊, T/I

sever, T/I

sew, ◊, T/I

sex (es), T

sextuple, T/I

shack, ◊, T/I

shackle, ◊, T

shade, ◊, T/I

shadow, T

shaft, ◊, T, C

shake, ◊, T/I

shall, A

sham (mm), T/I

shamble, ◊, I

shame, ◊, T, C

shampoo, T

shanghai, ◊, T, C

shape, ◊, T/I

share, ◊, T/I

sharp, T

sharpen, T/I

shatter, T/I

shave, ◊, T/I

shear, ◊, T/I

sheathe, ◊, T

shed (dd), ◊, T

sheer, ◊, I

sheet, ◊, T

shell, ◊, T/I

shelter, ◊, T/I

shelve, T / I
shepherd, ◊, T
shield, ◊, T, C
shift, ◊, T / I
shilly-shally (ie), I
shimmer, I
shin (nn), ◊, I
shine, ◊, T / I
shingle, T
shinny, T
ship (pp), ◊, T / I
shipwreck, T
shirk, T / I
shirr, T
shit (tt), I
shiver, ◊, T / I
shoal, T / I
shock, ◊, T, C
shoe, ◊, T
shoo, ◊, T / I
shoot, ◊◊, T / I
shop (pp), ◊, T / I
shore, ◊, T
short, T
shorten, T / I
should, A
shoulder, ◊, T
shout, ◊, T / I
shove, ◊◊, T / I
shovel (ll), ◊, T
show, ◊◊, T / I, C
shower, ◊, T / I
shred (dd), T
shriek, ◊, T / I
shrill, T / I
shrimp, I
shrink, ◊, T / I, C
shrive, T
shrivel (ll), ◊, T / I
shroud, ◊, T
shrug (gg), ◊, T / I

shuck, ◊, T
shudder, ◊, I
shuffle, ◊◊◊, T / I
shun (nn), T
shunt, T / I
shush (es), T
shut (tt), ◊, T / I
shuttle, ◊, T / I
shy (ie), ◊, I
sick, ◊, T
sicken, ◊, T / I, C
side, ◊, I
sidle, ◊◊◊, I
sieve, ◊, T / I
sift, ◊, T / I
sigh, ◊, I
sight, T
sign, ◊, T / I
signal (ll), ◊, T / I, C
signalise (am. -ize), T
signify (ie), T / I
signpost, T
silence, T
silhouette, ◊, T
silt, ◊, T / I
silver, T
simmer, ◊, T / I
simonize, T
simper, I
simplify (ie), T
simulate, T
sin (nn), ◊, I
sing, ◊, T / I
singe, T
single, ◊, T
singularise (am. -ize), T
sink, ◊, T / I
sip (pp), T
siphon, ◊, T
sir, T
sire, T

sit (tt), ◊◊, T / I
site, T
situate, T
size, ◊, T
sizzle, I
skate, ◊, I
skedaddle, I
skelp, T
skelter, ◊◊, I
sketch (es), ◊, T
skew, T / I
skewer, T
ski, I
skid (dd), I
skim (mm), ◊, T / I
skimp, ◊, T / I
skin (nn), ◊, T
skip (pp), ◊◊◊, T / I
skirmish (es), ◊, I
skirt, ◊, T / I
skitter, ◊◊◊, T / I
skive, ◊, T
skrag (gg), T
skulk, I
skunk, T
skurf, I
skyjack, T
skylark, I
skyrocket, I
slack, ◊, T / I
slacken, ◊, T / I
slag (gg) ◊, T
slake, T / I
slam (mm), ◊, T / I
slander, T
slang, T
slant, ◊, T / I
slap (pp), ◊, T
slash (es), T / I
slat (tt) T
slate, T

slaughter, T

slave, ◊, I

slaver, I

slay, T

sledge, ◊◊◊, T / I

sleek, T

sleep, ◊, T / I

sleet, I

sleigh, T / I

slenderise (am. -ize), T

sleuth, ◊, I

slew, ◊, T / I

slice, ◊, T

slick, ◊, T

slide, ◊◊◊, T / I

slight, T

slim (mm), ◊, T / I

sling, ◊, T

slink, ◊, I

slip (pp), ◊◊, T / I

slit (tt), ◊, T

slither, ◊◊◊, T / I

sliver, T / I

slob (bb), ◊, I

slobber, ◊, I

slog (gg), ◊◊◊, T / I

slop (pp), ◊, T / I

slope, ◊, T / I

slosh (es), ◊, T / I

slot (tt), ◊, T

slouch (es), ◊◊◊, T / I

slough, ◊, T

slow, ◊, T / I

slug (gg), T

sluice, ◊, T / I

slum, I

slumber, I

slump, ◊, I

slur (rr), ◊, T / I

slush, ◊◊, T / I

smack, ◊, T

smack, ◊, T / I

smarm, ◊, T / I

smart, ◊, I

smarten, ◊, T / I

smash (es), ◊, T / I

smatter, T

smear, ◊, T / I

smell, ◊, T / I, C

smelt, T

smile, ◊, T / I

smirch (es), T

smirk, I

smite, ◊, T

smoke, ◊, T / I

smooch (es), I

smooth, ◊, T

smother, ◊, T / I

smoulder, ◊, I

smudge, T / I

smuggle, ◊, T / I

snaffle, T

snag (gg), T

snake, I

snap (pp), ◊, T / I

snare, T

snarl, ◊, T / I

snatch (es), ◊, T / I

sneak, ◊◊◊, T / I

sneer, ◊, I

sneeze, ◊, I

snick, T

sniff, ◊, T / I

sniffle, I

snigger, I

snip (pp), ◊, T

snipe, ◊, I

snitch (es), ◊, I

snivel (ll), I

snog (gg), I

snoop, ◊, I

snoot, T

snooze, I

snore, I

snort, ◊, T / I

snow, ◊, T / I

snowball, T / I

snub (bb), T

snuff, ◊, T / I

snuffle, I

snug (gg), ◊, T / I

snuggle, ◊, T / I

soak, ◊, T / I

soap, ◊, T

soar, I

sob (bb), ◊, T / I

sober, ◊, T / I

socialise (am. -ize), T / I

sock, ◊, T

sod (dd), ◊, T

soften, ◊, T / I

solace, T

solder, T

soldier, ◊, I

sole, T

solemnise (am. -ize), T

solicit, ◊, T / I

solidify (ie), T / I

soliloquise (am. -ize), I

solve, T

soot, ◊, T

soothe, T

sop (pp), ◊, T

sorrow, ◊, I

sort, ◊, T

sough, I

sound, ◊, T / I

soup, ◊, T

sour, T / I

souse, ◊, T / I

south, I

sovietise (am. -ize), T

sow, ◊, T / I

space, ◊, T

spade, ◊, T

span (nn), T

spangle, ◊, T

spank, ◊, T

spar (rr), ◊, I

spare, ◊, T

sparge, T

spark, ◊, T/I

sparkle, ◊, I

spatter, ◊, T/I

spawn, ◊, T/I

spay, T

speak, ◊, T/I

spear, ◊, T

specialise (am. -ize), ◊, T/I

specify (ie), T, C

speck, T

speckle, T

spectacle, T

speculate, ◊, I

speechify (ie), I

speed, ◊, T/I

spell, ◊, T

spend, ◊, T

spew, ◊, T/I

spice, ◊, T

spiel, ◊, T/I

spike, T/I

spile, T

spill, ◊, T/I

spin (nn), ◊, T/I

spiral (ll), ◊, I

spirit, ◊, T

spit (tt), ◊, T/I

spit (tt), T

spite, T

splash (es), ◊, T/I

splatter, ◊, T

splay, ◊, T/I

splice, T

spline, T

splint, T

splinter, ◊, T/I

split (tt), ◊, T/I

splodge, T/I

splotch (es), ◊, T

splurge, ◊, I

splutter, ◊, T/I

spoil, ◊, T/I

spoke, T

sponge, ◊, T/I

sponsor, T

spook, T

spool, T

spoon, ◊, T/I

spoon-feed, T

spoor, T/I

sport, ◊, T/I

spot (tt), T

spotlight, T

spouse, T

spout, ◊, T/I

sprain, T

sprawl, ◊, I

spray, ◊, T/I

spread, ◊, T/I

sprig (gg), T

spring, ◊, T/I

sprinkle, ◊, T

sprint, ◊◊◊, I

sprout, ◊, T/I

spruce, ◊, T

spud (dd), T

spur (rr), ◊, T

spurn, T

spurt, ◊, T/I

sputter, ◊, T/I

spy (ie), ◊, T/I

squabble, ◊, T/I

squall, I

squander, ◊, T

square, ◊, T/I

squash (es), ◊, T/I

squat (tt), ◊, I

squawk, T/I

squeak, ◊, T/I

squeal, I

squeeze, ◊, T/I

squelch (es), T/I

squiggle, T/I

squint, ◊, T/I

squire, T

squirm, ◊, I

squirrel, ◊, T

squirt, ◊, T/I

squish (es), T/I

stab (bb), ◊, T/I

stabilise (am. -ize), T

stable, T

stack, ◊, T

staff, T

stage, T

stagger, ◊◊◊, T/I

stagnate, I

stain, ◊, T/I

stake, ◊, T

stale, T/I

stalk, ◊, T/I

stall, T/I

stammer, ◊, T/I

stamp, ◊, T/I

stampede, ◊, T/I

stand, ◊◊◊, T/I, C

standardise (am. -ize), T

staple, T

star (rr), ◊, T/I

starch (es), ◊, T

stare, ◊, T/I

start, ◊◊, T/I, C

startle, ◊, T

starve, ◊, T/I, C

stash (es), ◊, T

state, T, C
station, ◊, T
stave, ◊, T
stay, ◊◊, T/I
steady (ie), ◊, T/I
steal, ◊, T/I
steam, ◊, T/I
steel, ◊, T
steep, ◊, T/I
steepen, T/I
steer, ◊, T/I
stem (mm), ◊, T/I, C
stencil (ll), T
stenotype, T
step (pp), ◊◊, T/I
stereotype, T
sterilize, T
stet (tt), T
stew, ◊, T/I
stick, ◊◊, T/I, C
stickle, ◊, T/I
stickle, T, C
stiff, T
stiffen, ◊, T/I
stifle, T/I
stigmatize, T
still, T/I
stimulate, ◊, T
sting, ◊, T/I, C
stink, ◊, T/I
stint, ◊, T
stipple, T
stipulate, ◊, T/I
stir (rr), ◊, T/I
stitch (es), ◊, T/I
stock, ◊, T
stockade, T
stockpile, T/I
stoke, ◊, T/I
stomach, T
stomp, ◊◊◊, I

stone, T
stonewall, I
stooge, ◊, I
stoop, ◊, T/I
stop (pp), ◊◊, T/I, C
stopper, T
store, ◊, T
storm, ◊, T/I
stove, T
stow, ◊, T/I
straddle, T/I
strafe, T
straggle, ◊◊◊, I
straighten, ◊, T/I
strain, ◊, T/I
strand, ◊, T/I
strangle, T
strangulate, T
strap (pp), ◊, T
stratify (ie), T
stray, ◊◊◊, I
streak, ◊◊◊, T/I
stream, ◊◊◊, T/I
streamline, T
strengthen, T
stress (es), T
stretch (es), ◊, T/I
strew, ◊, T
stride, ◊◊◊, T/I
stridulate, I
strike, ◊◊, T/I, C
string, ◊, T
strip (pp), ◊, T/I
stripe, ◊, T
strive, ◊, I, C
stroke, T
stroll, ◊◊◊, I
strop (pp), T
struggle, ◊◊◊, I
strum (mm), ◊, T/I
strut (tt), ◊◊◊, I

stub (bb), ◊, T
stucco (es), T
stud (dd), ◊, T
study (ie), ◊, T/I
stuff, ◊, T
stultify (ie), T
stumble, ◊◊◊, I
stump, ◊◊◊, T/I
stun (nn), T
stunt, T/I
stupefy (ie), ◊, T
stutter, ◊, T/I
style, T
stylize, T
stymie / stymy (ie), T
sub (bb), T
subcontract, T/I
subdivide, ◊, T/I
subdue, T
subedit, T
subject, ◊, T
subjoin, T
subjugate, T
sublease, T/I
sublet (tt), ◊, T/I
sublimate, T
submerge, ◊, T/I
submit (tt), ◊, T/I, C
subordinate, ◊, T
suborn, T
subpoena, T, C
subrent, T
subrogate, T
subscribe, ◊, I
subserve, T
subside, ◊, I
subsidize, T
subsist, ◊, I
substantiate, T
substitute, ◊, T/I
subsume, T

subtend, T

subtilize, T/I

subtitle, T

subtract, ◊, T

suburbanize, T

subvert, T

succeed, ◊, T/I, C

succour, T

succumb, ◊, I

succuss (es), T

suck, ◊, T/I

suckle, T/I

sue, ◊, T/I

suffer, ◊, T/I

suffice, ◊, T/I

suffix (es), ◊, T

suffocate, T/I

suffuse, ◊, T

sugar, T

suggest, ◊, T, C

suit, ◊, T

sulk, I

sully (ie), T

sulphur, T

sum (mm), ◊, T

summarise (am. -ize), T

summer, I

summon, ◊, T, C

summons (es), T

sun (nn), T

sunbathe, I

sunder, ◊, T

sup (pp), ◊, T/I

superabound, ◊, I

superannuate, T/I

superheat, T

superimpose, ◊, T

superintend, T

superpose, ◊, T

supersaturate, T

superscribe, T

supersede, T

supervene, ◊, I

supervise, T/I

supplant, T

supple, T

supplement, ◊, T

supplicate, T/I, C

supply (ie), ◊, T

support, T

suppose, T, C

suppress (es), T

suppurate, I

surcharge, ◊, T

surf, I

surface, ◊, T/I

surfeit, ◊, T/I

surge, ◊, I

surmise, T, C

surmount, ◊, T

surname, T

surpass (es), ◊, T

surprise, ◊, T, C

surrender, ◊, T/I

surround, ◊, T

surtax (es), T

survey, T

survive, T/I

suspect, ◊, T, C

suspend, ◊, T

suss (es), ◊, T, C

sustain, T

swab (bb), ◊, T

swaddle, ◊, T

swagger, ◊◊◊, I

swallow, ◊, T/I

swamp, ◊, T

swank, ◊, I

swap (pp), ◊, T/I

swarm, ◊, I

swat (tt), T

swathe, ◊, T

sway, ◊◊◊, T/I

swear, ◊, T/I, C

sweat, ◊, T/I

sweep, ◊◊◊, T

sweeten, T/I

swell, ◊, T/I

swelter, I

swerve, ◊, T/I

swig (gg), ◊, T

swill, ◊, T

swim (mm), ◊◊◊, T/I

swindle, ◊, T

swing, ◊◊◊, T/I

swink, I

swipe, ◊, T/I

swirl, ◊◊◊, T/I

swish (es), ◊, T/I

switch (es), ◊, T/I

swivel (ll), ◊, T/I

swoon, I

swoop, ◊, I

swop (pp), T/I

swot (tt), ◊, T/I

syllogize, I

symbolize, T

sympathize, ◊, I

synchronize, T/I

syncopate, T

syndicate, T

synthetise, T

syringe, T

system(at)ise, T

table, T

taboo, T

tabulate, T

tack, ◊, T/I

tackle, ◊, T

tag (gg), ◊, T/I

tail, ◊, T/I

tailor, ◊, T

taint, ◊, T

take, ◊◊◊, T/I, C

talk, ◊◊, T/I, C

tally (ie), ◊, T/I

tame, T

tamp, ◊, T

tamper, ◊, I

tan (nn), T/I

tang, T/I

tangle, ◊, T/I

tango, I

tank, ◊, I

tantalize, T

tap (pp), ◊, T/I

tape, T

taper, ◊, T/I

tar (rr), T

tarnish (es), T/I

tarry (ie), I

tart, ◊, I

task, ◊, T

taste, ◊, T/I

tat (tt), T/I

tattle, I

tattoo, T

tauten, T/I

taw, T

tax (es), ◊, T, C

taxi, ◊, I

teach (es), T/I, C

team, ◊◊, T/I

tear, ◊◊, T/I

tease, ◊, T

tee, ◊, T/I

teem, ◊, I

teeter, I

teethe, I

telecast, T/I

telecopy, ◊, T

telegraph, ◊, T/I

telephone, ◊, T/I

telescope, ◊, T/I

teletype, ◊, T

televise, T

telex, ◊, T

tell, ◊◊, T, C

temper, ◊, T

temporise (am. -ize), ◊, I

tempt, ◊, T, C

tend, ◊, I, C

tend, T

tender, ◊, T/I

tense, ◊, T/I

term, T

terminate, ◊, T/I

terrace, T

terrify (ie), ◊, T, C

test, ◊, T

testify (ie), ◊, T/I, C

tether, T

thank, ◊, T, C

thatch (es), T

thaw, ◊, T/I

theorize, ◊, T/I

thicken, ◊, T/I

thieve, T/I

thin (nn), ◊, T/I

think, ◊◊, T/I, C

thirl, T

thirst, ◊, I

thole, T

thrash (es), ◊, T/I

thread, ◊, T

threaten, ◊, T/I, C

thresh (es), T

thrill, ◊, T/I

thrive, ◊, I

throb (bb), ◊, I

throng, ◊, T/I

throttle, ◊, T

throw, ◊◊, T/I

thrust, ◊◊, T/I

thud (dd), ◊, I

thumb, ◊, T

thump, ◊, T/I

thunder, ◊, T/I

thwack, T

tick, ◊, T/I

ticket, T

tickle, T/I

tide, ◊, I

tidy (ie), ◊, T/I

tie (yi), ◊, T/I

tighten, ◊, T/I

tile, T

till, T

tilt, ◊, T/I

timber, T

time, T, C

tin (nn), T

tincture, T

ting, T/I

tinge, ◊, T

tingle, ◊, I

tinker, ◊, T/I

tinkle, T/I

tin-plate, T

tinsel (ll), T

tint, T

tip (pp), ◊, T/I

tipple, I

tiptoe, ◊◊◊, I

tire, ◊, T/I, C

tithe, T

titillate, T

titivate, T/I

title, T

titrate, T

titter, I
tittle-tattle, I
toady (ie), ◊, T / I
toast, T
toboggan, I
toddle, ◊◊◊, I
toe, T
tog (gg), ◊, T / I
toil, ◊◊◊, I
tolerate, T, C
toll, ◊, T / I
tomahawk, T
tone, ◊, T / I
tongue, T
tool, ◊, T / I
toot, T / I
tooth, T
top (pp), ◊, T / I
topple, ◊, T / I
torch, T
torment, ◊, T
torpedo (es), T
torrefy (ie), T
torture, T
toss (es), ◊◊, T / I
tot (tt), ◊, T / I
total (ll), T / I
totalise (am. -ize), T
tote, T
totter, ◊, I
touch (es), ◊, T / I
toughen, ◊, T / I
tour, T / I
tourney, T
tousle, T
tout, ◊, I
tow, ◊, T
towel (ll), ◊, T
tower, ◊, I
toy, ◊, I
trace, ◊, T

track, ◊, T
trade, ◊, T / I
traduce, T
traffic, ◊, T / I
trail, ◊◊◊, T / I
train, ◊, T / I, C
traipse, ◊◊◊, I
tramp, T / I
trample, ◊, T / I
tranquilize, T
transact, ◊, T
transcend, T
transcribe, T
transfer (rr), ◊, T / I
transfigure, T
transfix (es), ◊, T
transform, ◊, T
transfuse, T
transgress (es), T / I
tranship (pp), T / I
translate, ◊, T / I
transliterate, T
transmit (tt), ◊, T
transmogrify (ie), T
transmute, ◊, T
transpierce, T
transpire, T / I
transplant, T
transport, ◊, T
transpose, ◊, T
transude, I
trap (pp), ◊, T, C
trash, T / I
travel (ll), ◊, T / I
traverse, T / I
travesty (ie), T
trawl, T / I
tread, ◊, T / I
treasure, ◊, T
treat, ◊, T / I
treble, T / I

tree, T / I
trek (kk), ◊, I
tremble, ◊, I
trench (es), ◊, T / I
trend, ◊, I
trepan (nn), T
trespass (es), ◊, I
trick, ◊, T, C
trickle, ◊, I
trifle, ◊, T / I
trig (gg), ◊, T
trigger, ◊, T
trill, T / I
trim (mm), ◊, T
trip (pp), ◊◊◊, T / I
triple, T / I
triplicate, T
trisect, T
triumph, ◊, I
troll, T / I
troop, ◊, T / I
trot (tt), ◊◊◊, T / I
trouble, ◊, T / I, C
trounce, T
truck, ◊, T / I
truckle, ◊, I
trudge, ◊◊◊, I
true, ◊, T
trump, ◊, T
trumpet, ◊, T / I
truncate, T
trundle, ◊◊◊, T / I
truss (es), ◊, T
trust, ◊, T / I, C
try (ie), ◊, T / I, C
tub (bb), T / I
tube, T
tuck, ◊, T / I
tuft, T
tug (gg), ◊, T / I
tumble, ◊, T / I

tumefy (ie), T / I
tune, ◊, T / I
tunnel (ll), ◊, T / I
tup (pp), I
turf, ◊, T
turn, ◊◊, T / I
tussle, ◊, I
tutor, ◊, T
twaddle, I
twang, T / I
tweak, T
tweet, I
twiddle, ◊, T
twig (gg), T
twin (nn), T
twine, ◊, T / I
twinge, I
twinkle, ◊, I
twirl, T / I
twist, ◊, T / I
twit (tt), ◊, T
twitch (es), T / I
twitter, I
two-time, T
type, ◊, T / I
type-cast, T
type-set, (tt) T
typewrite, T / I
typify (ie), T
tyrannise (am. -ize), ◊, T / I

U

ulcerate, T / I
ululate, I
umpire, T / I
unallocate, T
unbalance, T

unbar (rr), T / I
unbend, T / I
unbind, T
unblock, T
unbolt, T
unbosom, ◊, T
unbuckle, T
unburden, ◊, T
unbutton, T / I
uncap (pp), T
unchain, T
unclasp, T
unclench (es), T
uncloak, T
unclog (gg), T
unclothe, T
uncoil, T / I
uncork, T
uncouple, T
uncover, T
uncross (es), T
uncurl, T / I
undeceive, ◊, T
underbid (dd), T
undercall, T
undercharge, T
undercut (tt), T
underdo (es), T
underestimate, T
underfeed, T
undergird, T
undergo (es), T
underlie (yi), T
underline, T
undermine, T
underpin (nn), T
underplay, T
underquote, T
underrate, T
underscore, T
undersell, T

undershoot, T
understand, ◊, T / I, C
understate, T
understudy (ie), T
undertake, T
undervalue, T
underwrite, T
undo (es), T
undock, T / I
undress (es), T / I
undulate, T / I
unearth, T
unfasten, ◊, T
unfit (tt), ◊, T, C
unfix (es), T
unfold, ◊, T / I
unfreeze, T
unfrock, T
unfurl, T / I
unhand, T
unharness (es), T
unhinge, T
unhook, T
unhorse, T
unify (ie), ◊, T
unite, ◊, T / I
unkink, T / I
unknot (tt), T
unlace, T
unlash (es), ◊, T
unlatch (es), T
unleash (es), ◊, T
unlive, T
unload, ◊, T / I
unlock, T
unloose, T
unman (nn), T
unmask, T / I
unmoor, T / I
unnerve, T
unpack, T / I

unpick, T
unpin (nn), ◊, T
unplug (gg), T
unquote, I
unravel (ll), T/I
unreel, T/I
unriddle, T
unrobe, T/I
unroll, T/I
unsaddle, T
unsay, T
unscramble, T
unscrew, T/I
unseal, T
unseat, T
unsettle, T
unsex (es), T
unshackle, T
unsheathe, T
unship (pp), T
unsling, ◊, T
unsnarl, T
unstick, T
unstitch (es), T
unstop (pp), T
unstrap (pp), ◊, T
unstring, T
untangle, T
untether, T
unthread, T
untie (yi), T
untuck, T
untwine, T
untwist, T/I
unveil, T
unwind, T/I
unwrap (pp), T
unyoke, ◊, T
up (pp), T
upbraid, ◊, T, C
upchork, T

update, T
upend, T
upgrade, ◊, T
uphold, T
upholster, ◊, T
uplift, T
uproot, ◊, T
upset (tt), T/I
upshift, I
upstage, T
upturn, T
urbanize, T
urge, ◊, T, C
urinate, I
use, ◊, T, C
usher, ◊, T
usurp, ◊, T/I
utilize, ◊, T
utter, T

V

vacate, T
vaccinate, ◊, T
vacillate, ◊, I
vacuum, T/I
vail, T
valet, T
validate, T
value, ◊, T
vamoose, I
vamp, ◊, T/I
vandalize, T
vanish (es), ◊, I
vanquish (es), T
vaporize, T/I
vapour (am. -or), ◊, I
variegate, T

varnish (es), T
vary (ie), ◊, T/I
vat (tt), T
vaticinate, T/I, C
vault, ◊, T
vaunt, T/I, C
veer, ◊, T/I
veg (gg), ◊, I
vegetate, I
veil, T
vein, T
vend, T
veneer, T
venerate, T
vent, ◊, T
ventilate, T
venture, ◊, T/I, C
verbalize, T
verge, ◊, I
verify (ie), T
versify (ie), T/I
vest, ◊, T/I
vet (tt), T
veto (es), T
vex (es), ◊, T
vibrate, T/I
victimize, T
victual (ll), T/I
vie (yi), ◊, T/I
view, T
vignette, T
vilify (ie), T
vindicate, ◊, T
vintage, T/I
violate, T
visa, T
visit, ◊, T
visualize, T
vitalize, T,
vitaminize, T
vitiate, T

vitrify (ie), T / I
vituperate, T / I
vivify (ie), T
vivisect, T
vocalize, T / I
vociferate, ◊, T / I
voice, T
void, T
volatilize, T / I
volley, T / I
volunteer, ◊, T / I, C
vomit, ◊, T / I
vote, ◊, T / I, C
vouch (es), ◊, T / I
vouchsafe, T, C
vow, T, C
voyage, T / I
vulcanize, T / I
vulgarize, T

W

wad (dd), T
waddle, ◊◊◊, I
wade, ◊◊◊, T / I
waffle, ◊, I
wag (gg), T / I
wage, T
wager, ◊, T, C
waggle, T / I
wail, ◊, I
wainscot, T
wait, ◊, T / I, C
waive, T
wake, ◊, T / I
waken, ◊, T / I
wale, T
walk, ◊◊◊, T / I

wall, ◊, T
wallop, T
wallow, ◊, I
waltz (es), ◊◊◊, I
wander, ◊, T / I
wane, I
wangle, ◊, T / I
want, ◊, T / I, C
war (rr), ◊, I
warble, T / I
ward, ◊, T
warehouse, T
warm, ◊, T / I
warn, ◊, T, C
warp, T / I
warrant, T
wash (es), ◊, T / I
wassail, T
waste, ◊, T / I
watch (es), ◊, T / I, C
water, ◊, T / I
waterproof, T
wave, ◊, T / I
waver, I
wax (es), T
waylay, T
weaken, T / I
wean, ◊, T
wear, ◊, T / I
weary (ie), ◊, T / I, C
weather, ◊, T / I
weatherize, T
weave, ◊, T / I
wed (dd), ◊, T / I
wedge, ◊, T
weed, ◊, T
weep, ◊, T / I
weigh, ◊, T / I
weight, ◊, T
weird, ◊, I
welcome, ◊, T

weld, ◊, T / I
well, ◊, I
welsh (es), T / I
welt, T
welter, ◊, I
wench (es), I
wend, ◊◊◊, T / I
westernize, T
wet (tt), ◊, T
whack, ◊, T
whale, I
wharf, T / I
wheedle, ◊, T, C
wheel, ◊, T / I
wheeze, ◊, I
whelp, T / I
whet (tt), T
whicker, T
whiff, T / I
while, ◊, T
whimper, T / I
whine, T / I
whip (pp), ◊◊◊, T / I
whirl, ◊◊◊, T / I
whirr, ◊◊◊, I
whisk, ◊, T / I
whisper, ◊, T / I, C
whistle, ◊, T / I
white, ◊, T
whiten, T / I
whitewash (es), T
whittle, ◊, T / I
whizz (es), ◊, I
whomp, T
whoop, ◊, T / I
whop (pp), T
whore, ◊, I
wick, ◊, T
widen, ◊, T / I
wield, T
wig, ◊, T / I

wiggle, T/I
wile, T
will*, T, C
wilt, I
win (nn), ◊, T/I
wince, ◊, I
wind, ◊, T/I
wind, T
window, T
wing, T/I
winge, T
wink, ◊, T/I
winkle, ◊, T
winnow, ◊, T
winter, ◊, T/I
wipe, ◊, T
wire, ◊, T
wise, ◊, T
wish (es), ◊, T/I, C
withdraw, ◊, T/I
wither, ◊, T/I
withhold, ◊, T
withstand, T
witness (es), ◊, T/I, C
witter, ◊, T
wobble, ◊, I
wolf, ◊, T
womanize (am. -ize), I
wonder, ◊, T/I, C
woo, ◊, T, C
woof, I
word, T
work, ◊◊, T/I, C
worm, ◊, T
worry (ie), ◊, T/I
worsen, I
worship (pp), T/I
worst, T
would, A

wound, ◊, T
wrangle, ◊, I
wrap (pp), ◊, T
wreak, T
wreathe, ◊, T/I
wreck, T
wrench (es), ◊, T
wrest, ◊, T
wrestle, ◊, T/I
wrick, T
wriggle, ◊◊◊, T/I
wring, ◊, T
wrinkle, ◊, T/I
write, ◊◊, T/I, C
writhe, ◊, I
wrong, T

X

x, ◊, T
xerox, ◊, T
x-ray, T

Y

yacht, I
yackety-yak, T
yak, I
yammer, ◊, I
yank, ◊, T/I
yap (pp), ◊, I
yarn, I

yaw, I
yawn, T/I
yawp, I
yean, I
yearn, ◊, I, C
yeast, I
yell, ◊, T/I
yellow, T/I
yelp, I
yen (nn), I, C
yield, ◊, T/I
yip (pp), I
yock, I
yodel (ll), I
yoke, T
yomp, I
york, I
yowl, I

Z

zap (pp), ◊◊◊, T/I
zazz, ◊, T
zero (es), ◊, T/I
zigzag (gg), ◊◊◊, T/I
zing, ◊, T/I
zip (pp), ◊◊◊, T/I
zone, ◊, T
zonk, ◊, T/I
zoom, ◊◊◊, T/I

---

* Ne pas confondre l'auxiliaire et le verbe *to will* (vouloir, léguer). Voir p. 38.

Verbes à complémentation

Pour la grammaire des verbes à complémentation, voir p. 76-85.

a

abandon : + ing
abhor : + ing / + inf.
abominate : + ing
absorb : + part.
abstain : + part.
accept : + inf. / + that
account : + part.
accuse : + part.
accustom : + part.
ache : + inf.
acknowledge : + ing / + that / pass. imp.
add : + that
addict : + part.
adjure : + inf.
admit : + ing / + that
admonish : + inf.
adore : + ing / + inf.
advertise : + that / pass. imp.
advise : + ing / + inf. / + that
advocate : + ing / + inf. / + that
affirm : + that
afford : + inf.
agree : + inf. / + that / + part.
aid : + inf.
aim : + part.
allege : + that / pass. imp.
allocate : db. pass.
allot : db. pass.
allow : + inf. / db. pass.
amount : + part.
amuse : + part.
announce : + that / pass. imp.
annunciate : + that
answer : + that / db. pass. / + part.
anticipate : + ing

apologise : + part.
appeal : + inf.
apply : + inf. / + part.
appoint : + inf.
appreciate : + ing / + inf. / + that
approve : + part.
argue : + that / + part.
arraign : + part.
arrange : + inf.
ask : + inf. / + that / db. pass.
aspire : + inf.
assert : + that
asseverate : + that
assist : + inf. / + part.
associate : + part.
assume : + inf. / + that / pass. imp.
assure : + that / db. pass.
astonish : + that / + part.
atone : + part.
attempt : + inf.
attest : + that / pass. imp.
augur : + that
authorise : + inf.
aver : + that
avoid : + ing

b

badger : + into + ing
bait : + into + ing
bamboozle : + into + ing
bar : + part.
bark : + that
bear : + ing
beat : + into + ing

beg : + inf.
beguile : + into + ing
begin : + ing / + inf. / + part.
behove : + ing
believe : + that / pass. imp. / + part.
benefit : + part.
beseech : + inf.
beseem : + inf.
bet : + that
bethink : + that
bid : + inf.
bind : + inf.
blab : + that
blackmail : + inf. / + part.
blare : + that
blast : + that
bleat : + that
blubber : + that
bluff : + into + ing
blurt out : + that
blush : + inf.
boast : + that
bother : + inf.
brag : + part.
bribe : + into + ing
bring : + inf. / db. pass.
broadcast : + that
browbeat : + into + ing
bulldoze : + into + ing
bully : + into + ing
burn : + inf.
burst : + inf.
bust : + part.
busy : + ing

c

cable : + that
calculate : + that / + part.
care : + inf. / + int. ind. /
  + part.
cause : + inf.
caution : + inf. / + that /
  + part.
cease : + ing / + inf.
certify : + that / pass. imp.
chagrin : + part.
challenge : + inf. / pass. imp.
champion : + ing
chance : + inf.
charge : + part.
chastise : + part.
cheat : + into + ing
cheer : + inf.
chide : + into + ing / + part.
chi(v)vy : + into + ing
choose : + inf.
claim : + inf. / + that / pass.
  imp.
coax : + into + ing
coerce : + into + ing
cogitate : + that
come : + inf.
command : + inf.
commence : + ing / + inf.
commission : + inf.
commit : + inf. / + part.
compel : + inf.
complain : + that / + part.
compute : + that
con : + into + ing
concede : + that
conclude : + that / + part.
concur : + inf.
condemn : + inf.

condescend : + inf. / + part.
condition : + inf.
conduce : + part.
confess : + that / + part.
confide : + that
confine : + part.
confirm : + that / pass. imp.
confuse : + part.
congratulate : + part.
conjecture : + that
conjure : + inf.
consecrate : + part.
consent : + inf. / + part.
consider : + ing / + that /
  pass. imp.
consist : + part.
conspire : + inf.
constrain : + inf.
contemplate : + ing
contend : + that
content : + part.
continue : + ing / + inf.
contract : + inf.
contribute : + part.
contrive : + inf.
convey : + that
convict : + part.
convince : + inf.
cope : + part.
cosset : + into + ing
counsel : + inf.
count : + part.
court : + into + ing
covenant : + inf.
cow : + into + ing
credit : + part.
criticise : + ing / + part.
culminate : + part.

d

dare : + inf.
dawn : + that / + int. ind.
debar : + part.
debate : + int. ind.
deceive : + into + ing
decide : + inf. / + that / + int.
  ind. / + part.
declare : + that / pass. imp.
decline : + inf.
decorate : + part.
decoy : + into + ing
decree : + that
dedicate : + part.
deduce : + that
deem : + inf. / pass. imp.
defend : + part.
defer : + ing
defy : + inf.
degenerate : + part.
deign : + inf.
delay : + part.
deliberate : + int. ind.
delight : + part.
delude : + into + ing
demand : + inf. / + that
demonstrate : + that
deny : + ing / + that / db. pass.
depend : + int. ind.
deplore : + that
depose : + that
depute : + inf.
descend : + part.
deserve : + inf.
desire : + inf.
desist : + part.
despair : + that / + part.
despise : + ing / + part.

deter : + part.
determine : + inf. / + int. ind. /
  + part.
detest : + ing
devote : + part.
disagree : + inf. / + that /
  + part.
disappoint : + part.
disapprove : + part.
discourage : + part.
discover : + that
disdain : + ing / + inf.
disgust : + that / + part.
dislike : + ing / + inf.
dismay : + part.
dismiss : + part.
dispense : + part.
dispute : + int. ind.
disqualify : + part.
disremember : + inf. / + that
dissatisfy : + part.
dissuade : + part.
distract : + part.
do : + part.
doubt : + that / + int. ind.
dragoon : + into + ing
dread : + ing / + inf. / + that
dream : + that
drill : + part.

e

egg : + inf.
embolden : + inf.
employ : + part.
empower : + inf.
enable : + inf.
encourage : + inf.
end : + part.

endeavour : + inf.
endure : + ing
engage : + inf. / + part.
enjoy : + ing / + inf.
ensnare : + into + ing
enthral : + into + ing
entice : + inf.
entitle : + inf.
entrap : + into + ing
entreat : + inf.
escape : + ing
essay : + inf.
excel : + part.
exclaim : + that
excuse : + part.
exempt : + part.
exercise : + part.
exert : + inf.
exhort : + inf.
expect : + inf. / + that / pass.
  imp.
expend : + part.
explain : + that / + int. ind.
extend : + part.
exult : + part.

f

fail : + inf.
familiarise : + part.
fancy : + ing / + that
fathom : + int. ind.
fax : + that
fear : + ing / + that
feel : + that / + part.
find : + that / pass. imp.
finish : + ing / + part.

flatter : + that / + part.
fool : + into + ing
forbear : + inf. / + part.
forbid : + ing / + inf. / db. pass.
force : + inf. / + into + ing
foresee : + inf. / + that / db.
  pass. / + int. ind.
foretell : + inf. / + that / db.
  pass. / + int. ind.
forget : + ing / + inf. / + that /
  + int. ind.
forgive : + part.
frighten : + into + ing / + part.
fume : + part.
funk : + ing

g

get : + ing / + inf.
give : db. pass. / + part.
glory : + part.
go : + inf.
goad : + into + ing
grant : + that / db. pass.
guess : + that / + int. ind.
gull : + into + ing

h

habituate : + part.
happen : + inf. / + that
hasten : + inf.
hate : + ing / + inf.
hear : + ing / + inf. / + that /
  pass. imp. / + int. ind.

hector : + into + ing
help : + inf.
hesitate : + inf.
hint : + that
hoax : + into + ing
honour : + inf.
hoodwink : + into + ing
hope : + inf. / + that / pass.
imp.
humbug : + into + ing
humiliate : + into + ing
hustle : + into + ing
hypnotise : + into + ing

imagine : + ing / + inf. / + that
/ pass. imp. / + int. ind.
impeach : + part.
impel : + inf.
implore : + inf.
imply : + that
import : + that
imprecate : + that
impress : + that
include : + ing
indict : + part.
indispose : + part.
induce : + inf.
indulge : + part.
infer : + that
inform : + that
inhibit : + part.
inquire : + int. ind.
insinuate : + that
insist : + that / + part.
inspire : + inf.
instigate : + inf.
instruct : + inf. / pass. imp.

intend : + ing / + inf.
interdict : + ing
interest : + inf. / + part.
intimate : + that
inveigle : + into + ing
invite : + inf.
involve : + ing / + part.
irk : + inf.
itch : + inf.

jib : + part.
jockey : + part.
join : + part.
justify : + ing / + part.

keep : + ing / + part.
know : + that / pass. imp. /
+ int. ind.

labour : + part.
laugh : + into + ing
lay : + that
lead : + inf.
learn : + inf. / + that
leave : + inf.
lend : + part.

let : + inf.
license : + inf.
like : + ing / + inf.
limit : + part.
listen : + part.
loathe : + ing / + inf.
long : + inf.
look : + inf. / + ing
love : + ing / + inf.
lull : + into + ing
lure : + into + ing

m

maintain : + that
make : + inf.
manage : + inf.
mark : pass. imp.
marvel : + that
matter : + that
mean : + inf. / + that / pass.
imp. / + part.
meditate : + ing
mention : + that / pass. imp. /
+ int. ind.
mesmerise : + into + ing
mind : + ing
miss : + ing
motion : + inf.

n

need : + ing / + inf.
neglect : + inf.
nerve : + inf.
note : + that / + part.
notice : + that

O

object : + that / + part.
obligate : + inf.
oblige : + inf.
observe : + that
occupy : + ing
occur : + that
offer : + inf. / db. pass.
omit : + inf. / + that
opine : + that
oppose : + ing / + part.
order : + inf. / + that / db. pass.
owe : + inf.

p

pain : + inf.
pardon : + part.
pay : + inf. / db. pass.
penalise : + part.
perceive : + that
permit : + ing / + inf. / + that
persevere : + part.
persist : + part.
persuade : + inf. / + that
pester : + inf.
plan : + inf.
play : + part.
pledge : + inf.
plot : + inf.
plume : + part.
point : + that
postpone : + ing
praise : + part.
pray : + inf. / + that
preclude : + part.

predict : + that / pass. imp. / + int. ind.
prefer : + ing / + inf.
prejudice : + part.
premise : + that
prepare : + inf.
presage : + that
prescribe : + inf.
press : + inf.
pressure : + inf. / + into + ing
presume : + inf. / + that / pass. imp.
presuppose : + that / pass. imp.
pretend : + inf. / + that
prevent : + part.
pride : + part.
print : + that
privilege : + inf.
proceed : + inf.
prod : + into + ing
profess : + inf.
profit : + part.
prohibit : + inf.
promise : + inf. / + that / db. pass.
prompt : + inf.
prophesy : + that / + int. ind.
propose : + ing / + inf. / + that
proscribe : + ing
prosecute : + part.
protest : + part.
prove : + that / pass. imp. / + int. ind.
provoke : + inf. / + into + ing
punish : + part.
purport : + inf.
purpose : + ing / + inf.
put : + part.
puzzle : + int. ind.

q

quarrel : + part.
query : + int. ind.
question : + that / + int. ind.
quit : + ing

r

railroad : + into + ing
read : + that / db. pass.
realise : + that
reason : + that / + into + ing
rebel : + part.
rebuke : + part.
recall : + ing / + that
reckon : + that / pass. imp. / + part.
recoil : + part.
recollect : + ing
recommend : + ing / + inf. / + that
recompense : + part.
reconsider : + ing
recount : + that
reduce : + part.
reflect : + that / + int. ind.
refrain : + part.
refuse : + inf.
regret : + ing / + inf. / + that
rejoice : + inf. / + part.
relate : + that / + int. ind.
relish : + ing
remain : + inf. / + that
remark : + that
remember : + ing / + inf. / + that / pass. imp. / + int. ind.

remind : + inf. / + that / + int. ind. / + part.

remonstrate : + that

repeat : + that

repent : + ing

reply : + that

report : + that / pass. imp.

represent : + int. ind.

reprimand : + part.

reproach : + part.

reprove : + part.

repute : pass. imp.

request : + inf. / + that

require : + ing / + inf.

resent : + ing

resign : + part.

resist : + ing

resolve : + inf.

resort : + part.

restrain : + part.

restrict : + ing

result : + that / + part.

resume : + ing

retort : + that

reveal : + that

revel : + part.

revert : + part.

revolt : + part.

reward : + part.

rush : + into + ing

S

say : + that / pass. imp. / + int. ind.

scare : + into + ing

schedule : pass. imp.

scheme : + inf.

school : + inf.

scold : + part.

scorn : + ing / + inf.

scruple : + inf.

second-guess : + that / + int. ind.

seduce : + into + ing

see : + ing / + inf. / + that / + int. ind.

seek : + inf.

seem : + inf. / + that

sense : + that

set : + part.

shaft : + into + ing

shame : + into + ing

shanghai : + into + ing

shield : + part.

shock : + inf. / + into + ing

show : + that / db. pass. / + int. ind.

shrink : + part.

sicken : + part.

signal : + inf.

smell : + ing / + that

specify : + that

stand : + ing

start : + ing / + inf. / + part.

starve : + into + ing

state : + that

stem : + part.

stick : + part.

stickle : + that

sting : + into + ing

stop : + ing / + inf. / + part.

strike : + that / + part.

strive : + inf.

submit : + that

subpoena : + inf.

succeed : + part.

suggest : + ing / + that

summon : + inf.

supplicate : + inf.

suppose : + that / pass. imp.

surmise : + that

surprise : + inf. / + part.

suspect : + inf. / + that / + part.

suss : + that / + int ind

swear : + inf. / + that

t

take : + that / + part.

talk : + part.

tax : + part.

teach : + inf. / + that / db. pass. / + int. ind.

tell : + inf. / + that / db. pass. / + int. ind.

tempt : + inf. / + part.

tend : + inf.

terrify : + into + ing

testify : + that

thank : + part.

think : + inf. / + that / pass. imp. / + int. ind. / + part.

threaten : + inf.

time : + int. ind.

tire : + part.

tolerate : + ing

train : + inf.

trap : + into + ing

trick : + into + ing

trouble : + inf.

trust : + inf. / + that

try : + ing / + inf.

u

understand : + that / + int. ind.
unfit : + inf.
upbraid : + part.
urge : + inf. / + that
use : + part.

v

vaticinate : + that
vaunt : + that
venture : + inf.
volunteer : + inf.
vote : + that / + part.
vouchsafe : + inf.
vow : + inf. / + that

w

wager : + that
wait : + inf.
want : + inf.
warn : + inf. / + that / + part.
watch : + ing / + inf.
weary : + part.
wheedle : + into + ing
whisper : + that
will : + inf. / + that
wish : + inf. / + prét. mod.
wonder : + int. ind.
woo : + into + ing
work : + part.
write : + inf. / + that

y

yearn : + inf.
yen : + inf.

●

Verbes
à particules

●

Cet index comprend les verbes susceptibles de s'associer aux 30 particules les plus courantes, classées par ordre alphabétique.

Pour la grammaire des verbes à particules, voir p. 46.

L'abréviation (pass.) signale les verbes qui, avec la particule indiquée, sont généralement utilisés au passif.

L'abréviation (+ ing) indique que la particule peut être suivie d'un verbe à la forme en -*ing*.

a

abandon to
abash about (pass.)
abbreviate to
abet in
abide at, by, in, with
abound in, with
absent from
absolve from, of
absorb in (pass.) / (+ ing)
abstain from (+ ing)
abstract from
abut on, against
accede to
accept as
access to
acclimatise to
accommodate with, to
accord with, to
account to, for (+ ing)
accredit to
accrue to, from
accuse of (+ ing)
accustom to (pass.) / (+ ing)
ache for
acknowledge as
acquaint to (pass.), with (pass.)
acquiesce in, to
acquit of
act as, for, on, out, up, upon

adapt as, for, from, to
add up, in, to, on
addict to (pass.) / (+ ing)
address to
adhere to
adjourn for, to
adjudicate in, on
adjust to
administer to
admire for
admit of, to
adopt as
adorn with
advance on, to, towards, upon
advert to
advertise for
advise about, of, on, with
affect at (pass.)
affiliate to, with
affirm to
affix to
afflict with (pass.)
agglutinate to
agitate for
agree on (+ ing), to (+ ing), upon (+ ing), with
aim at (+ ing), for
airmail to
alarm at (pass.)
alert to
alienate from
alight from, on, upon
align with
allocate to

allot to
allow for, in, into, of, out, through, to, up
allude to
allure to
ally to, with
alternate with
amalgamate with
amaze at (pass.)
amble about, across, along, around, away, back, by, down, forth, forward, from, in, into, off, on, out of, out, over, round, through, to, towards, up, upon
amount to (+ ing)
amuse at (pass.) / (+ ing), by (pass.) / (+ ing), with (pass.) / (+ ing)
angle for, towards
animadvert on, upon
annex to
announce to
annoy about (pass.), at (pass.)
anoint with
answer back, for (+ ing), to
apologise for (+ ing), to
appal (l) at (pass.), by (pass.)
appeal against, for, to
appear at, for, in, on
append to
appertain to (+ ing)
apply to (+ ing)
appoint for, to
apportion to

appose to
apprentice to
apprise of
approach about, to
approbate of (+ ing)
appropriate to, for
approve of (+ ing)
approximate to
arbitrate in, on, for
arc around, away, back, down, into, over, round, through, towards, up
arch over
argue about (+ ing), against, back, down, for, in (+ ing), out of (+ ing), over (+ ing), with
arise for, out of
arm against, for, with
arouse from
arraign for (+ ing)
arrange about, for, with
arrive in, at
arrogate to
ascribe to
ask about, back, for, in, of, out, over, round, to, up
aspire to
assail with
assent to
assess at, in, upon
assign to
assimilate into, to, with
assist in (+ ing), with, at
associate in (+ ing), with
assort with
assure against
astonish at (pass.)
atone for (+ ing)
attach to
attain to
attend on, to, upon

attest to
attire in, with
attract to
attribute to
attune to
auction for
audition for
avail of
avenge of
average out
avert from
awake from, to
awaken from, to
award to
awe at (pass.)

babble out
back away, down, in, off, out, up
backdate to
badger into (+ ing), out of (+ ing)
bag up
bail out
bait into (+ ing), with
balance against, out, with
bale out
balk at (+ ing)
ball up
ballot against (+ ing), for (+ ing)
bamboozle into (+ ing), out of (+ ing)
band against
bandage up
bandy about

bang about, against, around, away, down, into, on, out, up, upon
banish from
bank on, up, with
bar from (+ ing), in, out, up
bare of
bargain about, away, for, on, over, with
barge about, across, along, around, away, back, by, down, forth, forward, from, in, into, off, on, out, out of, over, round, through, to, towards, up, upon
bark at
barricade against, in, into, out, out of, with
barter away, for, with
base on (+ ing)
bash about, in, up, upon
bask in
bat around
bathe in
batten back, down, on, upon
batter about, back, in, up
battle against, for, on, out, over, with
bawl out, for
bay at
be about, against, along, around, at, away, back, by, down, for, in, into, off, on, out, out of, over, round, through, up, upon, with
beam to, with
bear against, away, down, in, off, on, out, to, up, upon, with
beat about, against, at, back, down, in, into (+ ing), off, on, out, to, up, upon
beckon in, to

become of

bed down, in, with

bedew with (pass.)

beef up

beetle off

befoul with

befuddle with

beg for, from, of, off

begin as, on, with

begrime with

beguile into (+ ing), out of (+ ing), with

behave towards

belch forth, out

believe in (+ ing), of

bellow out

belly out

belong to

belt along, down, out, up

bend back, down, forward, in, on, over, to, upon

benefit by (+ ing), from (+ ing)

benumb with (pass.)

bequeath to

bereave of

beset with

besiege with

besmear with

besot with

bespatter with

besprinkle with

best at (+ ing)

bestow on, upon

bestrew with

bet into, on, with

bethink of

betray into (+ ing), out of (+ ing)

betroth to

beware of

bias against, towards

bicker about, over

bicycle about, across, along, around, away, back, by, down, forth, forward, from, in, into, off, on, out, out of, over, round, through, to, towards, up, upon

bid about, for, over

bike about, across, along, around, away, back, by, down, forth, forward, from, in, into, off, on, out, out of, over, round, through, to, towards, up, upon

bilk out of

billet in, on, with

billow to

bind down, off, out, over, up

bitch about

bite back, into, off, on

blab out

blabber about, on

black up, out

blacken out

blackmail into (+ ing), out of (+ ing)

blame for, on

blank out

blanket to

blare away, out

blaspheme against

blast off

blaze away, down, up, with

blazon forth, out

bleach out

bleat about

bleed for, to

blend in, into, with

bless with

blind to

blink away, back, at

block in, off, out, up

bloom into

blossom forth, into, out

blot up, out

blow about, around, away, back, down, in, into, off, on, out, over, round, to, up, upon

blubber out

bluff into (+ ing), out, out of (+ ing)

blunder away, on, out, through, upon

blur out, with

blurt out

blush for, with

bluster out

board in, out, up, with

boast about, of

bob down, to, up

bog down, off

boggle at

boil away, down, out, over, up

bolster up

bolt down, in, out

bomb up, out

bombard with

book up

boost up

boot out, out of

border on

bore for, out, through

borrow from, of

boss out of

botch up

bother about

bottle up

bottom up

bounce about, across, against, along, around, at, away, back, by, down, forth, forward, from, in, into, off, on, out, out of, over, round, through, to, towards, up, upon

bound away, with
bow away, with
bowl along, out, over
box in, off, up
brace up
brag about (+ ing), of (+ ing)
branch off, out
brand on, with
brazen out
break away, back, down, in, into, off, out, through, to, up, with
breakfast on, off
breathe down, in, into, on, out, upon
breeze in, through
brew up
bribe into (+ ing), out of (+ ing)
brick in, up
bridge over
bridle at, up
brighten up
brim over
bring about, along, around, away, back, down, forth, forward, in, off, on, out, over, round, through, to, towards, up, upon
brisk up
bristle up, with
broach to, with
broaden out
brood about, on, over, upon
browbeat into (+ ing), out of (+ ing)
brown off
browse on, through
brush away, down, off, over, up
brutalise with
bubble over, up
buck off, up

buckle down, to, up
budget for
buffet with
bug out
bugger about, around, off, up
build in, into, of, on, out, over, up, upon
bulge out
bulk up
bulldoze into (+ ing), out of (+ ing)
bully into (+ ing), out of (+ ing)
bum about, along, around
bump against, into, off, up
bunch up
bundle away, into, off, out, up
bung down, in, up
bunk up
buoy up
burden with
burn down, for, into, off, out, to, up, with
burp into
burrow into, out of, through
burst forth, in, into, on, out, through, upon, with
bury in
bust out, up
bustle up
busy with (+ ing)
butt in
butter up
button through, up
buttress up
buy back, in, off, out, over, up
buzz off

C

cable to
cadge from, off
cage up
cajole into (+ ing), out of (+ ing)
cake with
calculate for (+ ing), on (+ ing), upon (+ ing)
call about, away, back, by, down, for, forth, forward, in, into, off, on, out, over, round, to, up, upon
calm down
camp out, up
campaign against, for
canalize into
cancel out
cannon into, off
canvass for
cap with
capitalise on
capture from
care about (+ ing), for
career about, across, along, around, away, back, by, down, forth, forward, from, in, into, off, on, out, out of, over, round, through, to, towards, up, upon
carp at
carpet with
carry about, along, around, away, back, down, forward, in, off, on, out, over, through, with
carve up, out
cascade from, into, out, over, to
cash up, in

cast about, around, away, back, down, in, off, on, out, over, round, up, upon

catch at, in, on, out, up

cater to, for

caution about (+ ing), against (+ ing)

cave in

cavil at

cease from

cede to

censure for

center in, on, round

certify to

chafe to

chaffer over, with

chagrin at (pass.) / (+ ing)

chain down, to, up

chalk up, out

champ at

chance on, upon

change back, down, for, in, off, out of, over, round, to, up, with

channel off

charge across, along, around, away, back, by, down, for (+ ing), forth, forward, from, in, into, on, out, out of, round, through, to, towards, up, upon, with (+ ing)

charm with

chart out

chase about, around, down, up

chastise for (+ ing)

chat up

cheat into (+ ing), at, out of (+ ing)

check back, in, off, on, out, over, through, up

cheek up

cheer for, on, up

cheese off

chew away, on, out, over, up, upon

chide for (+ ing)

chime in

chip in, away

chisel in, out of

chivvy into (+ ing), out of (+ ing)

choke back, down, off, out of, up, with

choose as, for, from

chop about, around, away, down, into, off, round, up

christen after

chuck about, against, around, at, in, off, out, up

chuckle over, at

chug about, across, along, around, away, back, by, down, forth, forward, from, in, into, off, on, out, out of, over, round, through, to, towards, up, upon

churn into, out, to, up

circle about, around, over, round

circulate about, around, over, round

circumscribe to

cite for

claim against, back, for, from

clamber up, over

clamour against, back, for

clamp up

clap in, into, on, out, to, up

clash against, on, over, with

clasp to

class with

clatter about

claw at

clean down, of, off, out, up

clear away, of, off, out, up, with (pass.)

cleave to

click for, with

climb down, in, on, out, out of, over, up

cling to

clip on, out

clock in, off, on, out, up

clog up, with

clop about, across, along, around, away, back, by, down, forth, forward, from, in, into, off, on, out, out of, over, round, through, to, towards, up, upon

close about, around, down, in, off, on, out, round, up, upon, with

closet with (pass.)

clothe in, with

cloud over, up

clown about, around

club down, to, with

cluck over

clue in, up

cluster around, round

clutch at, to

clutter up, with

coach for

coast along

coat with

coax into (+ ing), out of (+ ing)

cock up

coerce into (+ ing), out of (+ ing)

coexist with

cogitate over (+ ing), upon (+ ing)

cohabit with
coil around, down, round, up
coin to
coincide with
collaborate with, on
collate with
collect up, from, for
collide with
collocate with
colour in, up
comb for, out, through
combat against, for, with
combine against, with
come about, across, along, around, at, away, back, by, down, for, forth, forward, from, in, into, of, off, on, out, out of, over, round, through, up, upon, with
commence as, on, with
commend to, for
comment on, upon
commentate on
commiserate with
commission for
commit for, on, to (+ ing)
commune with
communicate about, on, with
commute for, from, in, to
compact of (pass.)
compare with, to
compass by (pass.), with (pass.)
compel from
compensate for
compete against, for, in, with
complain about (+ ing), of, to
complicate with
compliment on
comply with
comport with

compose of (pass.)
compound with
compress in
comprise of (pass.)
compromise with
con into (+ ing), out of (+ ing)
concatenate to
conceal from
concede to
conceive as, of
concentrate at, on, upon
concern about, in, over, with
concert with
conclude with (+ ing)
concur in, with
condemn to, for, as
condescend to (+ ing)
condition to
condole with
conduce to (+ ing), towards (+ ing)
conduct away, out
confederate with
confer on, upon, with
confess to (+ ing)
confide in, to
confine to (+ ing)
confirm in
confiscate from
conflict with
conform to, with
confound with
confront with
confuse about (pass.) / (+ ing), with
congratulate on (+ ing), upon (+ ing)
conjure away, up, with
conk out
connect to, up, with
connive at, with

conscript into
consecrate to (+ ing)
consent to (+ ing)
consider as
consign to
consist in (+ ing), of (+ ing), with
console with
consort with
conspire against, with
constrain from
construct for, of, out of
construe as, with
consult about, with
consume away, with (+ ing)
contain for
contend against, for, over, with
content with (+ ing)
contest against, for, with
continue with
contract out, in, with, for
contrast with
contribute to (+ ing), towards
convalesce for
converge on
converse about, on, with
convert from, into, to
convey to
convict of (+ ing)
convince of
convulse with (pass.)
cook up, out
cool down, off, out
coop up
cooperate on, with
co-opt to
cop to
cope with (+ ing)
copulate with
copy down, out
cordon off

cork up
correlate to, with
correspond about, to, with
cosher up
cosset into (+ ing), out of (+ ing)
cost out
co-star in
cotton to, on
couch in
cough down, out, up
count against, as, down, for, from, in, off, on (+ ing), out, to, up, upon (+ ing), with
counter with
couple on, up, with
course through
court into (+ ing), out of (+ ing)
covenant for, with
cover against, for, in, over, up, with
cow into (+ ing), out of (+ ing)
cower away, back, down, forward
cozen into (+ ing), out of (+ ing)
crab about, against, along, around, at, away, back, by, down, for, forward, from, in, into, off, on, out, over, round, through, to, towards, up, upon
crack up
cram up, in, with, for
crane forward
crank up
crash about, around, down, in, out, with
crave for
crawl to, with
cream off
crease up
credit for (+ ing), to, with (+ ing)

creep about, across, along, around, away, back, by, down, forth, forward, from, in, into, off, on, out, out of, over, round, through, to, towards, up, upon
crib from
cringe before, from (+ ing), to
cripple with (pass.)
criticise for (+ ing)
crook up
crop up, out
cross in, off, out, over, with
crouch down
crow over
crowd in, into, out, round, with
crown with (pass.)
crumble up, away
crumple up
crunch up, down
crusade for, against
crush down, in, into, out, to, up
crust over
cry down, for, off, out, over, to, up
cuddle up
cue in
cull out, from
culminate in (+ ing)
cup round
curb down, up
cure of
curl up
curse with (pass.)
curtail of
curtain off
cut about (pass.), across, along, at, away, back, down, for, from, in, into, off, out, through, to, up, with

cycle about, across, along, around, away, back, by, down, forth, forward, from, in, into, off, on, out, out of, over, round, through, to, towards, up, upon

d

dab at, off, on, out
dabble at, in, with
dally over, with
dam up
damp down, off
dampen off
dance about, across, along, around, away, back, by, down, forth, forward, from, in, into, off, on, out, out of, over, round, through, to, towards, up, upon, with
dangle about, around, from, round
dart about, across, along, around, at, away, back, by, down, for, forth, forward, from, in, into, off, on, out, out of, over, round, through, to, towards, up, upon
dash about, across, along, around, away, back, by, down, for, forth, forward, from, in, into, off, on, out, out of, over, round, through, to, towards, up, upon
date back, from
daub on, over, up, with

dawdle along, away, over

dawn on, upon

daydream about

deaden with (pass.)

deal at, by, in, out, with

debar from (+ ing)

debate about, in, on, upon, with

debit against, to, with

decamp from

deceive in, into (+ ing), with

decide on (+ ing), for, upon (+ ing), against (+ ing)

deck out, up, with

declame against

declare against, for, off, on, to

decorate with, for (+ ing)

decoy into (+ ing)

decrease from

dedicate to (+ ing)

deduce from

deduct from

deed over, to

deface of

default on

defect from, to

defend against, from (+ ing)

define as

deflect from

defraud of

degenerate into (+ ing)

delay in (+ ing)

delegate to

delete from

deliberate about, on, over, upon

delight at (+ ing), by (pass.), in (+ ing), with (pass.)

deliver from, of, over, to, up

delude into (+ ing), out of (+ ing)

deluge with

delve into

demand from, of

demise to

demonstrate to

demote from, to

demur at, to

denounce for, to

denude of

deny to

depart from

depend on, upon

deplete of

depose to

deposit with, on

deprive of

depute to

deputise as, for

derive from

derogate from

descant on, upon

descend from, into, on, to (+ ing), upon

describe as, to

design for

designate as

desist from (+ ing)

despair of (+ ing)

despatch to

despise for (+ ing)

despoil of

destine for (pass.)

detach from

detail for, off

deter from (+ ing)

determine on (+ ing), upon (+ ing)

detract from

develop from, into

deviate from

devil for

devolve on, upon

devote to (+ ing)

devour with (pass.)

dice away, with

dictate to

diddle out

die away, back, by, down, for, from, in, of, off, out, with

differ about, from, in, on, with

differentiate from

dig at, down, for, in, into, out, over, up

digress from

dilate on, upon

dilute with

dim down, out, up

din in, into

dine at, off, on, out

dip in, into, to

direct to

dirty up

disabuse of

disagree about, on, over, with

disappear from, to

disappoint at (pass.), in (+ ing), with

disapprove of (+ ing)

disbar from

disbelieve in

disburden of

discern from

discharge from, into

disconnect with (pass.), from

discord with

discourage from (+ ing)

discourse on, upon

discriminate against, from

discuss with

disembark from

disembarrass from, of

disencumber from

disengage from

disentangle from

disguise as, in, with

disgust at (+ ing), by (pass.), with

dish out, up

dislodge from

dismantle of

dismay at (+ ing) / (pass.)

dismiss as, for (+ ing), from

dismount from

dispatch to

dispense from (+ ing), to, with

displease with, at (pass.)

dispose of, towards (pass.)

dispossess of

dispute against, at, over, with

disqualify for (+ ing)

dissatisfy at (pass.) / (+ ing), with

dissent about, from

dissociate from

dissolve in, into

dissuade from (+ ing)

distinguish from

distract from (+ ing)

distrain upon

distribute over, round, to

divagate from

dive in, into, off

diverge from, to

divert from, to, with

divest of

divide by, from, into, off, on, out, with

divorce from

divulge to

dizzy by, with

do about, as, by, down, for, in, of, out, out, over, to, up, with (+ ing)

dock off

dodder along

dole out

doll up

dolly in, out

dominate over

domineer over

donate to

doom to (pass.)

dope out, up

dose with

doss around, down, up

dot about, around, with

dote on, upon

double as, over, up, with

doubt of

dovetail into

doze off

draft out, to

drag at, away, down, in, into, off, out, through, up

dragoon into (+ ing)

drain away, from, into, of, off, out

drape in, over, round, with

draw at (+ ing), away, back, down, for, forth, from, in, into, off, on, out, over, to, up, upon

drawl out

dream about, away, of (+ ing)

dredge up, for

drench in (pass.), with

dress down, for, out, up

drift along, away, in, off, out, towards

drill in, down, into

drink away, down, in, off, to, up

drive about, across, along, around, at, away, back, by, down, for, forth, forward, from, in, into, off, on, out, out of, over, round, through, to, towards, up, upon

drivel on, about

drizzle down

drone out

drool over

droop down

drop across, around, away, back, by, down, in, into, off, on, out, over, round, through, to, up

drown out, in

drowse off, away

drum in, into, on, out of, up, upon

dry off, out, up

dub in

duck down, into, out

dull up

dump down, on

dun for

dunk in

dust down, off, out

dwell at, in, on, upon

dwindle away, down, to

earmark for

earth up

ease up, off, round, of

eat away, in, into, off, out, out of, through, up

eavesdrop on

ebb away

echo back, with

economise on

edge away, out, with

edit out

educate for, in

educe from

egg on

eject from

eke out

elaborate on

elate with (pass.)

elect as, to, with

elevate to

eliminate from

elope with

emanate from

emancipate from

embark for, on, upon

embed in

embellish with

emblazon with

embody in

embosom in, with

embrace in

embroil in

emerge from

emigrate from, to

emit from, into

empathize with

employ at, for, in (+ ing)

empty out, in

enamour of (pass.), with

encase in

enchant by, with

enclose in, with

encompass with

encourage in

encroach on, upon

encrust with

encumber with

end by (+ ing), in, up, with (+ ing)

endear to

endorse with

endow with

endue with

enfold in

enforce on

engage in (+ ing), to, with (pass.)

engorge with

engraft in, into, upon

engrave on, upon, with

engross in (pass.)

engulf in (pass.)

enjoin on

enlarge on, upon

enlighten on

enlist in

enmesh in (pass.)

enquire about, for, into, of

enrich with

enrol (I) for, in

ensconce in

enshrine in

ensnare into (+ ing), out of (+ ing)

ensue from, on

ensure against, from

entail on

entangle in (pass.), with

enter by, for, in, into, on, up, upon

entertain with, to

enthral (I) into (+ ing), out of (+ ing), with (pass.)

enthrone in

enthuse over, about

entice away, from, into, to

entitle to (pass.)

entomb in

entrap into (+ ing)

entreat of

entrust to, with

entwine about, around, round, with

envelop in

equal in

equate to, with (pass.)

equip with, for

erase from

err from

erupt into

escape from, out of, to

escort to, from

establish in

estimate at

estrange from (pass.)

etch away, in

evacuate to, from

evaluate at

evaporate down

even off, out, up

evict from

evolve from, out of

exact from

examine in, on

exasperate at (pass.), by

exceed by, in

excel at (+ ing), in

except from

excerpt from

exchange with, for

excite in

exclaim at, against

exclude from

excuse for (+ ing), from (+ ing)

exempt from (+ ing)

exercise in (+ ing)

exile from

exist by

exonerate from

exorcise from, out of

expand into, on

expatiate on, upon

expatriate from

expect from, of

expel from

expend in (+ ing), on (+ ing)

experiment in, on, upon, with

explain away, to
explode with
export to
expose to
expostulate with
expound to
express as, in, to
expropriate from
expunge from
expurgate from
extend across, over, to (+ ing)
extinguish by (pass.)
extort from, out of
extract from
extradite from
extricate from
extrude from
exult at (+ ing), in (+ ing), over
eye with

face about, away, down, forward, off, out, round, with
fade away, back, down, for, in, into, out, up
fag away, out
fail in, of
faint away, from, with
fake out, up
fall about, around, at, away, back, by, down, for, from, in, into, off, on, out, out of, over, through, to, towards, upon
falter out
familiarise with (+ ing)

fan out
fantasise about
fare forth
farm out
fashion from, on, out of, to, upon
fast from
fasten down, off, on, to, up, upon
father on, upon
fathom out
fatten on, out, up
favour with
fawn on, upon
fax back, from, to,
fear for
feather out
feature in
feed back, in, into, off, on, to, up (pass.), upon, with
feel about, for, like (+ ing), out, out of, towards, up, with
fence in, off, out, with
fend for, off
ferret about, around, out
ferry across, over
festoon with
fetch back, in, out, over, round, to, up
feud with
fiddle about, away, with
fidget about, with
fig out (pass.), up (pass.)
fight about, against, back, down, for, off, on, out, over, through, to, with
figure in, on, out, to, up
filch from
file away, down, for, out
fill away, in, out, up, with
film over

filter out, through
find against, for, in, out
fine down, for (+ ing)
finish in, off, up (+ ing), with (+ ing)
fire at, away, back, into, off, on, over, up, upon, with
firm up
fish for, in, out, up
fit for, in, into, on, out, round, to, up, with
fix for, on, over, up, upon, with
fizz up
fizzle out
flabbergast by (pass.)
flag down
flagellate for (+ ing)
flake out
flame out, up, with
flank on, upon, with
flap about, around, away
flare back, out, up
flash about, around, at, back, forward, on, out, through, up, upon
flatten out, in
flatter on (+ ing)
flavour with
fleck with
flee away, from, to
flesh up, out
flick away, off, over, through
flicker out
fling about, around, at, away, back, down, in, into, off, on, out, to, up
flip over, through
flirt with
flit about, through
float about, around, in, on, round, through, upon

flock in, into, round, to
flood in, into, out, with (pass.)
flop about, around, down, into
flounce in, out
flounder about, around, through
flow from, in, into, out, over, to, with
fluff up, out
flunk out
flush away, from, off, out, up, with
fluster up (pass.)
flutter about, across, along, around, away, back, by, down, forth, forward, from, in, into, off, on, out, out of, over, round, through, to, towards, up, upon
fly about, across, along, around, away, back, by, down, forth, forward, from, in, into, off, on, out, out of, over, round, through, to, towards, up, upon
foam at, up, with
fob off, on, with
focus on
foist in, into, off, on
fold away, back, down, in, up
follow about, in, on, out, through, up, upon
fool about, around, away, into (+ ing), out of, with
footle about, around
forbear from (+ ing)
force down, from, into (+ ing), on, out, upon
foreclose on
foregather with
forget about
forgive for (+ ing)

fork out, over, up
form from, into, up
fortify with, against
forward to
foul up
found on, upon
frame in, up
freak out
free from, of
freeze in, off, out, over, to, up
freshen up
fret about, into, on, over, upon
frig about, around
frighten away, from (+ ing), into (+ ing), off, out of (+ ing)
fringe with (pass.)
frisk about
fritter away
frog-march along, away, by, in, off, out of, to, towards
frolic about
front on, to, towards, upon
frost over, up
froth up, with
frown at, down, on, upon
fry up
fuck about, around, off, round, up
fudge on
fulminate against
fumble for, with
fume at (+ ing)
funk at
funnel into
fur up
furbish up
furnish to, with
fuse with
fuss about, around, over, up
fuzz out

g

gabble away, off, on, out
gad about, around
gain in, on, over, upon
gallivant about, off, around
gallop about, across, along, around, away, back, by, down, forth, forward, from, in, into, off, on, out, out of, over, round, through, to, towards, up, upon
galumph about, across, along, around, away, back, by, down, forth, forward, from, in, into, off, on, out, out of, over, round, through, to, towards, up, upon
galvanise with
gamble away, on
gambol about, across, along, around, away, back, by, down, forth, forward, from, in, into, off, on, out, out of, over, round, through, to, towards, up, upon, with
game away
gang up
gape at
garb in
garner up, in
garnish with
gas up
gasp at, for, out
gather from, in, round, to, up
gaze about, at, on, out, round, upon
gear down, to, up

gen up

generalise about, from

generate from

get about, across, along, around, at, away, back, by, down, for, from, in, into, off, on, out, out of, over, round, through, to, up

gibe at

giggle over, at

ginger up

gird up, on, for

girdle about, around, round

give away, back, for, forth, in, off, on, out, over, round, to, up (+ ing), upon

glance, at, back, down, off, over, round, through

glare at, down

glass in, over

glaze in, over

gleam with

glean from

glide about, around, away, back, down, from, in, into, off, on, over, through, to, upon, round, out of, by, along, towards, forward, forth, across

glisten with

glitter over, with

gloat over

glory in (+ ing)

gloss over

glow with

glower at

glue down, on, to

glut with

gnaw at, away, on

go about, across, against, along, around, at, away, back, by, down, forth, forward, from, in, into, off, on, out, out of, over, round, through, to, towards, up, upon, with

goad in (+ ing), on, out of (+ ing)

gobble down, up

goggle at

goof around, off, up

goose up

gorge with, on

gossip about, of

gouge out

grab for, away, at

grace with

grade up, down

graduate from, in, with

graft in, on, upon

grant to

graph out

grapple with

grasp at

grass on

grate on

gravitate to, towards

graze on

greet with

grieve about, for, over

grin at

grind away, down, in, into, on, out, to, up

gripe about, at

groan with

groom for

grope about, around, for

ground in (pass.), on

group about, around, round

grouse about, at

grout in

grovel in, to

grow back, down, from, in, into, on, out, out of, over, up, upon

growl out

grub about, around, up

grumble about, at, over

guarantee against, for

guard against, from

guess at

gull into (+ ing), out of (+ ing)

gulp back, down

gum down, on, up

gun down

gurgle with

gush forth, from, out, over, with

gussy up

guzzle down

habituate to (+ ing)

hack around, down, off, out, up

haggle about, for, over, with

hail from

hallo to

ham up

hammer at, down, in, into, on, out

hand back, down, in, off, out, over, round, to, up

hang about, around, back, by, down, from, off, on, out, over, round, up, upon, with

hanker for

happen to, on, upon

harden in, off, to (pass.) / (+ ing), up
hare off
hark at
harmonise with
harness up, to
harp on, about
hash out, over, up
hatch out
haul down, in, on, over, up
have about, against, around, at, away, back, by, down, for, in, off, on, out, over, to, up, upon, with
hawk about, round
haze over
head back, for, in, into, off, out, towards, up
heal up, over, of
heap on, up, upon, with
hear about, from, of, out, through
hearten up
heat up
heave about, in, on, to, up
hector into (+ ing), out of (+ ing)
hedge against, in
heel over, back
help along, back, down, forward, in, into, off, on, out, over, to, up
hem in, about, around, round
herd into, with
hesitate for
hew down, out
hide away, from, in, out, with
hinder from (+ ing)
hinge on, upon
hint to, at
hire out

hiss at, off
hit against, at, back, in, out, up, upon
hitch up, to
hitch-hike across, along, around, away, back, from, in, into, on, out, out of, through, to, towards
hive off
hoard up
hoax into (+ ing), out of (+ ing)
hobble across, along, around, away, back, forth, forward, in, into, off, out, out of, through, to
hobnob with
hoist up
hoke up
hold against, at, back, by, down, for, forth, in, off, on, out, out of, over, to, up, with
hole in, out, up
hollow out
home in
honour for (+ ing), with
hoodwink into (+ ing), out of (+ ing)
hoof out
hook up, on
hoot down, off
hop about, across, along, around, away, back, by, down, forth, forward, from, in, into, off, on, out, out of, over, round, through, to, towards, up, upon
hope in, for
horn in
horse about, around
hose down
hound down, out

house up
hover over, round
howl down, with
huddle up
hum with
humbug into (+ ing), out of (+ ing)
humiliate into (+ ing), out of (+ ing)
hump over
hunch up (pass.)
hunger for
hunker down
hunt down, for, out, over, through, up
hurl about, around, at, away, down, into, out
hurry along, away, back, down, forward, in, into, off, on, out, up
hurtle down, along
hush up
hustle on, into (+ ing), out of (+ ing)
hype up
hypnotise into (+ ing), out of (+ ing)

ice over, up
identify with
idle about, around, away
illuminate with
illumine with
illustrate with
imbue with (pass.)

I

MMERSE / ITCH

immerse in
immigrate into
immunise against
impale on
impart to
impeach for (+ ing)
impel to
impend over
impinge on, upon
implant in, into
implicate in
import from, into
impose on, upon
imprecate on, upon
impregnate with
impress by, on, upon, with
imprint on, with
imprison in
improve in, on, upon
impute to
incapacitate from (+ ing), for
incarcerate in
incite to
incline forward, to, towards
include in, out
incorporate in, into
increase for, in, to
inculcate in
indemnify against, for
indent for
indict for (+ ing)
indispose for (+ ing), towards
indoctrinate with
induce in
indulge in (+ ing)
infatuate with (pass.)
infect with
infer from
infest with
infiltrate into, through
inflate with

inflict on
inform on, against, of
infringe on, upon
infuse into, with
ingraft into, upon
ingratiate with
inhere in
inherit from
inhibit for (+ ing)
initiate into
inject into, with
ink in, over
inlay with
innovate in
inoculate against, with
input into
inquire about, for, into, of
inscribe with
insert in, into
inset in, into
insinuate into
insist on (+ ing), upon
inspire in, into, with
install in
instil in, into, with
institute against, into, to
instruct in, of
insulate from
insure against, for, with
integrate into, with
intend in, for, as
interact with
interbreed with
intercede with, for
interchange with
interdict from (+ ing)
interest in (pass.) / (+ ing)
interfere in, with
interlace with
interlard with
interleave with

interlink with
intermarry with
intermingle with
intern in
interpose in
interpret as
interrogate about
intersect by, with
intersperse with
intervene in
interview about
interweave with
intimate to
intimidate into (+ ing), out of (+ ing)
intoxicate with (pass.)
intrigue against, with
introduce into, to
intrude into, on, upon
intrust to, with
inundate with (pass.)
inure from, to
invalid out
inveigh against
inveigle into (+ ing), out of (+ ing)
invest in, with
invite in, out, over, round, to
invoke on, for, upon
involve in (pass.) / (+ ing), with (pass.)
iron out
irrigate with
isolate from
issue as, forth, from, out of, to, with
itch for

192

jab out, about, into
jack up
jam in, into, on, up, with
jangle on, upon
jar against, on, with
jaunt back , forth
jaw at
jazz up
jeer at
jerk away, off, out, up
jest about, at
jib at (+ ing)
jigger up
jink about, across, along, around, away, back, by, down, forth, forward, from, in, into, off, on, out, out of, over, round, through, to, towards, up, upon
job out
jockey for, into (+ ing), out of (+ ing)
jog about, across, along, around, away, back, by, down, forth, forward, from, in, into, off, on, out, out of, over, round, through, to, towards, up, upon
join in (+ ing), on, to, up, with
joke about, at, with
jolly along
jostle for, with
jot down
judge by, from
juggle with

jumble up
jump about, across, along, around, at, away, back, by, down, for, forth, forward, from, in, into, off, on, out, out of, over, round, through, to, towards, up, upon, with
justify in (pass.) / (+ ing), by (+ ing)
jut out

k

keel over
keep about, around, at, away, back, by, down, for, from (+ ing), in, off, on, out, out of, to, up, with
kick about, against, around, at, away, back, down, in, off, on, out, over, up
kid around, on, up
kill off
kindle with
kip down, out
kiss away, off
kit out, up
kneel down, to
knit up
knock about, against, around, at, away, back, down, for, in, into, off, on, out, out of, over, through, up
know about, as, by, for, from, of, to (pass.)
knuckle down
kowtow to

l

label as, with
labour at (+ ing), for, over (+ ing)
lace in, into, up, with
lack in, for
lade with
ladle for, out, out of
lag with
lam into, out
lament for, over
land in, on, up, upon, with
languish for, in, of, over
lap about, against, around, in, on, over, round, up
lapse for, into
lard with
lark about, around
lash about, against, at, down, into, out, round, to, up
last out, for
latch on
lather up
laugh about, at, away, down, into (+ ing), off, out of (+ ing), over
launch against, forth, into, on, out, upon
lavish on
lay about, against, along, at, away, back, by, down, for, in, into, off, on, out, over, up, with
laze away
leach about, from, out, out of
lead against, away, back, by, down, forth, in, into, off, on, out, to, up, with

leaf out, through

league against, with

leak away, in, out, to

lean against, back, down, forward, on, out, over, to, towards

leap at, forward, in, into, out, out of, up

learn about, by, from, of, off, up

lease back, out

leave about, around, at, down, for, in, off, on, out, out of, over, to, up, with

leaven with

lecture about, at, for, on, to

leer at

legislate against, for

lend out, to (+ ing)

lengthen out

let by, down, in, into, of, off, on, out, through, up

level against, at, down, off, out, up, with

lever against, out, up

levy on, upon

liaise with

liberate from

license for (pass.)

lick off, up

lie about, along, at, back, by, down, in, off, on, out, over, through, to, up, with

lie about, to

lift down, from, off, up

light up, with

liken to, with

limber up

limit to (pass.) / (+ ing)

limp along

line up, with

linger about, around, on, over

link to, up, with

lisp out

listen for, in, out, to (+ ing)

litter about, around, down, up

live at, by, down, for, in, off, on, out, out of, over, to, up, with

liven up

load down, into, up, with

loaf about, around

loan to

lob along, at

lobby against, for, through

lock away, in, into, on, out, up

lodge against, at, in, with

log off, on, out, up

loiter about, around, away, in, over

loll about, around, back, out

long for,

look about, around, at, away, back, down, for, in, into, on, out, over, to, up, through, upon, round, towards

loom up

loose from, off

loosen up

lop away, off

lope about, across, along, around, away, back, by, down, forth, forward, from, in, into, off, on, out, out of, over, round, through, to, towards, up, upon

lose at, by, in, on, out, over, to

lounge about, against, along, around, away

lour at, on, upon

louse up

lower at, on, upon

luff up

lug about, across, along, around, away, back, by, down, forth, forward, from, in, into, off, on, out, out of, over, round, through, to, towards, up, upon

lull into (+ ing), out of (+ ing)

lumber along

lump along

lunch in, off, out

lunge at

lure away, into (+ ing), on, out of (+ ing)

lurk about, around

lust for

luxuriate in

madden with (pass.)

mail to, from

maintain at

major in

make at, away, down, for, from, in, into, of (pass.), off, on, out, over, round, towards, up, with

man with

manage with

mangle up

manïuvre across, around, into, out of, through

mantle with, over

map up, out

march along, away, by, in, off, out of, to, towards

mark up, out, in, with, down, for, off

marry into, off (pass.), to (pass.), up, with (pass.)

marshal out, in

marvel at

mash up

mask out, with

masquerade as

match up, with, against

mate with

matter to

maul about, around

mean by (+ ing), for, to

measure against, off, out, up, with

meddle in, with

mediate between, in

meditate on, upon

meet up, with

melt away, down, in, into

mention in, to

merge in, into, with

mesh with

mesmerise into (+ ing), out of (+ ing)

mess up, about, around

metamorphose into, to

mete out

migrate from, to

militate against

mill about, around

mind out

mine out

mingle in, with

minister to

miscalculate about

misconceive of

miss out

mist up, over

mistake about (pass.), for

mix up, in, with

moan about

mock up, at

model on, upon

modulate to

moisten with

monkey about, around, with

mooch about

moon about, around, away

mop down, up

mope about, around, away

moralise about, on, over

motion away, to

mould from, out of

mount on, to, up

mourn for, over

move about, across, along, around, away, back, by, down, forth, forward, from, in, into, off, on, out, out of, over, round, through, to, towards, up, upon

mow down

muck about, along, in, out, through, up

muddle about, along, around, on, through, up

muddy up

muffle up

mug up

mulct of

mull over

multiply by

murmur against, at

muscle in

muse about, on, over, upon

muster up

mutiny against

muzz around, away, back, by, down, forth, forward, from, in, into, off, on, out, out of, over, round, through, to, towards, up

n

nag at

nail back, down, on, to, up

name as, to

narrow down

navigate about, across, along, around, away, back, by, down, forth, forward, from, in, into, off, on, out, out of, over, round, through, to, towards, up, upon

negotiate about, for, over, with

neighbour with

nerve for

nest in

nestle down, up

nettle at (pass.)

nibble at

nick up, in

niggle over

nip at, in, off

nod off, to

noise about, around

nominate for, to

nose about, around, into, out, round

notch up

note for (pass.) / (+ ing)

notify to, of

nourish with

numb with (pass.)

number off, with

nurse along, through

nurture on

nuzzle against, up

object to (+ ing)
oblige by, to (pass.), with
obscure from
observe on, to, upon
obsess with (pass.)
obtain for, from
obtrude on, upon
occupy in (+ ing), with
occur to
offend against, with
offer for, to, up
officiate as, at
ogle at
omit from
ooze out, away
open into, off, on, out, to, up
operate against, from, on
oppose to (pass.) / (+ ing)
opt for, in, out
order around, at, from, in, off, out, up
originate from, in, with
oscillate about, around
osculate with
oust from
overburden with
overcome by (pass.), with (pass.)
overcrowd with (pass.)
overflow with
overlay with
overpass in
overpower with (pass.)
overrun with (pass.)
overstock with
overweary with, of (+ ing)
overwhelm by (pass.), with (pass.)

owe to
own to, up

pace about, across, along, around, away, back, by, down, forth, forward, from, in, into, off, on, out, out of, over, round, through, to, towards, up, upon
pack away, down, in, into, off, out, up, with
pad about, across, along, around, away, back, by, down, forth, forward, from, in, into, off, on, out, out of, over, round, through, to, towards, up, upon, with
page up
paint in, on, out, over, upon
pair off, up, with
pal up
pale at
pall on, upon
palm off
palter with
pan out, in, for, off
pander to
pant for, out
paper over
parachute down
parcel up, out
parch up, with
pardon for (+ ing)
pare down, off
parley with

part from, over, with
partake in, of
participate in, with
partition off
partner off
pass along, away, back, by, down, for, forward, from, in, into, off, on, out, out of, over, round, through, up
paste up
pat down, on
patch up
patter about, around
pattern with, on, upon
pause on, upon
pave with
paw about, around
pay away, back, by, down, for, in, into, off, out, over, to, up, with
peach on
peak out
peal out
peck up, at
peek at
peel away, back, off
peep at, into, out, over, through
peer about, around, at, in, out, through
peg down, out
pelt along, at, down, out, with
pen in, up
penalise for (+ ing)
penetrate into, through, to, with
pension off
people with
pep up
pepper with
perch on

percolate through
perforate into
perform on
perish by, from, in, with
perk up
permeate through, with
permit in, into, of, out, through, up
persevere in (+ ing), with, at
persist in (+ ing), with
persuade of
pertain to
pervade with
pester with
peter out
petition for
phase in, out
philander with
philosophise about
phone for, in, up
pick at, away, from, in, off, on, up
picture to
piece up
pierce through
pig out
pile in, into, off, on, out, up, upon, with
pilfer from
pillow on
pilot in, into, out, through
pimp for
pin against, back, down, on, to, up
pinch back, off, out
pine away, for, over
pinion to
pink out
pipe away, down, in, into, up, with
pique on

piss about, around, off
pit against, with (pass.)
pitch forward, in, into, on, out, up, upon
pivot on
place at, back, down, in, on, out, to, with
plague with
plan for, on, out
plane away, down, off
plank down, on, out
plant in, on, out, with
plaster down, on, over, up, with
plate with
play about, against, along, around, as, at (+ ing), back, by, down, for, forward, in, off, on, out, over, round, through, to, up, upon, with
plead against, for, with
pledge to
plod about, across, along, around, away, back, by, down, forth, forward, from, in, into, off, on, out, out of, over, round, through, to, towards, up, upon
plonk down, out
plot against, on, out, with
plotz around
plough back, in, into, on, out, through, up
plow back, in, into, on, out, through, up
pluck from, off, out, up
plug in, up
plume on
plump against, down, for, out, up
plunge down, in, into

plunk down, for
ply with, across
poach on, for
point at, down, off, out, to, towards, up
poise on, over
poison against
poke about, along, around, at, forward, in, into, out, round, through, up
polish up, off
pollute with
ponder on, over, upon
poop out
pop across, along, back, down, in, into, off, on, out, over, round, up
pore on, over, upon
portion out, to
pose as, for
posh up
possess by (pass.), of (pass.)
post away, from, on, to, up
postpone to
postulate for
pot up, at
potter about, around
pounce on, upon
pound along, at, down, in, into, on, out, up
pour across, along, away, back, down, forth, in, into, off, on, out, over, through, with
powder with
power by (pass.), with (pass.)
powwow about
practise on, upon
praise for (+ ing), up
prance about, around
prate about

prattle about, away
pray to, over, for
preach against, at, to
precipitate into
preclude from (pass.) / (+ ing)
predestinate to
predestine for (pass.), to (pass.)
predispose to (pass.), towards (pass.)
predominate over
preface by with
prefer against, to
prefix to
prejudice against (pass.) / (+ ing)
prelude to
prepare for
preponderate over
prepossess against, with
presage from
prescribe for
present at, to, with
preserve for, from
preside at, over
press against, down, for, forward, in, into, on, out, round, to, towards, up, upon
pressure into (+ ing), out of (+ ing)
presume on, upon
pretend to
prevail against, on, over, upon
prevent from (+ ing)
prey on, upon
price out, up
prick down, off, on, out, up
pride on (+ ing)
prim up
prime with (pass.)
primp up

prink up
print in, off, out
prise for, off, out of, up
prize from, off, out of
probe into
proceed about, from, to, with
procure from, for
prod at, into (+ ing), out of (+ ing), with
produce from
profit by (+ ing), from (+ ing)
progress in, to, with
promise to
promote to
pronounce against, for, on, upon
prop up, against
propose to
prosecute for (+ ing)
prospect for
prosper from
protect against, from
protest against (+ ing)
protrude from
prove to
provide against, for, with
provision with
provoke into (+ ing)
prowl about, around, round
prune away, down, from, of
pry about, from, into, off, out of
psych out, up
pucker up
puddle about
puff about, across, along, around, away, back, by, down, forth, forward, from, in, into, off, on, out, out of, over, round, through, to, towards, up, upon, with

pull about, along, around, at, away, back, by, down, for, in, into, off, on, out, out of, over, round, through, to, towards, up
pulse through
pump in, into, out, through, up
punch down, in, on, out, up
punctuate with
punish for (+ ing), with
purge away, from, of, off, out
purify of
purse up
push about, against, along, around, at, away, back, by, down, for, forward, from, in, into, off, on, out, over, round, through, to, towards, up, upon
pussyfoot around, away, back, by, down, forth, forward, from, in, into, off, on, out, out of, over, round, through, to, towards, up
put across, against, along, as, at, away, back, by, down, forth, forward, in, into, off (+ ing), on, out, out of, over, through, to, up, upon
putter about, along, around, out
putty up
puzzle out, over

q

quail at
quake with
qualify as, for
quarrel about, for (+ ing), over, with
query with
question about
queue up
quibble about, over
quicken up
quiet down
quieten down
quit of
quiver with
quote from

r

rabbit on
race about, across, against, along, around, away, back, by, down, for, forth, forward, from, in, into, off, on, out, out of, over, round, through, to, towards, up, upon, with
rack up, with (pass.)
racket about
radiate from
raft down
rage against, at, out, through
rail against, at, in, off, on
railroad into (+ ing), out of (+ ing), through (pass.)

rain down, in, off (pass.), on, upon
raise from, to, up, with
rake about, around, in, off, out, over, round, through, up
rally from, on, round
ram down, into, through
ramble on
ramp about, around
rampage about, along, around
range against, from, in, over, through, to, with
rank with, as
rankle with
ransack for
rap at, on, out, over, with
rasp out
rat on
rate as, at, for (+ ing), up, with
ration out
rattle about, across, along, around, away, back, by, down, forth, forward, from, in, into, off, on, out, out of, over, round, through, to, towards, up, upon
rave over, about, at, against
ravel out
raze out
reach back, down, for, forward, into, out, to, towards, up
react to, on, upon, against
read about, around, as, back, for, from, in, into, of, out, out of, over, round, through, to, up
realise from, on
ream out
reap from
reapply upon
rear up

reason against, from, into (+ ing), out of (+ ing), with
reassure on, about
rebel against at (+ ing)
rebound from, on, upon
rebuke for (+ ing)
recall to
recast in
recede from
receive as, from, into
recite to
reck of
reckon as, for, from, in, on (+ ing), to, up, upon, with
reclaim from
recline on
recognise as, by, from
recoil on, for (+ ing), upon
recommend to
recompense for (+ ing)
reconcile with, to
reconstruct from
record from, on
recount to
recoup for
recover from
recriminate against
recruit from, into (+ ing)
recuperate from
recur to
redeem from
redirect to
redound to, on
reduce by, from, in, to (+ ing)
reef in
reek of, with
reel back, from, in, off, out, up
re-equip with
reeve through, to
refer back, to

refill with
refine on, upon
reflect in (pass.), on, upon
refrain from (+ ing)
refresh with
refuel with
refund to
refuse to
regain from
regale with
regard as, with
register as, for, in, on, with
regress to
regulate by
reign over
reimburse for, to
rein back, in, up
reinforce with
reingratiate with
reinstate in
reintegrate in
rejoice at, in (+ ing), over
rejoin to, with
relapse in
relate to
relax in, into
relay out, to
release to, from
relegate to
relieve from, of
rely on, upon
remain at, away, down, in, of,
    off, on
remand for, to
remark on, upon
remember as, in, to
remind of (+ ing)
reminisce about, with
remit to
remonstrate about, with
remove from

remunerate for
rend from, in, to
render up, to, down, for, into
renege on
rent at, out, to
repay by, for, with
repel from
repent of
repine at, against
replace with, by
replate with
replenish with
reply to, for
report back, for, on, out, to,
    upon
repose on, upon
reprehend for (+ ing)
represent to, as
reprimand for (+ ing)
reprint in, from
reproach for (+ ing), with
    (+ ing)
reproduce in, from
reprove for (+ ing)
repulse from
repute as
request from, of
require of
requisition as, for, from
requite with
rescue from
research into, on
reserve for
resettle to
reside in
resign to (pass.) / (+ ing), from
resolve into, on
resort to (+ ing)
resound in, through, with
respect for
respond to

rest up, in, with, on, from,
    upon, against
restitute to
restock with
restore to
restrain from (+ ing)
restrict to (pass.) / (+ ing)
result in (+ ing), from
retail to, for, at
retain on, over, upon
retaliate on, upon, against
retire from, in, on, to
retreat from, to
retrieve from
retroact against
return for, from, to
reunite with
rev up
reveal to
revel in (+ ing)
revenge on, upon
revert to (+ ing)
revile at, against
revolt against (+ ing)
revolve about, around
reward for (+ ing)
rhapsodise about, over
rhyme with
rid of
riddle with
ride about, across, along,
    around, away, back, by,
    down, forth, forward, from,
    in, into, off, on, out, out of,
    over, round, through, to,
    towards, up, upon
rifle through
rig out, up
ring about, around
ring about, back, for, in, off,
    out, round, through, up, with

rinse down, out

rip across, away, down, from, in, into, off, out, to, up

rise from, in, up

risk on

rivalise with

rivet to, on

roam about, around

roar at, down, out, with

rob of

rock about, around

rocket in

roll about, along, around, away, back, by, down, in, off, on, out, over, round, up

romp about, through

roof in, over

room with

root about, for, in, out, to, up

rope in, into, off, up

rot away, off, out

rough in, out, up

round down, in, into, off, on, out, up, upon

rouse from, to

rout out

route by, through

rove in, over

row about, across, along, around, away, back, by, down, forth, forward, from, in, into, off, on, out, out of, over, round, through, to, towards, up, upon

rub against, along, away, down, in, into, off, on, out, through, up

ruck up

ruckle up

ruffle up

rule against, off, on, out, over

rumble off

ruminate about, on, over, upon

rummage about, around, for, out, up

run about, across, against, along, around, away, back, by, down, for, forth, forward, from, in, into, off, on, out, out of, over, round, through, to, towards, up, upon, with

rush about, across, along, around, away, back, by, down, forth, forward, from, in, into, into (+ ing), off, on, out, out of, over, round, through, to, towards, up, upon

rust away, in

rustle up

sacrifice to

saddle on, up, upon, with

safeguard against

sag down

sail about, across, along, around, away, back, by, down, forth, forward, from, in, into, off, on, out, out of, over, round, through, to, towards, up, upon

sally forth, out

salt out, with, down, away

salute with

salvage from

sand down

sashay around, away, back, by, down, forth, forward, from, in, into, off, on, out, out of, over, round, through, to, towards, up, upon

satiate with

satisfy with (pass.), of

saturate with (pass.)

saunter across, along, back, into, out, out of, to

save for, from, up

savour of

saw down, into, off, through, up

say about, against, for, of, on, out, over, to

scab over

scale down, to, up

scamper about, across, along, around, away, back, by, down, forth, forward, from, in, into, off, on, out, out of, over, round, through, to, towards, up, upon

scandalise by (pass.)

scar over

scare away, into (+ ing), off, out of (+ ing)

scatter about, around, round, with

scent out

schedule as

scheme for

school in, to

scoff at

scold for (+ ing)

scoop out, up

scoot away, off, over

scope out

scorch along

score for, off, out, over, up

scour about, around, away, for, off, out

scout about, around, out

scowl at

scrabble about

scramble about, across, along, around, away, back, by, down, for, forth, forward, from, in, into, off, on, out, out of, over, round, through, to, towards, up, upon

scrape away, by, in, off, out, through, up

scratch about, along, away, from, out, up

scrawl over

scream down, for, out, with

screen out, from, off

screw down, on, out of, to, up

scribble away, down

scroll off, on, out

scrounge on

scrub away, down, out, round, up

scud about, across, along, around, away, back, by, down, forth, forward, from, in, into, off, on, out, out of, over, round, through, to, towards, up, upon

scuff up

scuffle through, with

sculpture out of

scurry about, across, along, around, away, back, by, down, forth, forward, from, in, into, off, on, out, out of, over, round, through, to, towards, up, upon

scuttle about, across, along, around, away, back, by, down, forth, forward, from, in, into, off, on, out, out of, over, round, through, to, towards, up, upon

scuzz out

seal up, off

seam up, with (pass.)

search for, out, through

season with

seat on

secede from

seclude from (pass.)

second to (pass.)

section off

secure against, from

seduce from, into (+ ing), out of (+ ing)

see about, across, against, around, as, back, in, into, off, out, over, round, through, to, up

seek out, from, for, into

seep away, in, through

seethe with

segregate against (pass.), from

seise of, with

seize on, up, upon, with (pass.)

select from, for, as (pass.)

sell at, down, for, on, out, to, up

send up, out, in, to, on, from, over, down, about, for, into, off, away, around, back, round, along, forward, forth, across

sentence to

separate from, into, off, out, up

serve as, for, in, on, out, round, to, up, with

set about (+ ing), across, against, along, at, back, by, down, for, forth, in, into, off, on, out, over, through, to, up, up, upon, with (pass.)

settle up, in, with, to, on, down, upon

sew up

shack along

shackle with (pass.)

shade from, in, into

shaft into, out of

shake down, off, out, out of, up, with

shamble along

shame into (+ ing), out of (+ ing)

shanghai into (+ ing)

shape into, to, up

share in, out, with

shave off

shear away, of (pass.), off

sheathe with

shed on, over, upon

sheer off

sheet down, in

shell out

shelter from

shepherd around, in, into, on, out, out of

shield against (+ ing), from (+ ing)

shift from, to

shin down, up

shine at, on, out, over, through, upon, with

ship out, off

shiver with

shock into (+ ing), out of (+ ing)

shoe with (pass.)

shoo away, off

shoot at, away, down, for, from, in, into, off, out, through, to, up, with (pass.)

shop around, on, round

shore up
shoulder in, into, out, out of
shout about, at, down, for, out
shove about, against, along, around, at, away, back, by, down, forward, in, into, on, out, over, to, towards, up
shovel down, in, into
show around, down, in, into, off, out, out of, over, round, through, to, up
shower on, upon, with
shriek out, with
shrink back, from (+ ing), up
shrivel up
shroud in
shrug off
shuck off
shudder at, with
shuffle about, across, along, around, away, back, by, down, forth, forward, from, in, into, off, on, out, out of, over, round, through, to, towards, up, upon
shut up, out, in, to, on, down, off, upon, of (pass.)
shuttle from, to
shy at
sick up
sicken at, for, of (+ ing)
side against, with
sidle about, across, along, around, away, back, by, down, forth, forward, from, in, into, off, on, out, out of, over, round, through, to, towards, up, upon
sieve out, through
sift out, through
sigh about, away, for, over

sign away, for, in, off, on, out, over, up
signal to
silhouette against (pass.)
silt up
simmer down, with
sin against
sing along, away, out, to, up, with
single out
sink back, down, in, into, to
siphon on
sit about, around, at, back, by, down, for, in, on, out, through, to, up, upon
size up
skate over, around, round
skelter around, away, back, by, down, forth, forward, from, in, into, off, on, out, out of, over, round, through, to, towards, up, upon
sketch out, in
skim off, over, through
skimp for
skin over, through
skip about, across, along, around, away, back, by, down, forth, forward, from, into, off, on, out, out of, over, round, through, to, towards, up, upon
skirmish with
skirt along, around, round
skitter around, away, back, by, down, forth, forward, from, in, into, off, on, out, out of, over, round, through, to, towards, up, upon
skive down, off
slack about, off

slacken away, off, up
slag off
slam down, in, on, to
slant against, towards
slap down, on, up
slave at, over
sledge about, across, along, around, away, back, by, down, forth, forward, from, in, into, off, on, out, out of, over, round, through, to, towards, up, upon
sleep around, away, in, off, on, out, over, through, with
sleuth around
slew around, round
slice in, on, through, up
slick down, up
slide about, across, along, around, away, back, by, down, forth, forward, from, in, into, off, on, out, out of, over, round, through, to, towards, up, upon
slim down
sling up, out, at
slink off, away
slip away, back, by, down, from, in, into, off, on, out, out of, over, through, up
slit up
slither about, across, along, around, away, back, by, down, forth, forward, from, in, into, off, on, out, out of, over, round, through, to, towards, up, upon
slob about, around
slobber over
slog about, across, along, around, away, back, by, down,

forth, forward, from, in, into, off, on, out, out of, over, round, through, to, towards, up, upon

slop about, around, out, over

slope down, off, towards, up

slosh on, about, around

slot in

slouch about, across, along, around, away, back, by, down, forth, forward, from, in, into, off, on, out, out of, over, round, through, to, towards, up, upon

slough off, over

slow down, up

sluice down, out

slump down, over

slur over

slush in, up

smack down (pass.)

smack of

smarm down, over, up

smart for

smarten up

smash against, in, up

smear on, with

smell at, of, out, up

smile at, on, upon

smite on, upon, with (pass.)

smoke out, up

smooth away, back, down, in, on, out, over

smother in, up, with

smoulder with

smuggle, in, out, through

snap at, back, off, on, out, out of, up

snarl at, up

snatch at, away, from, out of, up

sneak about, across, along, around, away, back, by,

---

down, forth, forward, from, in, into, off, on, out, out of, over, round, through, to, towards, up, upon

sneer at

sneeze at

sniff up, out, at

snip off

snipe at

snitch on

snoop around, into

snort at

snow up, in (pass.), off

snuff out

snug down

snuggle down

soak in, into, off, out, through, up, with

soap down

sob out

sober down, up

sock away, in (pass.)

sod off, over, up

soften up

soldier on

solicit for

soot up

sop up

sorrow about, at, over

sort out

sound out, off

soup up

souse in, with

sow with

space off, out

spade up

spangle with

spank along

spar with

spare for

spark off

---

sparkle with

spatter on, over, up, with

spawn from

speak about, against, for, from, of, on, out, to, up, upon

spear up

specialise in

speculate about, in, on

speed along, up

spell for, out

spend for, in, on, up (pass.)

spew forth, out, up

spice up, with

spill out, over

spin along, off, out, round

spiral down, up

spirit away, off

spit at, back, in, on, out, up, upon

splash about, around, down, on, over, up, with

splatter about, around, over, with

splay out

splinter off

split into, off, on, up

splotch with

splutter out

spoil for

sponge away, down, from, off, on, out, up

spoon out, up

sport with

spout from, off

sprawl about, out

spray on, with

spread about, around, on, out, over, to

spring at, back, from, on, out, to, up, upon

sprinkle with

sprint about, across, along, around, away, back, by, down, forth, forward, from, in, into, off, on, out, out of, over, round, through, to, towards, up, upon

sprout up

spruce up

spur on

spurt out

sputter out

spy into, on, out, upon

squabble about, over

squander away, on, upon

square away, off, round, up, with

squash in, up

squat down

squeak by, out, through

squeeze by, from, in, out, through, up

squint at

squirm out of, with

squirrel away

squirt out, in

stab in, at

stack up

stagger about, across, along, around, away, back, by, down, forth, forward, from, in, into, off, on, out, out of, over, round, through, to, towards, up, upon

stain with (pass.)

stake out, on, upon

stalk out, in, into, out of, along

stammer out

stamp as, on, out, upon, with

stampede for, in, towards

stand about, across, against, along, around, as, at, away, back, by, down, for, in, off, on, out, out of, over, to, up, upon

star in

starch up

stare out, down, at

start up, out, in, with, on, from, over, for, off, away, back, out of, as (+ ing)

startle out of

starve for, into (+ ing), out, out of (+ ing)

stash away

station in, on, at

stave in, up

stay at, away, back, by, down, for, in, off, on, out, out of, over, to, up

steady down

steal away, from, over

steam into, off, out, over, up

steel against, for

steep in

steer for, in, through, towards

stem from (+ ing)

step back, down, forward, in, into, off, on, out, over, up, upon

stew in

stick about, around, at, by, down, for (pass.), in, into, on, out, to (+ ing), up, with

stickle at

stiffen up

stimulate in, to

sting into (+ ing), out of (+ ing) with (+ ing)

stink of, out, up, with

stint of

stipulate for

stir about, around, in, to, up

stitch up

stock up, with

stoke up

stomp about, across, along, around, away, back, by, down, forth, forward, from, in, into, off, on, out, out of, over, round, through, to, towards, up, upon

stooge about, around

stoop to, down

stop at, away, by, down, for, from (+ ing), in, off, on, out of, over, to, up, with

store away, in, up

storm at, in, out

stow away, into, with

straggle about, across, along, around, away, back, by, down, forth, forward, from, in, into, off, on, out, out of, over, round, through, to, towards, up, upon

straighten out, up

strain at, away, off, on, through

strand on

strap down, in, on

stray about, across, along, around, away, back, by, down, forth, forward, from, in, into, off, on, out, out of, over, round, through, to, towards, up, upon, with

streak about, across, along, around, away, back, by, down, forth, forward, from, in, into, off, on, out, out of, over, round, through, to, towards, up, upon, with

stream about, across, along, around, away, back, by, down, forth, forward, from, in, into, off, on, out, out of, over, round, through, to, towards, up, upon

stretch away, forth, out

strew on, over, with (pass.)

stride about, across, along, around, away, back, by, down, forth, forward, from, in, into, off, on, out, out of, over, round, through, to, towards, up, upon

strike as (+ ing), at, back, down, for, in, into, off, on, out, over, through, up, upon

string along, up, with

strip away, down, from, of, off

stripe against, from, over, towards

strive against, for, with

stroll about, across, along, around, away, back, by, down, forth, forward, from, in, into, off, on, out, out of, over, round, through, to, towards, up, upon

struggle about, across, against, along, around, away, back, by, down, for, forth, forward, from, in, into, off, on, out, out of, over, round, through, to, towards, up, upon

strum on

strut about, across, along, around, away, back, by, down, forth, forward, from, in, into, off, on, out, out of, over, round, through, to, towards, up, upon

stub up, out

stud with (pass.)

study for

stuff up, in, with, down

stumble about, across, along, around, away, back, by, down, forth, forward, from, in, into, off, on, out, out of, over, round, through, to, towards, up, upon

stump about, across, along, around, away, back, by, down, forth, forward, from, in, into, off, on, out, out of, over, round, through, to, towards, up, upon

stupefy with (pass.)

stutter out

subdivide into

subject to

sublet to

submerge in

submit to

subordinate to

subscribe to

subside in

subsist in, on

substitute for

subtract from

succeed at, in (+ ing), to

succumb to

suck up, down, at

sue to, for

suffer from, for

suffice for

suffix to

suffuse with (pass.)

suggest to

suit for, to, up, with

sum up

summon up, to

sunder from

superabound in, with

superimpose on

superpose on, upon

supervene on

supplement by

supply from, to, with

surcharge with

surface with

surfeit with

surge in, out, up

surmount with (pass.)

surpass in

surprise at, in (+ ing), out of (+ ing), with

surrender to

surround with

suspect of (+ ing)

suspend from

suss out

swab down, out

swaddle with

swagger about, across, along, around, away, back, by, down, forth, forward, from, in, into, off, on, out, out of, over, round, through, to, towards, up, upon

swallow up, down

swamp with (pass.)

swank about

swap around, for, over, round, with

swarm over, round, through, up, with

swathe in

sway about, across, along, around, away, back, by, down, forth, forward, from, in, into, off, on, out, out of, over, round, through, to, towards, up, upon

swear out, in, on, for, off, at, upon, by
sweat for, off, out
sweep about, across, along, around, away, back, by, down, forth, forward, from, in, into, off, on, out, out of, over, round, through, to, towards, up, upon
swell out, up, with
swerve from
swig at, off
swill down, out
swim about, across, along, around, away, back, by, down, forth, forward, from, in, into, off, on, out, out of, over, round, through, to, towards, up, upon
swindle out of
swing about, across, along, around, away, back, by, down, forth, forward, from, in, into, off, on, out, out of, over, round, through, to, towards, up, upon
swipe at
swirl about, across, along, around, away, back, by, down, forth, forward, from, in, into, off, on, out, out of, over, round, through, to, towards, up, upon
swish off, through
switch back, from, off, on, out, over
swivel round
swoop on, upon
swot for, up
sympathise with

t

tack about, down, on, to
tackle about, on, over
tag along, on, out
tail away, back, off, on
tailor to
taint with (pass.)
take about, across, against, along, around, as, at, away, back, by, down, for, from, in, into, off, on, out, out of, over, round, through, to (+ ing), up (+ ing), upon
talk about, around, at, away, back, down, for, into (+ ing), of, on, out, out of (+ ing), over, round, through, to, up, upon
tally with
tamp down
tamper with
tangle up (pass.), with
tank up
tap at, down, for, in, off, on, out
taper off
tart up
task with
taste of
tax with (+ ing)
taxi up, down, along
team up
tear about, across, along, around, at, away, down, from, in, into, off, out, to, up
tease out
tee off, up

teem in, with
telecopy to
telegraph to
telephone in, to
telescope into
teletype to
telex to
tell about, against, by, from, of, off, on, over, to, with
temper against
temporise with
tempt from, in (+ ing), out of (+ ing), to
tend towards
tender for
tense up, for
terminate at, in
terrify into (+ ing), out of (+ ing)
test for, out
testify against, for, to
thank for (+ ing)
thaw out
theorise about
thicken up
thin down, out
think about (+ ing), back, for, of (+ ing), on, out, over, through, to, up, upon
thirst for
thrash about, around, out, through
thread through
threaten with
thrill with, to (pass.), at (pass.)
thrive on, upon
throb away, with
throng in, into, out
throttle back, down
throw about, around, at, away, back, down, in, into, off, on, out, over, to, up, upon

thrust against, at, away, back, down, forward, from, in, into, on, out, through, towards, up, upon

thud against, into

thumb through

thump on, out

thunder against, out

tick away, off, over

tide over

tidy up, out away

tie up, in, with, to, on, down, into, back

tighten up

tilt back, up

tinge with

tingle with

tinker about, around, with

tip in, into, off, out, over, up, with

tiptoe about, across, along, around, away, back, by, down, forth, forward, from, in, into, off, on, out, out of, over, round, through, to, towards, up, upon

tire of (pass.) / (+ ing), out

toady to

toddle about, across, along, around, away, back, by, down, forth, forward, from, in, into, off, on, out, out of, over, round, through, to, towards, up, upon

tog up, out

toil about, across, along, around, away, back, by, down, forth, forward, from, in, into, off, on, out, out of, over, round, through, to, towards, up, upon

toll for

tone down, in, up

tool up

top off, out, up

topple down, from, over

torment with (pass.)

toss up, in, down, about, for, into, off, away, around, back, at

tot up

totter in, into, out, out of, to

touch down, for, in, off, on, to, up, upon

toughen up

tout about, around, as (pass.), for

tow away

towel down, off

tower over

toy with

trace back, out, over, to

track down, in, up

trade down, for, in, off, on, upon

traffic in

trail about, across, along, around, away, back, by, down, forth, forward, from, in, into, off, on, out, out of, over, round, through, to, towards, up, upon

train up, on, for, upon

traipse about, across, along, around, away, back, by, down, forth, forward, from, in, into, off, on, out, out of, over, round, through, to, towards, up, upon

trample down, in, on, out, upon

transact with

transfer to, from

transfix with (pass.)

transform into

translate in, to, from

transmit to

transmute in

transport to, with (pass.)

transpose into

trap in, into (+ ing)

travel by, from, in, on, over, to

tread down, in, into, on, out, upon

treasure up

treat as, for, of, to

trek to

tremble at, for, from, with

trench on, towards

trend to, towards

trespass against, on, upon

trick into (+ ing), out, out of (+ ing), up

trickle away, down, in, into, out, out of

trifle away, with

trig out, up

trigger off

trim away, down, off

trip about, across, along, around, away, back, by, down, forth, forward, from, in, into, off, on, out, out of, over, round, through, to, towards, up, upon

triumph over

troop

trot about, across, along, around, away, back, by, down, forth, forward, from, in, into, off, on, out, out of, over, round, through, to, towards, up, upon

trouble with (pass.), over, about, for

truck in, for
truckle to
trudge up, out, in, to, on, from, over, down, about, into, off, away, around, back, through, upon, round, out of, by, along, towards, forward, forth, across
true up
trump up
trumpet forth
trundle about, across, along, around, away, back, by, down, forth, forward, from, in, into, off, on, out, out of, over, round, through, to, towards, up, upon
truss up
trust in, with, to, for
try for, on, out, over
tuck up, in, down, into, away
tug at
tumble down, for, into, off, on, out, over, to, upon
tune up, out, in
tunnel into, through
turf out
turn about, against, away, back, down, from, in, into, off, on, out, round, to, towards, up, upon
tussle with
tutor in
twiddle with
twine around, round
twinkle with
twist around, into, off, round, up
twit with
type as, in, out, up
tyrannise over

unbosom to
unburden to, of
undeceive of
understand by
unfasten from
unfit for
unfold to
unify into, with
unite in, into, with
unlash from
unleash on, upon
unload on, upon
unpin from
unsling from
unstrap from
unyoke from
upbraid with, for (+ ing)
upgrade to
upholster in, with
uproot from
urge along, forward, on, to, upon
use as, for, to (pass.) / (+ ing), up
usher in, into, out, out of
usurp from
utilise for

V

vaccinate against
value as, at, for
vamp up
vanish away, from
vapour about

vary from, in, to, with
vault over
veer to, from, off, round
veg out
vent on, upon
venture forth, on, out, upon
verge into, on, upon
vest with
vex at (pass.), with
vie for, in
vindicate to, for
visit on, upon, with
vociferate against
volunteer for (+ ing)
vomit out
vote against (+ ing), down, for (+ ing), in, on, through, upon
vouch for

W

waddle about, across, along, around, away, back, by, down, forth, forward, from, in, into, off, on, out, out of, over, round, through, to, towards, up, upon
wade about, across, along, around, away, back, by, down, forth, forward, from, in, into, off, on, out, out of, over, round, through, to, towards, up, upon
waffle about
wager on
wail over, for
wait about, around, for, in, on, out, up, upon

 209

wake from, to, up
waken from, to
walk about, across, along, around, away, back, by, down, forth, forward, from, in, into, off, on, out, out of, over, round, through, to, towards, up, upon
wall up, in, on, round
wallow in
waltz about, across, along, around, away, back, by, down, forth, forward, from, in, into, off, on, out, out of, over, round, through, to, towards, up, upon
wander about, around, from, on
wangle out of
want back, in
war against, over
ward from, off
warm over, up
warn about, against (+ ing), of, off
wash away, down, off, out, over, up
waste away, on
watch for, out, over
water down
wave about, around, at, away, on, to
wean from
wear away, down, off, on, out, through, up, upon
weary with, of (+ ing)
weather through
weave from, in, through
wed to (pass.)
wedge in, up
weed out

weep about, away, for, over
weigh against, down, in, on, out, up, upon, with
weight against, down
weird out
welcome back, in, to, with
weld on, throughout, together
well out, over, up
welter in
wend about, across along, around, away, back, by, down, forth, forward, from, in, into, off, on, out of, out, over, round, through, to, towards, up, upon
wet down, off, out
whack off, up
wheedle into (+ ing), out, out of (+ ing)
wheel about, around, away, in, out, round
wheeze out
while away
whip about, across, along, around, away, back, by, down, forth, forward, from, in, into, off, on, out, out of, over, round, through, to, towards, up, upon
whirl about, across, along, around, away, back, by, down, forth, forward, from, in, into, off, on, out, out of, over, round, through, to, towards, up, upon
whirr about, across, along, around, away, back, by, down, forth, forward, from, in, into, off, on, out, out of, over, round, through, to, towards, up, upon

whisk away, off
whisper about, around
whistle for, up
white out
whittle down
whoop up
wick away
widen out
wig out
will to, away
win out, over, away, around, back, at, through, round
wince at
wind back, down, in, into, off, on, through, up
wink at, away, back
winkle out of
winnow out
winter in, over
wipe up, out, over, off, away
wire up, in, for, off
wise on, to
wish away, for, on, upon
withdraw from, in
wither away, up
withhold from
witness to
witter about
wobble about, around
wolf down
wonder about, at
woo away, into (+ ing), out of (+ ing)
work against, as, at (+ ing), away, by (pass.), in, into, off, on, out, over, round, through, to, towards, up, upon
worm in, out of, through
worry about, along, at, out, over, through
wound in

wrangle over, about
wrap around, in, round, up
wreathe about, in (pass.), into, round
wrench from, off
wrest for, off
wrestle into, with
wriggle about, across, along, around, away, back, by, down, forth, forward, from, in, into, off, on, out, out of, over, round, through, to, towards, up, upon
wring out, from
wrinkle up
write against, away, back, down, for, in, into, of, off, on, out, to, up, upon
writhe at

x out
xerox to

yammer for
yank at, away, in, off, on, out, up
yap away
yearn for
yell for, out, with
yield to, up

Z

zap about, across, along, around, away, back, by, down, forth, forward, from, in, into, off, on, out, out of, over, round, through, to, towards, up, upon
zazz up
zero in
zigzag about, across, along, around, away, back, by, down, forth, forward, from, in, into, off, on, out, out of, over, round, through, to, towards, up, upon
zing past
zip about, across, along, around, away, back, by, down, forth, forward, from, in, into, off, on, out, out of, over, round, through, to, towards, up, upon
zone for, off
zonk out
zoom about, across, along, around, away, back, by, down, forth, forward, from, in, into, off, on, out, out of, over, round, through, to, towards, up, upon

Verbes irréguliers

Vous trouverez une classification des verbes irréguliers p. 104.

a

arise	arose	arisen
awake	awoke (awaked)	awoke (awaked)

b

baby-sit	baby-sat	baby-sat
backslide	backslid	backslid
be	was/were	been
bear	bore	born/bore
beat	beat	beat/beaten
become	became	become
befall	befell	befallen
beget	begot	begotten
begin	began	begun
behold	beheld	beheld
bend	bent	bent
bereave	bereft (bereaved)	bereft (bereaved)
beseech	besought (beseeched)	besought
beset	beset	beset
bespeak	bespoke	bespoken
bestrew	bestrewed	bestrewn (bestrewed)
bestride	bestrode	bestridden
bet	bet	bet
betake	betook	betaken
bethink	bethought	bethought
bid	bade/bid	bidden/bid
bind	bound	bound
bite	bit	bit/bitten
bleed	bled	bled
blow	blew	blown
bottle-feed	bottle-fed	bottle-fed
break	broke	broken

breast-feed	breast-fed	breast-fed
breed	bred	bred
bring	brought	brought
broadcast	broadcast	broadcast
build	built	built
burn	burnt (burned)	burnt (burned)
burst	burst	burst
buy	bought	bought

C

caretake	caretook	caretaken
cast	cast	cast
catch	caught	caught
chide	chid (chided)	chidden (chided)
choose	chose	chosen
cleave	cleft (clove/cleaved)	cleft (cloven/cleaved)
cling	clung	clung
clothe	clad (clothed)	clad (clothed)
come	came	come
cost	cost	cost
countersink	countersank/countersunk	countersunk
creep	crept	crept
crossbreed	crossbred	crossbred
crosscut	crosscut	crosscut
cut	cut	cut

d

deal	dealt	dealt
defreeze	defroze	defrozen
dig	dug	dug
do	did	done
draw	drew	drawn
dream	dreamt (dreamed)	dreamt (dreamed)
drink	drank	drunk
drive	drove	driven
dwell	dwelt	dwelt

e

eat	ate	eaten

f

fall	fell	fallen
feed	fed	fed
feel	felt	felt
fight	fought	fought
find	found	found
flee	fled	fled
fling	flung	flung
fly	flew	flown
forbear	forbore	forborne
forbid	forbade	forbidden
force-feed	force-fed	force-fed
forecast	forecast	forecast
forego	forewent	foregone
foresee	foresaw	foreseen
foretell	foretold	foretold
forget	forgot	forgotten/forgot
forgive	forgave	forgiven
forgo	forwent	forgone
forsake	forsook	forsaken
forswear	forswore	forsworn
freeze	froze	frozen

g

gainsay	gainsaid	gainsaid
get	got	got/gotten
ghost-write	ghost-wrote	ghot-written
gild	gilt (gilded)	gilt (gilded)

gird	girt (girded)	girt (girded)
give	gave	given
go	went	gone
grave	graved	graven (graved)
grind	ground	ground
grow	grew	grown

h

hang	hung (hanged)	hung (hanged)
have	had	had
hear	heard	heard
heave	hove (heaved)	hove (heaved)
hew	hewed	hewn (hewed)
hide	hid	hidden
hit	hit	hit
hold	held	held
hurt	hurt	hurt

i

inlay	inlaid	inlaid
input	input	input
inset	inset	inset
interbreed	interbred	interbred
interweave	interwove	interwoven

k

keep	kept	kept
kneel	knelt	knelt
knit	knit (knitted)	knit (knitted)
know	knew	known

l

lade	laded	laden
lay	laid	laid
lead	led	led
lean	leant (leaned)	leant (leaned)
leap	leapt (leaped)	leapt (leaped)
learn	learnt (learned)	learnt (learned)
leave	left	left
lend	lent	lent
let	let	let
lie	lay	lain
light	lit (lighted)	lit (lighted)
lose	lost	lost

m

make	made	made
mean	meant	meant
meet	met	met
misbecome	misbecame	misbecome
miscast	miscast	miscast
misdeal	misdealt	misdealt
misdo	misdid	misdone
misfeed	misfed	misfed
misgive	misgave	misgiven
mishear	misheard	misheard
mishit	mishit	mishit
misknow	misknew	misknown
mislay	mislaid	mislaid
mislead	misled	misled
misread	misread	misread
misspell	misspelt (misspelled)	misspelt
misspend	misspent	misspent
mistake	mistook	mistaken
misunderstand	misunderstood	misunderstood
mow	mowed	mown (mowed)

O

outbid	outbade/outbid	outbid/outbidden
outbreed	outbred	outbred
outdo	outdid	outdone
outfight	outfought	outfought
outgo	outwent	outgone
outgrow	outgrew	outgrown
outride	outrode	outridden
outrun	outran	outrun
outshine	outshone	outshone
outspeak	outspoke	outspoken
outspend	outspent	outspent
outspread	outspread	outspread
outstand	outstood	outstood
outthink	outthought	outthought
outwear	outwore	outworn
overbear	overbore	overborne
overbid	overbade/overbid	overbid/overbidden
overbuild	overbuilt	overbuilt
overcast	overcast	overcast
overcome	overcame	overcome
overdo	overdid	overdone
overdraw	overdrew	overdrawn
overdrive	overdrove	overdriven
overeat	overate	overeaten
overfeed	overfed	overfed
overfly	overflew	overflown
overgrow	overgrew	overgrown
overhang	overhung	overhung
overhear	overheard	overheard
overlay	overlaid	overlaid
overlie	overlay	overlain
overpay	overpaid	overpaid
override	overrode	overridden
overrun	overran	overrun
oversee	oversaw	overseen
oversell	oversold	oversold
overset	overset	overset
oversew	oversewed	oversewn (oversewed)

overshoot	overshot	overshot
oversleep	overslept	overslept
overspend	overspent	overspent
overstrew	overstrewed	overstrewn (-strewed)
overtake	overtook	overtaken
overthrow	overthrew	overthrown
overwind	overwound	overwound
overwrite	overwrote	overwritten

p

partake	partook	partaken
pay	paid	paid
photoset	photoset	photoset
prepay	prepaid	prepaid
pre-shrink	pre-shrank	pre-shrunk
put	put	put

q

quit	quit (am.) / quitted	quit (am.) / quitted

r

read	read	read
rebind	rebound	rebound
rebroadcast	rebroadcast	rebroadcast
rebuild	rebuilt	rebuilt
recast	recast	recast
reclothe	reclad/clothed)	reclad/clothed)
recut	recut	recut
redo	redid	redone
redraw	redrew	redrawn
reeve	rove (reeved)	rove (reeved)
refeed	refed	refed

regrind	reground	reground
rehear	reheard	reheard
re-lay	re-laid	re-laid
relearn	relearnt (relearned)	relearnt (relearned)
relet	relet	relet
remake	remade	remade
rend	rent	rent
repay	repaid	repaid
reread	reread	reread
rerun	reran	rerun
resell	resold	resold
reset	reset	reset
retake	retook	retaken
retell	retold	retold
retread	retrod	retrodden
rewind	rewound	rewound
rewrite	rewrote	rewritten
rid	rid (ridded)	rid
ride	rode	ridden
ring	rang	rung
rise	rose	risen
run	ran	run

S

saw	sawed	sawn (sawed)
say	said	said
see	saw	seen
seek	sought	sought
sell	sold	sold
send	sent	sent
set	set	set
sew	sewed	sewn (sewed)
shake	shook	shaken
shear	sheared	shorn (sheared)
shed	shed	shed
shine	shone	shone
shoe	shod	shod
shoot	shot	shot

show	showed	shown (showed)
shrink	shrank	shrunk
shrive	shrove (shrived)	shriven (shrived)
shut	shut	shut
sing	sang	sung
sink	sank	sunk
sit	sat	sat
slay	slew (slayed)	slain
sleep	slept	slept
slide	slid	slid
sling	slung	slung
slink	slunk	slunk
slit	slit	slit
smell	smelt (smelled)	smelt (smelled)
smite	smote	smitten
speak	spoke	spoken
speed	sped (speeded)	sped (speeded)
spell	spelt (spelled)	spelt (spelled)
spend	spent	spent
spill	spilt (spilled)	spilt (spilled)
spin	spun	spun
spit	spat	spat
split	split	split
spoil	spoilt (spoiled)	spoilt (spoiled)
spoon-feed	spoon-fed	spoon-fed
spread	spread	spread
spring	sprang	sprung
stand	stood	stood
steal	stole	stolen
stick	stuck	stuck
sting	stung	stung
stink	stank	stank
strew	strewed	strewn (strewed)
stride	strode	stridden
strike	struck	struck/stricken
string	strung	strung
strive	strove	striven
sublet	sublet	sublet
swear	swore	sworn
sweep	swept	swept
swell	swelled	swollen

swim	swam	swum
swing	swung	swung

t

take	took	taken
teach	taught	taught
tear	tore	torn
telecast	telecast	telecast
tell	told	told
think	thought	thought
thrive	throve (thrived)	thriven (thrived)
throw	threw	thrown
thrust	thrust	thrust
tread	trod	trodden
type-cast	type-cast	type-cast
type-set	type-set	type-set
typewrite	typewrote	typewritten

u

unbend	unbent	unbent
unbind	unbound	unbound
unclothe	unclad	unclad
underbid	underbid/underbade	underbid/underbidden
undercut	undercut	undercut
underdo	underdid	underdone
underfeed	underfed	underfed
undergird	undergirt (girded)	undergirt (girded)
undergo	underwent	undergone
underlie	underlay	underlain
undersell	undersold	undersold
undershoot	undershot	undershot
understand	understood	understood
undertake	undertook	undertaken
underwrite	underwrote	underwritten
undo	undid	undone
unfreeze	unfroze	unfrozen

unsay	unsaid	unsaid
unsling	unslung	unslung
unstick	unstuck	unstuck
unstring	unstrung	unstrung
unwind	unwound	unwound
uphold	upheld	upheld
upset	upset	upset

W

wake	woke (waked)	woken (waked)
waylay	waylaid	waylaid
wear	wore	worn
weave	wove	woven
weep	wept	wept
win	won	won
wind	wound	wound
withdraw	withdrew	withdrawn
withhold	withheld	withheld
withstand	withstood	withstood
wring	wrung	wrung
write	wrote	written

Imprimé en France par I.M.E. - 25110 Baume-les-Dames
Dépôt légal n° 18741 - Juin 2007